the art of
DIVING
and adventure in the underwater world

the art of
DIVING
and adventure in the underwater world

Written by
Nick Hanna

Photographed by
Alexander Mustard

ULTIMATE SPORTS®

THE LYONS PRESS
Guilford, Connecticut
An Imprint of The Globe Pequot Press

To buy books in quantity for corporate use
or incentives, call **(800) 962–0973**
or e-mail **premiums@GlobePequot.com**.

For more information, see www.artofdiving.com

Planned and produced by Ultimate Sports Publications
Limited
Publisher: David Holyoak
Project Manager: Richard Watts
Design: Paul Phillips
Editor: Mike Unwin
Indexer: Janet Dudley

Ultimate Sports would like to thank Nick Hanna and Alex
Mustard for their excellent work and helpful feedback,
David Doubilet and Tim Ecott for their reviews. Thanks to
Richard Watts and each of the team members mentioned
above for their individual and collective contributions, also
to Graeme Gourlay and Paul Critcher at DIVE magazine
and everyone else who has helped in the making of *The
Art of Diving*.

Reprographics by PDQ Digital Media Solutions Ltd. and
Adelphi Graphics Ltd.

ISBN: 978-1-59921-227-2

Library of Congress Cataloging-in-Publication Data is available on file.

SECRETARY BLENNY (TURTLE FARM, GRAND CAYMAN)

Acknowledgements

Alex Mustard

The photography in this book is the culmination of my life's work to date. I took my first undersea photos when I was snorkelling at nine years old, and took my first breath of "sweet, effortless air" on scuba at the bottom of the school swimming pool aged 13. At the time I remember wondering if I would be doing this for the rest of my life, and by the following summer, when I first dived in the ocean, I was lucky enough to know that my life had changed and I was ready to "run headlong down an immutable course."

Most of the images in this book were taken during 2004 and 2005. And while my general dive travels have contributed images, most of the key images come from three trips that Nick and I made; to Dahab, diving with Reef 2000; to Grand Cayman, diving with Ocean Frontiers and Dive Tech; and to the Maldives, diving with Maldives Scuba Tours.

Taking pictures in the ocean requires specialist equipment and I am most grateful to the manufacturers who allow me to do what I love. Almost all the images here were taken with Nikon SLR cameras (D2X, D100, D70 and F100) in underwater housings made by Subal, Austria. Lighting was usually from flashguns made by Subtronic, Germany. I am particularly grateful to Ocean Optics, London, who supply and maintain all my underwater equipment, and to London Camera Exchange, Southampton, UK, who I rely on for all my cameras and lenses. On a personal level, I am indebted to Peter Rowlands, who has been an influential mentor. His insightful critique has been responsible for turning many of my crazy ideas into the finished images you see here. Finally I would like to thank my friends and peers in the British Society of Underwater Photographers and the online community Wetpixel.com for their encouragement, education and for filling me with a desire to continue to improve my photography.

There are many images in this book featuring divers. These people are not in these images by chance. I would like to thank the following for their patience and elegance underwater: Anna Hickman, Nick Hanna, Henny Van den Burgh, Kim Paumier, Giles Shaxted, Peter Rowlands, Kirk Krack, Denis Antippa, Brian Corryer, Dawn Deydey, Steve Schultz, Monica Farrell, Patrick Weir, Anna Yunnie, Claire Nichols, Annelise Hagan, Cindy Abgarian, Mandy-Rae Cruickshank, Martin Stepanek, Mon Pongsum, Chris Brandson, J.P. Trenque and Charles Hood. I am also grateful to underwater photographer Eric Cheng for providing three shark images that give Chapter Five extra bite. Although these come from Eric's stock I feel that in style they could have been taken specifically for this book. Thank you.

I would also like to thank my friend, Nick Hanna, for thinking of me when he sent the email that started this project. I have greatly enjoyed travelling and diving with Nick and also being able to ask him to interview many of my diving heroes and heroines for this book, and to include many of my favourite quotes about scuba.

Finally, I would like to thank my family and friends for their love and support. Photography frequently takes me away from the UK, yet I always look forward to returning home to their warm friendship and perhaps a chilled bottle, waiting in The Platform. I would especially like to thank my father for his constant support of my obsession with the ocean, despite his own lack of comfort beneath (or on) the waves. I hope that this book reveals the details of a passion that for me is expressed so much better in images than in words.

Nick Hanna

I would like to thank Kim Paumier for her constant love and support, Charlotte Parry-Crooke of Creative Projects Consultancy for her wise advice and loyal friendship, and my nephew Hugh Williamson for his work transcribing tapes. Thanks are also due to Dive Sportif for enabling my trip to Dahab, and to Regaldive, Emperor Divers and NoTanx Diving for making it possible for me to undertake a free-diving course in the Red Sea. Thanks also to Sue Wells, consultant to UNEP/WCMC in Cambridge, for her insightful comments on Chapter Eight.

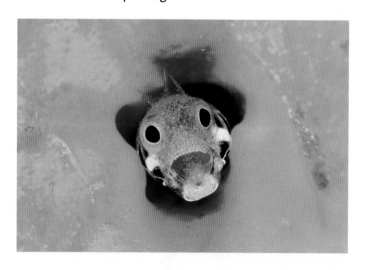

www.artofdiving.com

The Art of Diving website has been specially created to enhance your enjoyment of this book.

Packed full of beautiful images and useful information it will appeal to all who are interested in the underwater world, whether an advanced diver, aspiring beginner or somewhere in between.

And for the keen underwater photographers among you the site features technical details and extended captions for all of the images in this book and more.

If you are not yet a diver we hope this book will inspire you to learn to dive. Begin your own underwater adventures by visiting **www.artofdiving.com** which includes helpful advice and information for newcomers to the sport.

Special features include:

• Photo gallery featuring all the images in this book

• Technical photographic data for each image

• Alex Mustard's favourite 20 images and his reasons for choosing them

• Behind the scenes images from the making of book

• Guest photographer images

• Free downloads of desktop pictures and screen savers

• Links to partner sites and special offers

• Advance news of other publications

Your access password for the members only zone is:

vnw5-2a1c-84xr

Visit **www.artofdiving.com** and enter your password to activate your FREE membership.

➔ ➔ MANY HOST GOBY ON A SEA WHIP.
(RAYMOND POINT, MANADO, INDONESIA)

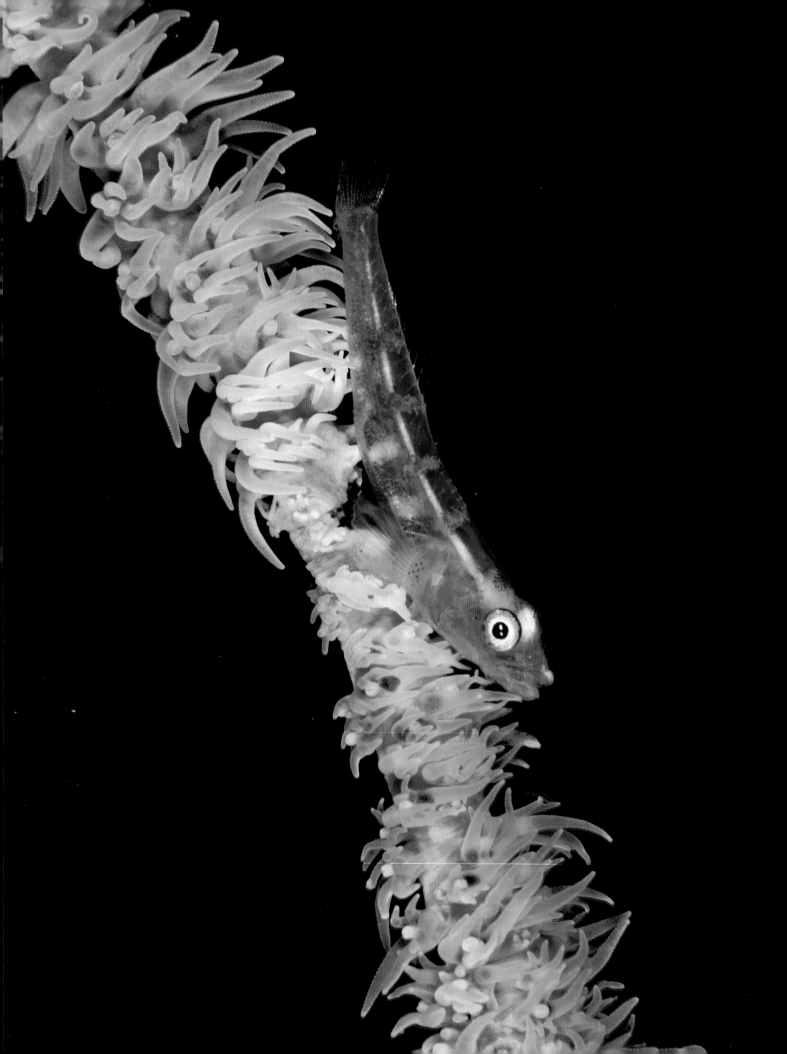

contents

↑ SOUTHERN STINGRAY (STINGRAY CITY, GRAND CAYMAN)

"Buoyed by water, he can fly in any direction – up, down, sideways – by merely flipping his hand. Underwater man becomes an archangel."

Jacques Cousteau

introduction

THIS BOOK STARTED OUT AS A FEATURE CALLED 'THE ZEN OF DIVING', WRITTEN FOR A SPECIAL EDITION OF THE 'BODY & SOUL' SECTION OF *THE TIMES* ON HOLISTIC HOLIDAYS. THE FEATURE FOCUSED ON MONICA FARRELL'S YOGA DIVING COURSES IN THE RED SEA RESORT OF DAHAB AND STEVE SCHULTZ'S PADI COURSE ON MIND, BODY, SPIRIT SCUBA AND, AFTER APPEARING IN *THE TIMES*, WAS SYNDICATED TO A HANDFUL OF DIVING MAGAZINES AROUND THE WORLD. DURING THE RESEARCH, I HAPPENED TO COME ACROSS ALEX'S WORK AND WAS IMMEDIATELY TAKEN WITH THE FRESHNESS AND CREATIVE DEPTH OF HIS UNDERWATER PHOTOGRAPHY. I E-MAILED HIM ASKING IF HE WAS INTERESTED IN CO-OPERATING ON THE PROJECT, HAVING NO IDEA WHERE HE MIGHT BE IN THE WORLD. A COUPLE OF DAYS LATER ALEX REPLIED FROM THE CAYMAN ISLANDS AND SENT ME THE PICTURE OF A WOMAN ON THE SEABED BLOWING BUBBLES, WHICH APPEARS ON PAGE 188. WHEN I OPENED HIS E-MAIL I HAD THAT 'WOW' SENSATION THAT MANY OF ALEX'S PICTURES EVOKE, BUT ALSO A FAMILIAR TINGLING OF THE SPINE TELLING ME THAT THIS PROJECT WAS GOING TO BE SOMETHING SPECIAL. ALEX HAD NOT ONLY GRASPED THE CONCEPT PERFECTLY, BUT INTERPRETED IT THROUGH HIS OWN PARTICULAR TALENT. A PARTNERSHIP WAS BORN.

Since then it has been – as they say – a long road, as we have navigated the choppy waters of the publishing world to bring this book to fruition. Over the last two years Alex and I have worked and dived in many different parts of the world – sometimes together, sometimes in the same place but at different times. We have shared words and images across continents and oceans and, rather like Osha Gray Davidson's 'enchanted braid', have interwoven our concepts and ideas into a larger whole. The final result is not simply an illustrated 'how to' guide, with each stage accompanied by a picture; rather it's an expression of our own subjective interpretations – each one's overflowing into the other's.

As the book developed it took on a life of its own. The scope became broader and more colourful, and the central thesis expanded from 'Zen Diving' into 'The Art of Diving'. Scuba diving is now one of the most popular holiday activities in the world. In the past two decades it has grown from a minority interest into a mainstream activity that anyone – and their grandmother – can enjoy. Today there are an estimated fifteen to twenty million qualified divers worldwide.

With this growth in popularity, it has become clear that diving offers something more than simply a sporting challenge. Diving conveys you effortlessly into another dimension, a liquid world of fabulous habitats and bizarre creatures whose magnetic allure draws you back again and again. Once a sport dominated by macho feats of endurance, it has since matured into something much more meaningful: an art form requiring grace and agility, a waltz with water and the creatures who live in it. And every dive, like every painting or piece of music, is different – a fresh creation that enthralls us all the more.

Our book is a voyage into the soul of diving. We hope that it will open your eyes and your imagination to new ways of being underwater – ways that are based as much on kinesthetic awareness as on what's in your logbook. Of course technical skills and know-how are important. But this book is not the place to look for an explanation of the intricacies of Nitrox or the causes of nitrogen narcosis – although we do hope that you will come away with some taste of the 'rapture of the deep'.

⊙ FROGFISH (BALI, INDONESIA)

↑ DIVER EXPLORING A CORAL REEF AT RAS MUHAMMED, EGYPT.

The art of diving is more down to attitude than technique. It embodies a certain approach, an ability to embrace the spirit of the sea, which was evident in the words of the earliest pioneers but since then seems somehow to have been lost along the way. Today we see this approach resurfacing – a fact that emerged with one-hundred-foot visibility when we began talking to the people featured in this book. Underwater photographers, naturalists, filmmakers, journalists, marine biologists, divemasters – these are people who spend more time underwater than anybody else. We discovered a clear consensus amongst these professionals about what diving really means and where it's heading.

As friends and collaborators, Alex and I have derived huge pleasure in diving together for this book, and have learned from each other in the process. As many divers will confirm, to be able to share the underwater world with people close to you – your friends, your family, your partner and frequently nowadays your children – brings enormous joy. It is one of the many benefits of the democratization that has swept our sport in recent decades. Another is the ability to share our underwater experiences with the wider world, particularly our sense of wonder at being able to meet marine wildlife in its own backyard.

I don't think there can be any diver who hasn't at some point emerged from a dive with a sense of privilege at what they have witnessed underwater. But marine creatures and their habitats are increasingly under threat. The causes are well known, and, as divers, we are uniquely placed to influence change. Today the diving community is becoming increasingly conscious of the fact that what's happening underwater is connected to our own lifestyles.

This book is about the joys of diving and the exhilaration of animal encounters – dances with fishes, if you like. But we all know it's impossible to dive and be unaware of the human impact on the oceans. As divers we owe it to the world of fishes, from which we derive so much pleasure, to call for changes that respect their magical underwater home.

We hope you enjoy this journey into the soul of diving as much as we have.

⊕ SEAHORSE
(BALI, INDONESIA)

the lure of the
underwater world

"He goes on a great Voyage, that goes to the bottom of the Sea."

Anon, 17th century

EVERYBODY REMEMBERS HIS OR HER FIRST DIVE. FUELLED BY A HEADY MIX OF APPREHENSION AND EXCITEMENT, IT HERALDS YOUR EVOLUTION FROM A NATURALLY AIR-BREATHING MAMMAL TO *HOMO AQUATICUS*, WHOSE LIFE SUPPORT IS SCUBA GEAR.

I was fortunate enough to make mine in the Red Sea, and I can still vividly recall that moment when I deflated my buoyancy jacket and sank slowly beneath the surface. Fear of drowning soon gave way to awe, as amazing scenes unfolded in front of me.

Seen from below, the surf frothing over the reef crest looked like a champagne whirlpool. I felt as though I had dropped through a watery ceiling into someone else's universe, populated by a weird and wonderful cast of thousands. There was so much to see, so many bright colours, fabulous plants and bizarre creatures.

Even now, many years later, I still have a sense of wonder at leaving the surface world and descending into this other dimension. It's a glorious feeling, that first dive of the holiday or season. You may have travelled thousands of miles to reach your destination, or you may simply be diving off your local beach. Either way, the point of your painstaking preparations becomes clear as soon as your field of vision changes from sky to sea.

That wonderful sensation of being in another world has captivated divers ever since someone first worked out how to see (and later, how to breathe) underwater. People have been plunging underwater for centuries – but even though Greek sponge divers and Asian pearl divers managed to stay underwater for long periods, they still had to come back to the surface to breathe after a few minutes.

"I sank gently to the sand. I breathed sweet, effortless air. The sand sloped down into a clear blue infinity. The sun struck so brightly I had to squint. My arms hanging at my sides, I kicked the fins languidly and travelled down, gaining speed, watching the beach reeling past."

Jacques Cousteau

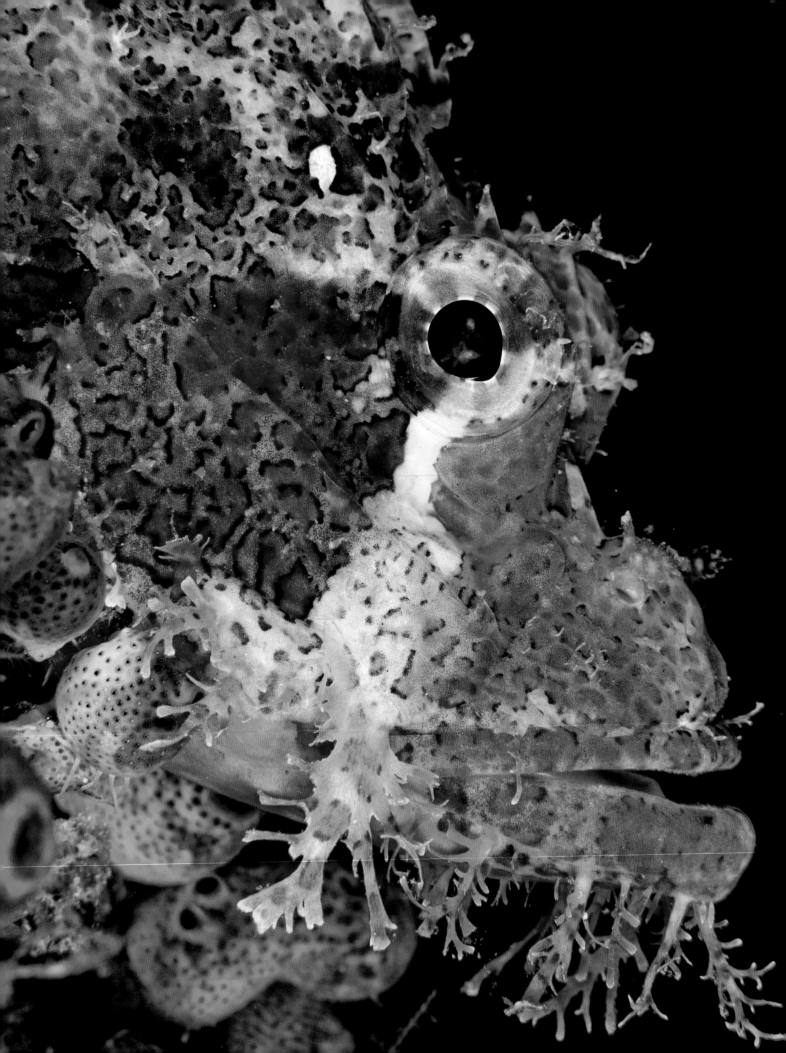

Sinking scientists

The first proper diving devices were bell-shaped jars that divers had to climb inside, which were used for salvage work in the 16th century. Around the beginning of the 18th century, the scientist Edmund Halley (of comet fame) refined the principle further in his treatise, *The Art of Living under Water.* His idea was to lower fresh barrels of air down to the divers, allowing them to stay underwater much longer. The promise of retrieving treasure hoards from sunken ships led to many more 'diving engines' over the following decades.

By the beginning of the 19th century, strange-looking diving suits were in use in various countries. In 1865 two Frenchmen, mining engineer Benoît Rouquayrol and naval officer Auguste Denayrouze, designed a system which began the process of liberating divers from surface-supplied air: it utilised an air cylinder, strapped to the diver's back, which was supplied by an air hose from the surface – but the diver could also disconnect the air hose and walk around freely on the seabed. Also, crucially, this rig included a simple regulator which could level the air pressure in the lungs with the pressure in the surrounding water. It was to be another 77 years before Emile Gagnan, a French engineer, was to rediscover the same principle and create the technology for scuba diving.

During the 20th century scientists began to make detailed studies of the causes and symptoms of decompression sickness, and soon discovered the joys of diving. In 1923 Roy Miner, a curator of zoology with the American Museum of Natural History in New York, set off on an expedition to study coral reefs in the Bahamas. They took with them an underwater tube with a metal sphere hanging beneath it, which was lowered beneath the surface from a barge. "I shall never forget my first view of the barrier reef seen through the window of the tube," said Miner. "Great trees of reef-forming coral, a veritable stone forest with closely interlacing branches...a marble jungle which melted into the pearly haze."[1]

One of the first divers to capture the popular imagination with his startling descriptions of marine life was the American zoologist William Beebe, whose underwater adventures were published in several volumes during the 1920s. Beebe devised a copper helmet with two windows in the front, fed by a garden hose from a hand pump on the surface. "The first time I climbed down my submerged ladder, I knew I had added thousands upon thousands of miles to my possible joy of earthly life," he wrote. "From the moment one is submerged, the reality of the absolute apartness of the place is apparent. Here miracles become marvels, and marvels recurring wonders."[2]

Beebe had a gift for publicity and managed to finance scientific expeditions to the Galapagos, Baja California and the Caribbean. In *Beneath Tropic Seas,* his excitement at being underwater is infectious:

The general impression of hours and days spent on the bottom of the sea is its fairy-tale unreality. It is an Alice's Wonderland, where our terrestrial experiences and terms are set at nought. The flowers are worms, and the boulders living creatures; here we weigh but a fraction of what we do on land; here distance is sheer color and the sky is a glory of rippling light...Until we have found our way to the surface of some other planet, the bottom of the sea will remain the loveliest and strangest place we can imagine.[3]

Despite being tethered by a hose, Beebe was the first to describe the delights of weightlessness in the water, where "one can leap twelve feet, or lift oneself with a crook of a finger." He liked to sit on the seabed six metres (20 feet) down and simply experience the surge pulling him backwards and forwards, along with "every fish in sight, every bit of weed or hydroid." He found the best technique (and it's still good advice today) was not to resist and cling to the reef, but instead "to balance carefully and let oneself be wafted

"The general impression of hours and days spent on the bottom of the sea is its fairy-tale unreality. It is an Alice's Wonderland, where our terrestrial experiences and terms are set at nought."

William Beebe

A SCORPIONFISH USES ITS CAMOUFLAGE TO LAY AN AMBUSH ON THE REEF. (SOUTH MALI ATOLL, MALDIVES)

⬀ A SQUADRON OF SOUTHERN STINGRAYS GLIDE OVER THE SEABED. (STINGRAY CITY, GRAND CAYMAN)

"Sometimes we are lucky enough to know that our lives have changed, to discard the old, embrace the new, and run headlong down an immutable course."

Jacques Cousteau

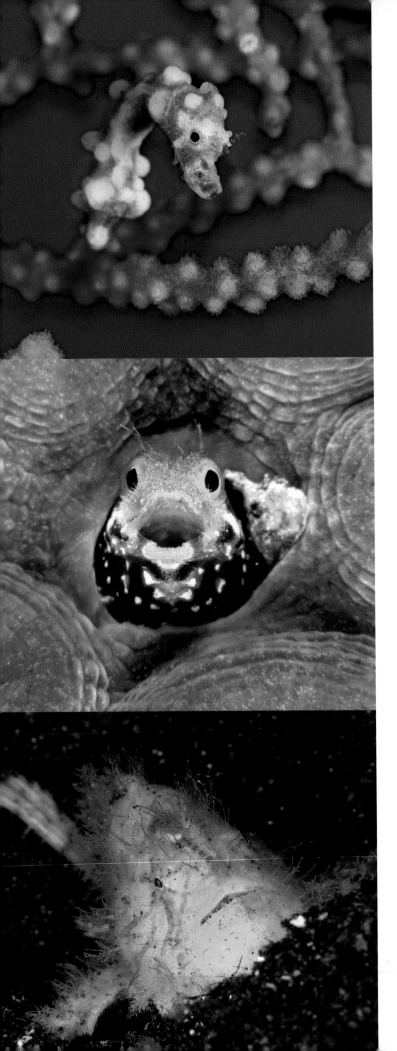

through space and deposited safely on the next rock."4

Like so many of the pioneers of diving, Beebe sometimes talked more about the sensation of being underwater than he did about what he saw down there. Many marine biologists and explorers who followed him were similarly moved to communicate their joy at being in this weightless world – without perhaps spending quite as much time as they might have done pondering serious issues of science.

William Beebe urged the public not to die before "having borrowed, stolen, purchased, or made a helmet of sorts to glimpse for yourself this new world,"5 and his writings on ocean life inspired a whole generation of scientists. One of them was Rachel Carson, who wrote *Silent Spring*, became one of the best-known naturalists of her generation with her writings on the ocean environment. Another was Eugenie Clark, who had a huge success with her books about the underwater world, the first of which was *Lady with a Spear*.

Mad about fishes, Clark majored in zoology. While working towards her PhD, she got a job as part-time research assistant to Dr Carl Hubbs at the Scripps Institute of Oceanography at La Jolla, California, one of the world's greatest marine research laboratories. It was here that she had her own baptism into diving:

> *When I reached the bottom rung of the ladder I could see... I was over a thick bed of kelp. The ends of the long strands of orange-brown seaweed reached up through the murky green water just to my feet, as if I were standing on the tops of sinuous trees in this strange underwater forest. What a lot of fish down there, and how close they came to inspect this slow-moving intruder they did not seem to fear. One bold fish came right up to my helmet and looked in my face. "Shoo!" I said, rather startled.6*

After wandering through the kelp beds, Eugenie finds a large mass of rock festooned with shells, which she likens to "a gingerbread house in this underwater forest." But her fairytale walk is interrupted by a problem with her air supply, forcing her to bail out and make an emergency ascent to the surface. After the helmet is fixed Eugenie has another go: "I went down again – this time, as with the dozens of helmet dives I have done since, with no mishaps."7

Ⓚ DENISE'S PYGMY SEAHORSE (BALI, INDONESIA)
Ⓚ SECRETARY BLENNY (TURTLE FARM REEF, GRAND CAYMAN)
Ⓔ YELLOW HAIRY FROGFISH (LEMBEH STRAIT, INDONESIA)
Ⓔ FUSILIERS STREAM PAST (ARI ATOLL, MALDIVES)

Goggling in the Med

In the 1920s the development of scuba had been gathering pace on the other side of the Atlantic. In 1925 a French inventor, Yves Le Prieur, witnessed a demonstration in Paris in which a diver swam around a tank wearing just a pair of goggles and a nose clip, breathing from a tube supplied by a pump from the surface. Devised by fellow Frenchman Maurice Fernez, this system was popular with Mediterranean sponge divers since it allowed them to move around much more freely in the water than the traditional diving helmets had. Le Prieur adapted the system, using bottles of compressed air supplied by the Michelin tyre company, and made his first successful sorties underwater in the South of France.

In 1933 a fellow Frenchman, Louis de Corlieu, patented the first flippers, or rubber foot fins. He invited Le Prieur to try them out, and the marriage of the two technologies created the basis for contemporary diving equipment.

The warm waters of the French Riviera were also the birthplace of the newly fashionable sport of spearfishing. One of its chief proponents was an American writer called Guy Gilpatric, whose tongue-in-cheek manual, *The Compleat Goggler*, sub-titled *'the First and Only Exhaustive Treaty on the Art of Goggle Fishing'*, was published to great acclaim in 1938. He plunged underwater wearing 'water-tight eye-glasses', the first pair of which he made himself "from an old pair of flying goggles, plugging up the venti-

lating holes with putty and painting over them." Gilpatric is hugely enthusiastic about his underwater excursion:

I was unprepared for the breathtaking sensation of free flight which swimming with goggles gave me... The bottom was fifteen feet below me now, but every pebble and blade of grass was distinct as though there was only air between. The light was a soft bluish-green – even restful, and somehow wholly appropriate to the aching silence which lay upon those gently waving meadows.[8]

At this time Jacques Cousteau was a young Naval gunner and keen swimmer, stationed further east along the coast, who had acquired a pair of the newly fashionable Fernez goggles solely with the aim of keeping salt water out of his eyes as he perfected his crawl style. In *The Silent World* he describes how, the minute he took a look underwater, he realised his life had been changed irrevocably by the sight of the 'jungle' he found there.

One Sunday morning in 1936 at Le Mourillon, near Toulon, I waded into the Mediterranean and looked into it through Fernez goggles. I was astounded by what I saw in the shallow shingle at Le Mourillon, rocks covered with green, brown and silver forests of algae and fishes unknown to me, swimming in crystal-clear water. Standing up to breathe I saw a trolley-bus, people, electric street lights. I put my eyes under again and civilisation vanished with one last bow. I was in a jungle never seen by those who floated in the opaque roof.[9]

Cousteau had no doubt that this was a pivotal moment. "Sometimes we are lucky enough to know that our lives have changed," he wrote, "to discard the old, embrace the new, and run headlong down an immutable course."[10]

He spent the next two years skin diving along the coastline and tailoring and vulcanising rubberised garments in order to stay warm in the water. In 1938 he met Frédéric Dumas (who was to become his life-long diving partner) and, along with another spearfisherman whom he already knew, Philippe Tailliez, formed his first diving team.

Coincidentally, another of the 20th century's great ocean explorers, Hans Hass, ran into Gilpatric on the Riviera. In 1937 Hass was a footloose 18 year-old taking a post-exam holiday on the Riviera. Spurned by a girlfriend, he was sitting on a rock near Juan-les-Pins staring morosely out to sea

"At night I had often had visions of flying by extending my arms as wings. Now I flew without wings."

Jacques Cousteau

"... live – live in the bosom of the waters! There is only independence! There I recognise no masters! There I am free!"

from *20,000 Leagues Under the Sea* **by Jules Verne**

↗ A HAWKSBILL TURTLE OVER SAND. (HEPP'S WALL, GRAND CAYMAN)

when he happened to spot Gilpatric spearfishing. Hass was captivated as he watched the undersea hunter surface with a large fish attached to his spear, and after a conversation with the sunburned American, he rushed off to buy goggles and a speargun. "When I held my first underwater goggles in my hands that day in Antibes, that little contraption of glass and rubber, I little suspected how many wonderful hours it would give me," wrote Hass. "I spent hours swimming along the coast of Antibes, diving, never tiring of all the new things I saw."[11] It wasn't until a year later that Hass began to use 'rubber foot fins' to help him in his diving.

The birth of the aqualung

Cousteau tried out several diving systems, including one that used a cylinder of compressed air strapped to the chest and another with a pipe carrying oxygen from the surface. But on two occasions the pipe ruptured at depth, placing both him and Dumas in mortal danger. Although they worked on the equipment to make it more reliable, Cousteau recognised its limitations: "It fastened us on a leash and we wanted freedom," he said. "We were dreaming about a self-contained compressed-air lung."[12]

"I shall never forget my first view of the reef... great trees of reef-forming coral, a veritable stone forest with closely interlacing branches..."

Roy Miner

⊛ A SCHOOL OF PADDLETAIL SNAPPERS. (FELIDHOO ATOLL, MALDIVES)

Cousteau travelled to Paris looking for someone to build it and met Emile Gagnan, an engineer who worked for his father-in-law's industrial gas company. In December 1942, Gagnan presented Cousteau with a demand valve, which he had designed to regulate gas intake. Within a few weeks, they had come up with the first automatic regulator and had tested it in a river, but it was not until the following summer that Cousteau tried it out in the sea. "No children ever opened a Christmas present with more excitement than we did when we unpacked the first 'aqualung'," he wrote. "If it worked, diving could be

revolutionized."[13] Revolutionized it was, although it was Cousteau, not Gagnan, who took the credit. (Cousteau had also met Le Prieur, who by then had developed a full-face mask with a continuous flow of air to the diver's lungs – but it was Gagnan's gadget that won the day.)

Hurrying off to a sheltered cove where they could play with their new toy undisturbed by the German occupying forces, Cousteau was strapped into the equipment and walked into the sea.

I sank gently to the sand. I breathed sweet, effortless air. The sand sloped down into a clear blue infinity. The sun struck so brightly I had to squint. My arms hanging at my sides, I kicked the fins languidly and travelled down, gaining speed, watching the beach reeling past. I stopped kicking and the momentum carried me on a fabulous glide.[14]

Cousteau learned to adjust his buoyancy with his breathing, equalised the pressure in his ears, and compared himself favourably with clumsy helmet divers, linked to the surface by an air pipe. "To swim fishlike, horizontally, was the logical method in a medium eight hundred times denser than air. To halt and hang attached to nothing, no lines or air pipe to the surface, was a dream. At night I had often had visions of flying by extending my arms as wings. Now I flew without wings."[15] An elated Cousteau described his excitement with this invention, wondering how far down he would be able to go, and what might happen as he got deeper. His exuberance knew no bounds on this epoch-making, first ever scuba dive.

I could attain a speed of almost two knots without using my arms; I soared vertically and passed my own bubbles; I went down to sixty feet. I experimented with all possible manoeuvres of the aqualung – loops, somersaults, and barrel rolls. I stood upside down on one finger and burst out laughing – a shrill, distorted laugh. Whatever I did, nothing altered the automatic rhythm of air. Delivered from gravity and buoyancy I flew around in space.[16]

⊕ DIVERS ON SCOOTERS (TURTLE FARM REEF, GRAND CAYMAN)

Cousteau, ever the visionary, started a trend for divers to bounce around on the seabed like over-excited Tiggers. Meanwhile Philippe Tailliez recounted how perfectly the new regulator functioned:

It kept its promises magnificently. For the first time skin divers, who up to that time had to come up to the surface for lack of breath, experienced in a three-dimensional space the free intoxication of diving without a cable. Back on the shore, we danced for joy. We were already certain that this was really the discovery which a few years later was to inaugurate, in France and the world over, the age of undersea exploration. [17]

By 1940 Hans Hass had already led an expedition to Curaçao, in the Dutch Caribbean, and had made his first films and a book about the underwater world. But his team was still essentially spearfishing using just goggles and fins. It wasn't until 1941 that Hass settled on a proper diving system - an early version of a rebreather. He carried out his first experimental descent with the new gear on July 12th 1943, in Greece. "I was completely overwhelmed by this first hour of virtual transformation into a fish-like being," he wrote. "In my elation I stood on my head at a depth of 50 feet, turned somersaults, and like a demented predator fish, darted through shoals of fish which lined my route like a horrified and respectful guard of honour ... The return to the upper world was like a blissful flight."[18]

The arrival of scuba

By 1943 Cousteau had produced his first underwater films and begun to realise the military potential of the aqualung. In November 1944, as the war began to turn in the Allies' favour, he travelled to London to try and convince the British navy of the value of his equipment in attacking enemy shipping and penetrating harbours undetected. The naval commanders weren't interested, but with typical military passion for acronyms they dubbed his invention the Self-Contained Underwater Breathing Apparatus, which soon became shortened to Scuba.

By 1946 the first sets of equipment were on sale in France. The 1950s were a decade of explosive growth for scuba diving: in November 1950 *Life* published a major feature on Cousteau and his work, with *National Geographic*

A DIVER EXPLORES THE WRECK OF THE *GIANNIS D.* (ABU NUHAS, EGYPT)

A PYGMY SEAHORSE, ABOUT A CENTREMETRE LONG, DANCES ACROSS A SEAFAN. (LEMBEH STRAIT, INDONESIA)

following suit in 1951. The first issue of *Skin Diver* magazine appeared in the same year.

Cousteau was actively marketing his new system, trying to sell it for commercial applications such as marine salvage, offshore oil work, mining the ocean floor and seafloor surveys. Bizarrely, according to biographer Axel Madsen, "one commercial area that didn't immediately occur to him was diving gear for amateurs."[19] Meanwhile Cousteau had bought the *Calypso*, an old minesweeper, and converted her for expedition work. She left Toulon harbour on her

first journey to the Red Sea in November 1951, the first of many expeditions were to be filmed and eventually broadcast worldwide on television. The *Calypso* was to become a familiar sight to spellbound audiences of the television series *The Undersea World of Jacques Cousteau,* which ran for over a decade.

Hans Hass had already made a name for himself and his glamorous wife, Lotte, with the appearance of his film *Red Sea Adventure,* which won a prize at the Venice Film Festival in 1950. English-language editions of his book

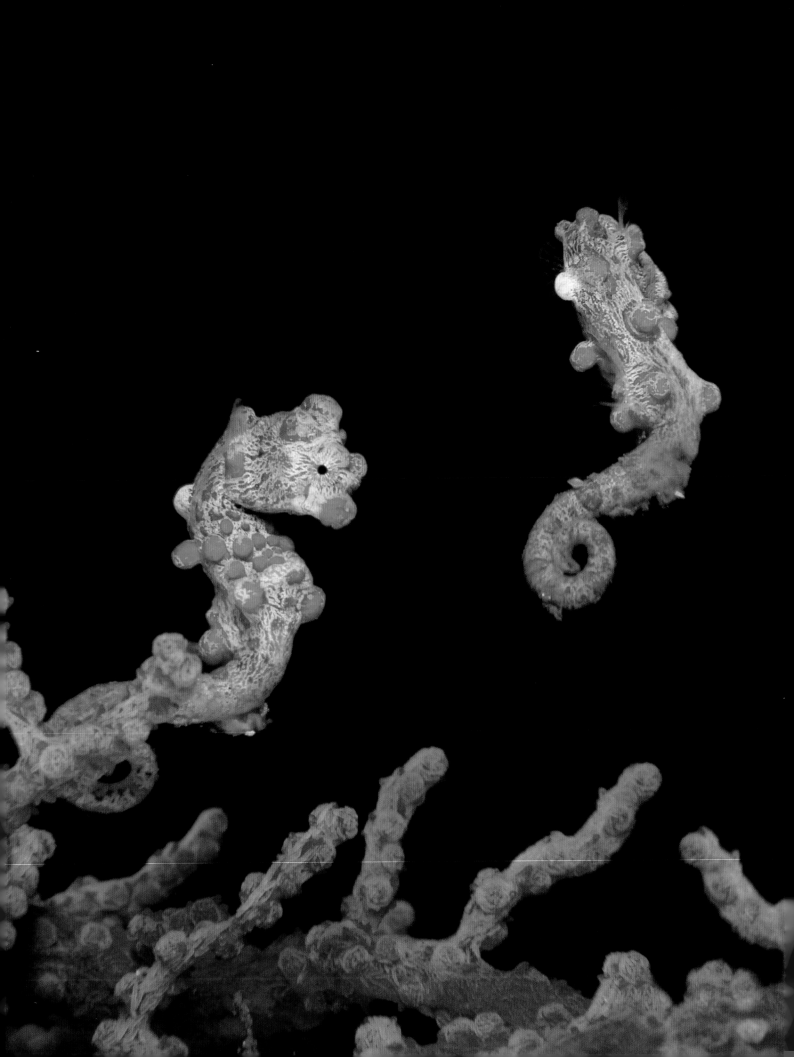

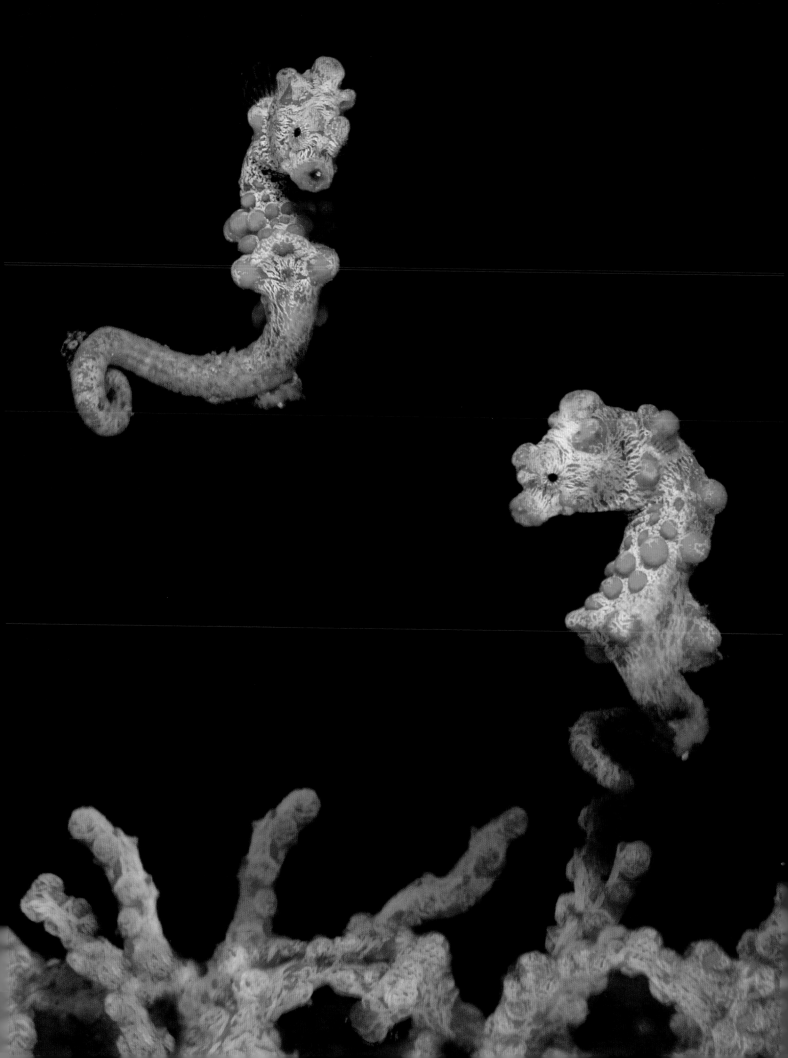

appeared in 1951 and a further volume, *Under the Red Sea*, was published the following year. Hans and Lotte became household names when the BBC had a major success with the television series *Diving to Adventure* in 1956.

Just ten years after his first experiments, Cousteau saw that diving had become all too easy for those who followed him. "Today, a decade after our hesitant penetration of the one hundred and thirty foot zone," he wrote in 1952, "women and old men reach that depth on their third or fourth dive." Cousteau admits to ambivalent feelings about this new phenomenon, particularly while watching a certain Monsieur Dubois renting out an aqualung along the Riviera during the summer: "Hundreds of people put on the lung and plunge confidently," he observes. "Recalling the ominous struggles [we] had, my pride in Monsieur Dubois's outfit is not unmixed with resentment."[20]

In February 1953 *The Silent World* was first published, collated from the logs that Cousteau and Dumas had kept since their first early experiments. The book charted the development of the 'aqualung diving apparatus', according to the publisher's foreword in the first British edition, breathlessly declaring that "this self-contained device, with which Captain Cousteau himself has made more than a thousand dives, enables a nearly naked man, without lines to the surface, to swim down to 300 feet and stay under for up to two hours at a time."[21] Worldwide sales went on to exceed five million copies.

Scuba was becoming increasingly popular, and most divers and scientists were making the transition from old-fashioned, tethered diving. Veteran oceanographer Sylvia Earle, who went on to log many thousands of hours underwater, took her first dive using a copper diving helmet, borrowed from a friend's father. Aged just sixteen, she went down into the waters of a Florida river, "a venture I looked forward to with pleasure spiced with fear." The experience left her enraptured: "For twenty blissful minutes," she declared, "I became one with the river and its residents, bending with the current, blending in – and breathing!"[22] The following year, while enrolled in a marine biology class at Florida State University, Earle got her first chance to try scuba gear. She soon discovered the joys of underwater weightlessness:

> *I hovered, blending with the sea like a jellyfish and then, inspired by the athletic grace of every other creature in sight, tried something I imagined to be impossible: a midwater slow-motion back flip. No problem! Forward, then soaring, rolling, swimming upside down, then a spin. The fish were almost certainly perplexed by the large mass thrashing about in their midst, but in my mind I was dolphinlike.*[23]

Earle was not alone in her excitement. People responded in their thousands to the new wonders of breathing underwater. The first public diver education programme was developed in 1954 by diving pioneer Al Tillman and his fellow Los Angeles County employee Bev Morgan; it later became a model for diving certification in the US. In Britain the first diving courses were being operated by a maverick ex-RAF officer, Captain Trevor Hampton, who claimed he could train recruits to the navy's standards of 'frogging'

Ⓚ ORANGUTAN CRAB (MANADO, INDONESIA)

Ⓔ FROMIA STARFISH (RAS MUHAMMED, EGYPT)

Ⓔ SWALLOW REEF REFLECTIONS. (SHARM EL SHEIKH, EGYPT)

"It was all a bit daft. They were all headed for Wetropolis, with divers living in these underwater bungalows and they'd just trot out to feed the caged fish outside the front door..."

Professor Trevor Norton

at his dive school in Warfleet Creek, near Dartmouth in the West Country. Reg Vallintine, who in his turn went on to become a well-known national instructor, was among those trained by Hampton. "He put you down on your first dive straight into the sea, alone – but with a line to the surface," Reg told me. "His motto was 'Keep some energy in reserve and come back slowly to the surface: if you can do that, you'll probably come back alive'."

Vallintine later became a director of the British Sub-Aqua Club (BSAC), which was formed in 1953. The first issues of its magazine, *Neptune*, appeared in 1954 and just two years later it had two thousand members.

By the middle of the 1950s around 25,000–30,000 sets of equipment had been sold worldwide, with at least three-quarters of these being sold in California. The first series of *Sea Hunt* aired on US television, starring Lloyd Bridges as Mike Nelson, underwater adventurer; it ran for over 150 episodes. In 1959 the YMCA began the first nationally organised course for diver certification in the US, and in 1960 Al Tillman was instrumental in founding the National Association of Underwater Instructors (NAUI).

Dreams beneath the sea

The 1960s is better known as the decade of space exploration, but it was also a key period in ocean exploration. In 1960 Jacques Picard and Don Walsh descended 10,868 metres (35,830 feet) in the bathyscape *Trieste* to the deepest point of the world's oceans, the Marianas Trench. At the beginning of the decade there were just three manned deep submersibles – by 1970 this figure had grown to nearly fifty.

There were also numerous experiments involving divers living in underwater habitats, such as Ed Link's pioneering attempt off Villefranche in the South of France in 1962, and Cousteau's Conshelf experiments, which included the Diogenes project off Marseilles and, later, his more ambitious Starfish House at Shaab Rumi in the Sudanese Red Sea. Set on the seabed at ten metres (33 feet), Starfish House had an annexe, the Deep Cabin, at 27 metres (88 feet). A US Navy Captain, George Bond, also undertook various experiments in which volunteers lived in a pressurized container for a fortnight. Eventually, more than fifty undersea habitats were built around the world.

Alina Szmant, now Professor of Biology at the University of North Carolina Wilmington, was a researcher in several undersea habitats, including Tektite II in the 1970s and Hydrolab in the 1980s, both in the Virgin Islands. Tektite II, with its television, hot showers and carpets, was considered fairly luxurious. Hydrolab, though rather more basic, had something unique: underwater loudspeakers to provide music to the scientists working on the reef outside. As Alina explained to me, it also had no toilet, so you had to take a hookah, or air pipe, and swim outside if you needed to go:

I remember there was some kind of harp music playing and I was swimming out there with just a diving mask and the hookah belt – there was no inside toilet so that's how we went to the bathroom. It was incredible, this feeling of swimming out there naked with this beautiful music playing underwater – it was very existential!

Underwater habitats allowed scientists to carry out intensive work at depths they wouldn't have otherwise been able to maintain for such long periods. Alina Szmant recalls the sensation of being *inside* an aquarium, with the fish looking in through the portholes at the scientists. Sylvia Earle was similarly taken with the poetic possibilities of life underwater while in Tektite:

On full-moon nights, silhouettes of large, sleek predators – amberjack and tarpon – arched and turned, silver on silver, attracted to the clouds of small fish who in turn were attracted to the hordes of minute crustacea drawn to the lights of the habitat. Sometimes scientific detachment was put aside in favour of joining in the exuberant rush of fins and scales, not as predator, but as an active witness and benign participant in the ebb and flow of life.[24]

Scientists dreamed of living underwater. Even William Beebe mused about how people would tend their undersea gardens, with future hosts and hostesses taking their guests "to row with them off-shore, put on helmets, dive, and inspect at leisure the new coral plantings and beds which a seascape gardener has lately arranged."[25] But Professor Trevor Norton, an authority on scientific diving and author of *Stars Beneath the Sea*, says that these were just pipe dreams. "It was all a bit daft," he told me. "They were all headed for Wetropolis, with divers living in these underwater bungalows, and they'd just trot out to feed the caged fish outside the front door, scoop up some manganese nodules off the seabed, and then inspect the oilrig."

The logistics and expense of supporting static structures on the seabed eventually made them untenable, and scarcely a handful remain today. One of these is now a small underwater hotel, the Jules Verne Lodge in Florida, where you can pretend to be an aquanaut for a night or two. A new generation of underwater buildings is being created, but they're connected to the surface: the world's first all-glass underwater restaurant opened at the Hilton

resort on Rangalifinolhu island in the Maldives in 2005, and a German entrepreneur, Joachim Hauser, has announced ambitious plans for a huge underwater hotel complex called Hydropolis, which is to be built five kilometres (three miles) offshore from the Gulf state of Dubai.

As a teenager Jean-Michel Cousteau had witnessed his father's team beat all records by occupying Starfish House for a whole month, and by staying for one entire week in the Deep Cabin. He decided to study architecture because he reckoned more and more people would be living underwater, and he worked in the St-Nazaire naval shipyards to gain some experience of marine architecture. Alas, submersibles and remote-operated vehicles (ROVs) took over from fixed habitats. "I had all the necessary knowledge to build cities underwater," recalls Jean-Michel, "but I'm still waiting for my first client." He now believes the era of underwater habitats has passed:

Although we will explore more and more underwater, basically we're land animals. We have no reason to settle on the seabed unless it's for research and eventually, in the somewhat distant future, mining. There aren't going to be villages underwater – we like the sun, we don't want to go all wrinkly from living underwater.

NEON TRIPLEFIN ON PINK SPONGE. (LEMBEH STRAIT, INDONESIA) ⓘ

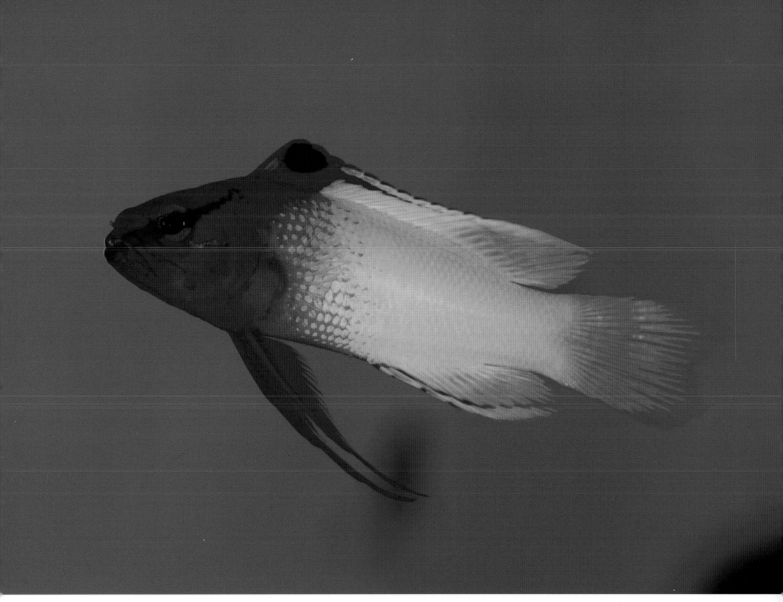

⊕ A FAIRY BASSLET DARTS INTO OPEN WATER AT MAGGIE'S MAZE, GRAND CAYMAN.

But getting wrinkly for an hour or so was growing enormously in popularity during the 1960s, a trend that was accelerated by the creation of the Professional Association of Dive Instructors (PADI) in 1966. Founders John Cronin and Ralph Ericson designed an open water diving course with just 32 hours of instruction, and in 1967, its first full year of operation, PADI trained 3,226 divers.

Lambasted by die-hards as the McDonalds of diving, PADI nonetheless opened up scuba diving as a recreational sport to the general public and helped turn it into the worldwide industry that it is today. The PADI system of standardised modules divided into the theory and practice of diving ranges from entry-level through to advanced courses and instructor certificates. By 2005, PADI had issued more than fourteen million certifications, and it's estimated that the organisation now trains more than half of the world's divers through 4,300 PADI dive centres worldwide.

Before Certification

Although PADI and BSAC were becoming well established, in the 1960s and 1970s there were still plenty of divers just taking the plunge with bits of homemade kit and little or no training. Renowned fish behaviour specialist Ned DeLoach was one of them. Raised in south-west Texas, he had been on the college swimming team, but he had no scuba training whatsoever when he decided to give it a go while on holiday in Cozumel, Mexico, in 1967. "We just went down there, rented the gear, and went overboard," he explained to me. "I remember one of us out of the group of three had a depth gauge and we immediately went down to 30–34 metres, like everybody had to do in those days – I mean you weren't diving if you were above 30 metres."

Ned was lucky enough to be diving on Palancar Reef before divers had really discovered Cozumel:

We were on Palancar, which is probably one of the most beautiful of all the reefs in the Caribbean, we had visibility which must have been around 60 metres, we saw Jewfish which must have been 400 pounds and I remember thinking 'Wow! this is better than I thought it would be – I can't wait until I get to the good stuff!' Little did I know I was in the good stuff!

He and his college buddies ended up going all the way to Central America, hitch-hiking their way in search of dive sites. "It was quite a memorable trip," he says. "Most of the time we were free diving and 'of course' spear-fishing, as everyone did in those days."

Another diver who plunged in at the deep end was German author and photographer Helmut Debelius. He was a keen snorkeller when he went on holiday to the Canary Islands, where he took his first dive on Christmas Eve 1972. "I was down at 40 metres with this beautiful false coral with the long polyps, that impressed me very much," he recalls. Astonishingly, this wasn't even part of a dive course: it was Helmut's 'try dive'. "They did that then," he explains. "Today I would be a little scared, but then I was crazy: I couldn't get deep enough." Debelius survived this experience and has spent the last thirty years publishing field guides to the marine life of the Red Sea, Indian Ocean and elsewhere.

Cousteau's television films were an inspiration for a whole generation of divers, among them Charles Hood, now senior correspondent of Britain's *Dive* magazine. He started out by snorkelling in Kuwait, where his family was based, and then a Navy colleague of his father's gave him a small cylinder and told him as he went into the water 'don't go deeper than nine metres, your air will run out before you get decompression sickness." "That was my training!" says Charles. "There wasn't a lot to see but it was tremendous fun being able to stay down rather than snorkel. It was the Cousteau era and you felt very much part of it, and very privileged because very few people dived in those days."

Not everyone's first dive, of course, goes entirely according to plan. Diving journalist John Bantin, formerly a commercial photographer, recalls his first immersion in Antigua. Despite not knowing how to swim, he decided to give diving a go while killing time on a photo shoot waiting for the weather to clear. "I had lots of difficulties with water filling my mask and so forth," he told me, "but the instructors said 'don't worry - it'll be easy in the sea'." The experience proved eventful:

The next day I found myself in the sea, at 30 metres deep, in a cave, with a nurse shark. I thought 'bloody hell, this is a shark!' I wasn't sure, having never seen one before – and of course sharks ate people in those days, back in the 1970s. Then I ran out of air, so I had to do a bit of a quick swim back, and got told off for it. "Why did you swim back to the surface, it's not necessary – I have plenty of air!" said the instructor. So I would have been sharing air with him, in the cave, at 30 metres, with the shark – on my first dive.

Despite this inauspicious start, he hasn't stopped diving since and now logs hundreds of dives annually on assignment for Britain's *Diver* magazine. "I never get bored with diving," says Bantin. "The world is as varied underwater as it is on the surface."

The scuba boom

At a congress in Barcelona in 1970 the Confédération Mondiale des Activités Sousmarines (CMAS – the nearest thing there was to a world governing body at the time) adopted the system of internationally accepted hand signals, which all divers use today. During the following decade there were significant advances relating to dive safety, such as the adoption of certification cards to indicate a minimum level of training, a switch to single-hose regulators as standard, and the widespread use of the BCD – or buoyancy control device.

The first generation of truly recreational divers also began to show more of an interest in seeing fish alive rather than impaled on the end of a spear. It wasn't until 1980, though, that the BSAC formally adopted a motion that it would no longer support spearfishing competitions.

"There'll probably be a particular moment when you realise you're hooked, when the marine world has got you in its grip."

"Thirty feet down, I stayed put... and then it suddenly sank in: I am underwater and breathing!"

Sylvia Earle

In America, advances in diver safety included the launching in 1980 of a national telephone help-line to give divers access to a diving medicine specialist twenty-four hours a day. Originally called the National Diving Network, it was re-christened the Diver's Alert Network (DAN) in 1983. Today this non-profit organisation has over 200,000 members and still provides round-the-clock assistance to divers and as well as promoting diving safety through research and education.

The first commercially available electronic dive computer was the Orca Edge, introduced in 1983. Now used by almost everybody in recreational and technical diving, dive computers have taken over the functions of decompression tables and conventional dive planners in working out your dive profiles and surface intervals and making other critical safety calculations. They are indispensable if you're diving more than once a day and indeed computers are now usually compulsory on most live-aboard dive boats.

Throughout the 1980s and 1990s scuba diving boomed alongside the growth in international air travel and the development of dive centres in tropical destinations with coral reefs. New developments and improvements in the sport, including the uses of gases other than air (such as Nitrox), were eagerly taken up by the diving public.

Underwater photography and video continued to be popular, but their appeal remained largely a minority interest due to the skill levels required and the high costs involved. That all changed at the beginning of this century with the introduction of digital underwater cameras. Smaller, cheaper and more lightweight than their traditional counterparts, digital cameras have also taken most of the guesswork out of snapping our favourite fishes.

Rebreathers, which prolong the time you can spend underwater by recycling your exhaled air, have also entered the mainstream in the last few years. But whatever advances technology can offer today's diver, from fancy fins to wing-style BCDs, the essential principle remains the same as it was for the pioneers of scuba: namely, strapping a tank on your back and getting underwater for an hour or so of fun.

Once bitten

Any diver can tell you of that one magical moment when you first realize that you're hooked; when the marine world has you in its grip. It could be your first Spanish Dancer on a night dive, an eagle ray gliding past, a shipwreck looming out of the blue or the thrill of your first shark. It could be just the utter sense of freedom, floating in the deep blue – or it could be a shared moment with your dive buddy, as the two of you witness something extraordinary, seen by nobody else.

These peak experiences are what set diving apart from other sports, lifting us from the realms of the everyday into the celestial, and gaining a deeper sense of our own humanity in the process. They bring a sense of privilege, stemming sometimes from a magnificent display of nature in the raw and sometimes simply from the joy of being alive, at this moment, underwater. Few people, once initiated, can resist the siren call of the underwater world, and with millions of recreational scuba divers enjoying the sport today, its allure is clearly stronger than ever. "Once you have a taste of the ocean," says Trevor Norton, "the intoxication lasts a lifetime."[26]

"These peak experiences are what set diving apart from other sports, lifting us occasionally out of the realms of the everyday and into the celestial – touching nature in the raw, and gaining a deeper sense of our own humanity in the process."

A SCHOOL OF BOHAR SNAPPERS AT RAS MUHAMMED, EGYPT.

A LARGE SCHOOL OF BOHAR SNAPPER GATHERS EACH JUNE AT RAS MUHAMMAD TO SPAWN.

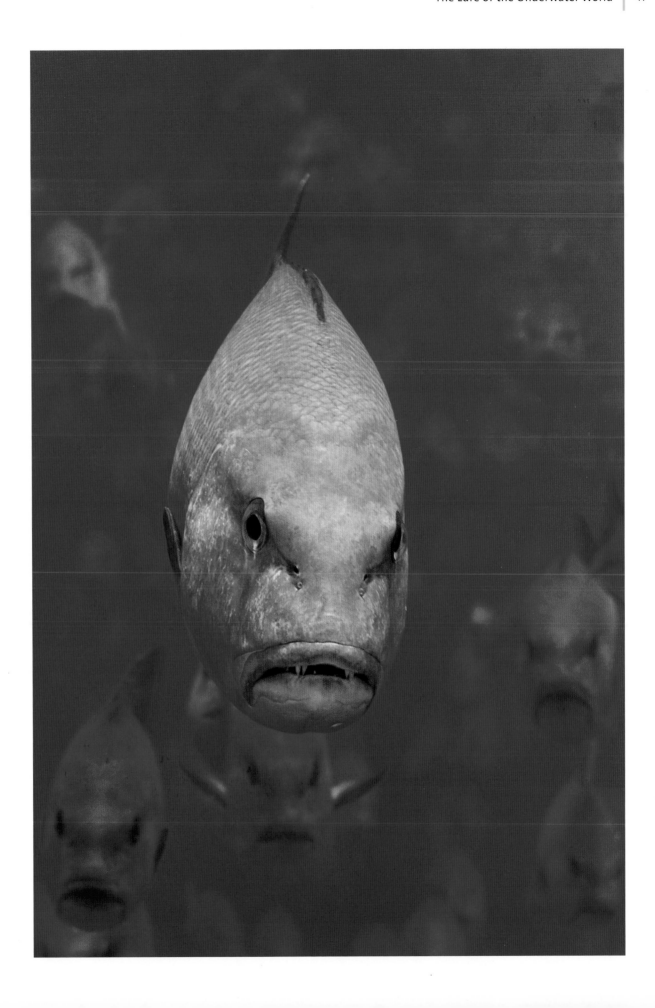

underwater landscapes:
where we dive

*"How inappropriate to call this planet Earth,
when quite clearly it is Ocean."* **Arthur C. Clarke**

STEPPING OFF THE BACK OF A DIVE BOAT AND DESCENDING THROUGH A CLEAR BLUE TROPICAL SEA, ALL I CAN SEE BENEATH ME IS WHAT LOOKS LIKE A SERIES OF UNDULATING BROWN HILLS ON THE SEABED SOME 15 METRES (49 FEET) BELOW. BUT AS I GET CLOSER, COLOURS AND FORMS START TO MATERIALISE AND THE UNMISTAKABLE OUTLINES OF A CORAL REEF TAKE SHAPE. HERE ARE THE BRIGHT BLUE FINGERS OF AN *ACROPORA* CORAL, GREEN MOUNDS OF *PORITES* CORAL AND THE CONVOLUTED CONTOURS OF A BRAIN CORAL. THERE ARE GIANT CLAMS NESTLING BETWEEN THE CORALS, AND VIVID SPONGES COLONISING OTHER SURFACES. SEA WHIPS AND BUSHY GORGONIANS WAVE GENTLY BACK AND FORTH IN THE CURRENTS.

As I go deeper, the inhabitants of this undersea garden begin to reveal themselves: blue-and-silver fusiliers hovering in shoals just off the reef; pairs of butterflyfish flitting coquettishly between the corals; a moray eel slithering stealthily between coral outcrops.

The current propels me gently over the reeftop. Below me, a tumble of corals covers the reef slope like a shantytown, its communities teeming with inhabitants at every level. As I peer down at all the different strata of fish society, it strikes me, yet again, how privileged I am to have been born in the age of recreational scuba. This amazing spectacle is something that previous generations can only have dreamed about.

The world of the reef

Coral reefs are the best known of many diving environments, and for both Alex Mustard – who took the remarkable photographs in this book – and myself, they remain a firm favourite. Their popularity is hardly surprising, given that the colour and exuberance of a healthy coral reef makes it surely one of the most glorious sights on the planet. Today, there are dive centres in most regions with reefs, and dive tourism is now well established in over 90 countries worldwide.[1] Alex has no doubts about the attractions of reefs:

Coral reefs are, in my opinion, the finest environment for observing wildlife on the planet. Not only are the animals painted from the most staggering palette of colours, there are so many of them packed densely into every ecological niche on the reef. Reefs reward you on every level: at first they're a kaleidoscope of confusing colours; then you get to know the critters and appreciate more what's going on down there.

Ⓔ RED ROPE SPONGE AT BABYLON, GRAND CAYMAN.

Once you start to dig deeper into their behaviour you soon realise that the kind of things reef animals get up to is even more fascinating than what they look like. There's always something new to see.

Coral reefs are among the world's most ancient ecosystems, having first emerged more than 200 million years ago. These beautiful, labyrinthine structures are, amazingly, built out of limestone deposited by living creatures, the most important of which are hard (or 'stony') corals. They are built to last: most of today's reefs have developed over the last 5,000 to 10,000 years, with a few thought to be more than two million years old.

So what kind of creature is coral? Well, confusingly, it is part animal, part plant. The ones we see underwater in the shape of tables, boulders, branches and so forth are actually colonies of thousands and thousands of tiny, individual animals called coral polyps. These are pretty simple animals: each one little more than a short tube with a ring of tentacles around its mouth at one end and a primitive stomach in the middle. They sit on their own limestone skeletons, into which they retreat by day.

At night corals emerge from their skeletons to feed on microscopic marine organisms called zooplankton. Their tentacles are armed with stinging nematocysts – coiled, thread-like filaments that shoot out like barbed darts to paralyse and capture the drifting plankton. *The Diver's Universe* suggests a trick with a torch that allows you to watch this process in action:

Hold the light steady for a few seconds to attract a concentration of planktonic creatures. Then move the light with the plankton cloud towards the open polyps without touching them and watch the corals gorge! The tiny tentacles grab at the miniature morsels just as effectively and relentlessly as those of the big sea anemones.[2]

FISH SCHOOLS CAN BE SO THICK THAT THEY
COMPLETELY OBSCURE THE REEF BELOW. (ARI ATOLL, MALDIVES)

"*Coral reefs are the finest environment for observing wildlife on the planet – not only are the animals painted from the most staggering palette of colours, but they're also packed in like sardines.*"

Alex Mustard

This elaborate mechanism only accounts for a tiny portion (around two per cent) of the polyp's needs – but the zooplankton contains important nutritional compounds for the coral's growth. The rest of the polyp's food comes from a form of algae, called zooxanthellae, which live within the coral tissue. Invisible to the human eye, zooxanthellae live on the carbon dioxide and nitrogen produced as waste by the coral polyp: like other plants, they harness sunlight in order to photosynthesize organic compounds and convert them into carbohydrates and oxygen. This is a symbiotic relationship: the polyp uses the excess carbohydrates to make calcium carbonate or limestone (a process known as calcification), and with this builds the stony corallite skeleton in which it lives; the zooxanthellae, in turn, gain important nutrients and find a safe home in the coral's tissues from herbivorous predators. A microscopic look at a coral polyp would reveal several million zooxanthellae in just one square inch of coral; it's these that add the colour to transparent coral tissue.

Reef-building

In Osha Gray Davidson's evocative natural history of coral reefs, *The Enchanted Braid*, he explains that this strange 'animal-plant' should really be called an 'animal-plant-mineral' because each of the three elements (coral, zooxanthellae and corallite) plays a critical role in the survival of the others:

> *Nowhere in nature are the three basic elements of the planet woven together in such close fashion – nor with such spectacular results. The coral polyp – this diminutive and deceptively simple creature, this enchanted braid of animal, mineral and vegetable – is responsible for the largest biogenic (made by living organisms) formation on the planet and the most complex ecosystem in the sea: the coral reef.* 3

Coral colonies grow at different rates, depending on factors such as water temperatures, turbidity, salinity and so forth. The slowest are the massive corals, which grow between five and 25 millimetres per year. The quickest are the branching and staghorn corals, which can add 20 centimetres (eight inches) per year – ten times faster than the massive corals, although they break more easily. Building a reef can take centuries, a fact which was appreciated by Darwin: "We feel surprise when travellers tell us of the vast

dimensions of the Pyramids and other great ruins," he noted, "but how utterly insignificant are the greatest of these, when compared to these mountains of stone accumulated by the agency of various minute and tender animals!" 4

Hard or stony corals, also known as hermatypic corals, are the main architects of the reef. Soft (or ahermatypic) corals don't usually have resident zooxanthellae and therefore can't secrete enough limestone to build reefs. Instead of creating a stony skeleton, soft corals – such as sea whips and sea fingers – develop horny, protein-based cores and look more like trees or bushes. They tend to thrive in areas with plenty of currents, extending their tentacles to feed on passing plankton.

Where reefs grow

Coral reefs will only grow in warm, shallow and clear water. They need sunlight in order for the zooxanthellae to function, so they won't grow in muddy estuaries or sediment-rich seas, and rarely develop at depths of below 50 metres (160 feet). Ideally, corals prefer a temperature of around 26 to 27 degrees Celsius (79 to 80 degrees Fahrenheit). These conditions mean they mostly grow within the tropics, although they do also grow where warm currents flow out further from the equator: the Gulf Stream allows reef growth around Florida and the Kuroshio current creates similar conditions around southern Japan. Corals aren't the only reef builders, though: calcareous algae, forams (amoeba-like organisms with shells), solid sponges, and molluscs such as giant clams all contribute to these amazing structures. Film-maker Howard Hall is equally at home in kelp forests and in the cold waters of British Columbia but coral reefs, he says, are something special:

> *What I like most about coral reefs is that the enormous biodiversity found in coral habitats has precipitated really dramatic specialisation. Many of the animals have evolved into really weird morphologies and have come to exhibit very bizarre behavioural strategies. Capturing these unusual behaviours on film or video is fascinating and great fun.*

Coral reefs are found in over 100 countries worldwide, the main areas being the Indian Ocean, the Pacific Ocean, the Caribbean, the Red Sea and the Arabian Gulf. The richest reefs are in the Indo-Pacific: of the 700 or so corals known in the world, 600 occur in this region. Sometimes

up to several hundred corals can occur on a single reef in South-east Asia.

Covering a total area of around 284,000 square kilometers (111,000 square miles), reefs are one of the most biologically rich ecosystems on the planet and, collectively, are believed to harbour more than a million marine species. Around a quarter of all the oceans' fishes spawn, feed, grow, fight and flee among the labyrinths of nature's most dazzling aquarium. "The relationships between the teeming organisms of the coral reef are among the most complex of any on the planet," writes Davidson. "Coral reefs are the Russian novels of the sea world, full of passion and avarice, convoluted and interweaving story lines, and colourful characters by the dozens." 5

Not forgetting sex, of course. Most of the big corals you see on a reef reproduce themselves in a mass orgy, which takes place just once a year in one of the most astounding acts of synchronicity in the natural world. Trillions of eggs and sperm are simultaneously released into the water during these events. Incredibly, it wasn't until 1982 that this phenomenon was discovered, and since then, scientists have been amazed to find that 85 per cent of corals studied are spawners. "Corals are animals, but they do spend most of their year making a damn fine impression of a rock," comments Alex, "so it's wonderful to dive on that one night when they're spawning and realise that they are living creatures after all."

Life and death strategies

It's the sheer complexity of reefs and the mesmerising combinations of animals, colours, shapes and scenery that pull us back again and again. "Dive a healthy coral reef and you are witnessing a complex animal interaction that has been going on unabated for millions of years," says diving journalist John Bantin. "From the tiniest coral polyp to the most magnificent whaleshark, it's all there." There is always something new to discover, some weird creature or wonderful scenario you haven't previously spotted. "I love seeing things that I have never seen before," says photographer Cathy Church. "Just the other day on Cayman, where I have dived for 37 years, I saw a tiny nudibranch that I hadn't come across before," she adds. "I am curious about everything down there, and it's a place where you can dive forever and still not get it all."

"Nowhere in nature are the three basic elements of the planet woven together in such close fashion – nor with such spectacular results. The coral polyp – this diminutive and deceptively simple creature, this enchanted braid of animal, mineral and vegetable – is responsible for the largest biogenic formation on the planet and the most complex ecosystem in the sea: the coral reef"

Osha Gray Davidson

With so much packed into such a concentrated ecosystem, competition for space on the reef is intense. Corals, sponges and algae are all fighting for surfaces on which to settle and grow. Corals also have to compete among themselves for the available space: two corals may appear to be living happily side by side on the reef, but in reality they're engaged in a marathon (albeit slow-motion) struggle, which may have been going on for centuries.

Marine animals defend themselves and their territories with an impressive armoury of techniques. Poison is a common weapon. The stinging nematocysts of corals are used not only to capture food but also to ward off enemies. They can even give the unwary diver a painful injury, which is just one of many reasons why we shouldn't touch corals).

Numerous other species, from starfish and sponges to lionfish and sea anemones, use chemical warfare to protect themselves from predators. Because the toxins are diluted by vast amounts of seawater they have to be incredibly powerful. The Blue-ringed Octopus, for instance, is only the size of golf ball but produces enough venom in its saliva to kill a human being within minutes.

If you're carrying chemical weapons it makes sense to advertise the fact – after all, they wouldn't be much use if your predator only finds out that you're poisonous after having eaten you. Seaslugs are, literally, brilliant at advertising their toxicity, coating themselves in gorgeously flamboyant colours that shout 'poisonous – not edible!' Being totally blind, they use their colours only for deterring predators. But other creatures use bright colours to send various messages to their own kind, such as what sex they

Warning colours underwater are often similar to those on land: for instance, yellow and black stripes and spots (think bees and wasps) are used to good effect by the Valentine Pufferfish. And those without nasty weapons of their own can always improvise: hermit crabs, for instance, will attach stinging anemones to their shells, and as they grow larger and move into new shells they will often transfer their anemones from the old one.

Body armour – like that of the turtle, the Queen Conch, the Giant Triton or the Crown-of-thorns Starfish – provides another defence against being eaten. And those without any can create a personal fortress by hiding inside some part of the reef structure where their predators can't reach.

Hide and Seek

Camouflage is another popular strategy for escaping detection – as much for predators as prey, of course, since it often helps to remain hidden when you're trying to capture your lunch. Some of the best camouflage artists, including scorpionfishes, frogfishes and flounders, are ambush predators. Flounders can match the colours and patterns of their surroundings within seconds of settling in a new location. (Other fish take longer – up to a week or so in the case of Ghost Pipefish.) Frogfish adapt to their new environment within hours, their colour patterns and shapes mimicking whatever surface they've settled

A *HYPSELODORIS BULLOCKII* NUDIBRANCH, OR SEASLUG, ADVERTISES IT.

⬆ A FLAMBOYANT CUTTLEFISH CRAWLS ACROSS THE SEABED WITH AN EMPEROR SHRIMP. (LEMBEH STRAIT, INDONESIA)

⬇ THE MIMIC FILEFISH AVOIDS PREDATORS BY IMITATING THE POISONOUS VALENTINE PUFFERFISH. (MANADO, INDONESIA)

on, from Sargassum weed to sponges. Even experienced divers find frogfish hard to spot, but one animal that never fail to amuse is the trumpetfish, which stalks its prey by hanging in a head-down, vertical position among branching gorgonians or sponges.

Living in close association with a particular part of the reef can also be helpful: Slender Filefish, for instance, blend in impeccably among the branches of gorgonians or algal bushes, and small gobies become nearly invisible against the backdrop of the soft corals where they like to hide. Another camouflage artist is the tiny Pygmy Seahorse, which can match its host seafan in both colour and texture. In fact, this species was only discovered by accident when marine biologists collecting seafans found the seahorses among their branches.

The true masters of disguise, however, are octopuses and cuttlefish, which have had to evolve this ability because their lack of an external skeleton leaves them extremely vulnerable to attack. Both can alter their appearance in an instant by manipulating a sophisticated range of coloured skin patches. By contracting their muscles to squeeze pigment through the skin cells, they can change colour, pattern and texture in order to blend seamlessly into the background. Although often compared to chameleons, they are in fact far more sophisticated: chameleons change colour with mood, whereas octopuses and cuttlefish change theirs at will whenever they move into a different environment.

The amazing thing about reefs is that these body types have remained virtually unchanged for around 50 million years. We know this because of an incredible collection of fish fossils found near a small mountain village in northern Italy called Monte Bolca. Some 227 species from 80 families have been described from these rocks, and today's coral reef-fish community hardly differs from them at all. A snapshot in time preserved in limestone, the Bolca fishes even show the same species schooling in groups as their descendants do today. It's a humbling thought that *Homo sapiens* has only evolved within the last 200,000 years – a mere drop in the ocean compared to the 50 million years for which coral reefs have been functioning.

The reef by night

A coral reef at night is a strange place. Some divers are passionate about night diving, and go whenever the opportunity arises. Others don't like it at all, finding it disori-

entating to be down in the dark with their field of vision reduced to the sweep of an underwater torch beam and who knows what else lurking unseen beyond. Either way, the reef is just as busy by night as it is by day, only with a different cast on the stage.

In the late 1960s Cousteau was on another expedition aboard *Calypso*, this time down through the Red Sea and exploring the Maldives, Seychelles and Madagascar. "There are laws here, and secrets," he remarked of the reef on this trip, "but they are not the laws and secrets of the world above." It was during the hours of darkness that he found the reef most intriguing:

Under our lights, coral tentacles wave about, forming halos around sea fans and on the downy branches of the madreporarians. Some of the Alcyonium swell up in the darkness, sometimes quadrupling their size to form plump, transparent, pink tree shapes in which their mouths are clearly visible. These nighttime dives into the coral world teach us a great deal by showing us a new aspect of what we see during the day. For marine life exhibits, in those magic hours of darkness, the fullness of its wealth. [6]

"Corals are animals, but they do spend most of their year making a damn fine impression of a rock. It's wonderful to dive on that one night when they're spawning and see them so alive."

Alex Mustard

⬆ WHITE TIP REEF SHARKS COME UP ONTO MAAYA THILA, IN ARI ATOLL
IN THE MALDIVES, TO HUNT SLEEPING FUSILIERS AT NIGHT.

Some people still can't bear the thought of being underwater in the dark, Hans Hass among them. "I admit frankly that diving by night fills me with fear," he confesses in *Conquest of the Underwater World*. "We made our first such descent in 1954 in the Caribbean, where we dived on a reef with five-kilowatt floodlights," he wrote. "I knew this reef like the back of my hand, but at night everything was changed; we saw only the narrow cone illuminated by the floodlights and were completely surrounded by pitch black." The darkness became menacing: "We knew how sharks behave by day, but who could know what came out of the depths by night?" [7]

But Hans and Lotte found nothing more threatening than snoozing parrotfish: "We swam through the reef with the floodlights and looked at fish sleeping peacefully on the seabed. We got so close to many of them that we could touch them with our hands," recalled Hass. "Other denizens of the sea which we hardly ever saw by day had now left their hiding places and were moving busily about the seabed," he observed. Despite emerging from this ordeal-by-parrotfish unscathed, Hass could not overcome his unease with night diving: "Unless I can see around me clearly my imagination tends to run wild," he admitted.

Howard Hall, writing about the shooting of his new documentary *Deep Sea 3D* (2006), the long-awaited sequel to his phenomenal 1994 IMAX film *Into the Deep*, confesses to a feeling of unease as his team manoeuvred 700kg (1,500lb) of equipment into place to film squid off San Marcos Island, California:

Diving at night is most disquieting when you're in the open sea hanging far above the ocean floor many fathoms beyond diving range, and even more forbidding when the water is murky. You feel exposed hanging in the dark murk, easily disoriented, largely blind, and knowing that all sorts of creatures with more sophisticated senses are watching from below. [8]

Lonely Planet publisher Tony Wheeler is one of those who can't get enough of night diving. "I've never done a night dive I've been disappointed in," he told me. "They've always been something special for me." One favourite night dive was off Heron Island, Australia:

a number of cuttlefish and turtles. I've met turtles fairly regularly at Heron but several at night definitely felt unusual. Plus we had a White-tip Reef Shark coming by for a look. All in all it was a busy and interesting dive but it was the bull ray which just came right by us, as if we weren't there, which was the high point. We all came back afterwards and just said 'wow'!

Newcomers to night diving will find that it's always a good idea to go back to a reef that you're already familiar with – say a dive site you've visited earlier that day. You'll be familiar with the topography and therefore much more relaxed about diving in the dark. You'll also have a much better idea about what to look for and where. Dive sites with minimum wave and current action are ideal.

Reef topography

Thirty yards behind me the bow of the yacht was attached to the shallow mooring, but the stern diving platform had drifted over the edge of the perpendicular reef wall which plummeted into the abyss. Six thousand feet of blue water. At the edge of my vision I could just make out the wall, its sheer vertical face of coral plunging downwards, a mass of life hanging out over the depths, fish moving between its plant growth, and who knew what ready to swim up its face from the reaches of the ocean. [9]

Tim Ecott's classic description of a wall dive off Little Cayman captures that wonderful sensation of drifting out over the reef edge to be confronted with the dizzying magic of a coral wall. If you're in a relaxed, comfortable frame of mind, the experience can flood your mind with endorphins, creating a natural high that is further enhanced by your weightlessness. No wonder people pay good money for their fix of wall diving.

Reef walls generally occur where reefs are growing on the edge of an ocean trench such as – in the case above – the Cayman Trench. The Red Sea, famous for its wall diving, is the northern extremity of the Great Rift Valley, a geologi-

FLOATING ABOVE
A COLOURFUL REEF
IN THE STRAIT OF
TIRAN, RED SEA.

⬆ DIGITAL CAMERAS HAVE MADE UNDERWATER PHOTOGRAPHY AVAILABLE TO EVERYONE. (SOUTH MALE ATOLL, MALDIVES)

There are many other types of reef. The simplest are fringing reefs, which grow on shelving coastlines. These are often separated from the shoreline by a shallow lagoon, and because they are so near the surface, they are among the prettiest and easiest for snorkelling, free-diving and shallow scuba dives. Eugenie Clark recalls 'goggling' at Shark's Bay, just south of Hurghada in the Red Sea, where the desert shore slopes straight down to a short fringing reef. "My first look at this unusually gorgeous reef is still a vivid picture in my mind," she wrote. "You could see a thousand fishes at a glance." 10

Barrier reefs are found further offshore and rise from a deeper base than fringing reefs, often growing along the edge of the continental shelf. They're often separated from land by a wide, deep lagoon. The best known is the Great Barrier Reef, although this is actually a string of ribbon reefs rather than one long barrier. The Great Barrier Reef comprises just under 3,000 individual reefs and supports over 1,500 species of fish and more than 4,000 species of mollusc. It is one of the world's major destinations for reef tourism, logging as many as ten million visitors annually with an overall value of more than US$ one billion to the country's economy.

Atolls are the most unusual of reef structures, roughly circular in shape and enclosing a wide lagoon. In the early days of reef science no one could work out how these great structures grew in the middle of the sea, thousands of metres above the ocean floor. Darwin was the first to solve this puzzle: he suggested that as volcanic islands slowly sank, their fringing reefs grew upwards at the same rate. Eventually just a ring of reef – the atoll – was left behind, with the island totally submerged. It wasn't until over a century later, when test drillings made at Enewetak Atoll in the Pacific reached a volcanic base at 1,405 metres (4,600 feet), that Darwin's theory was proved correct.

Most atolls are in the Pacific, although there's also a long chain in the Indian Ocean, which includes the Maldives (the word atoll comes from the Maldivian *atolu*) and the Chagos Archipelago.

↑ ON THE REEF EVERY AVAILABLE SURFACE IS COLONISED BY LIFE. (ARI ATOLL, MALDIVES)
⊕⊕ BARRACUDA HUNTING SILVERSIDES IN A LAGOON. (EAST END SOUND, GRAND CAYMAN)

Coral reefs come in many other different shapes and sizes, including patch reefs, bank reefs, platform reefs and table reefs. They are also closely connected to two other important tropical ecosystems, mangroves and seagrass beds. Like coral reefs, mangroves are among the world's rarest ecosystems. They are home to numerous fish, birds and invertebrates, and provide an important nursery habitat for juvenile reef fish, which are able to feed and grow to maturity beneath the protective shelter of their roots. Seagrass beds are more widespread, often growing on sandy flats next to reefs. They stabilise the seabed and act as huge filters, removing particles from the water and depositing them as fine sediment. The sediment provides a rich source of food, which attracts fish, conch, lobster, turtles and manatees for feeding and breeding. Reef fish also use seagrass beds as a nursery, sheltering from predators amidst the grasses.

All three habitats – reefs, mangroves, and seagrass beds – are tied together in a circle of interdependence, providing sustenance and life to many tropical coastal habitats.

Into ice, caves and kelp

Given the fabulous diversity of coral reefs and the sheer joy that is to be had from diving around them, it's not surprising that they're so popular with divers. But not everyone can afford to travel to the tropics, and many divers in temperate climates are just as happy exploring the inland lakes, flooded quarries, or coastal waters of their own countries. These are often rich environments that can bring great rewards to those who dive them.

Even the strange, eerie world of ice diving has its fans, Cousteau having reputedly been among them. Phoebe Rudomino-Duscaska was the 2004 Rolex European Scholar for the Our World-Underwater Scholarship Society, an amazing charity that aims to foster future leaders of the marine environment by sponsoring them to experience different kinds of diving. She spent her year diving all around the world, acquiring 18 diving certifications in the process, and what she loved most was diving beneath the ice in the White Sea near Murmansk, Russia. "It was fantastic,"

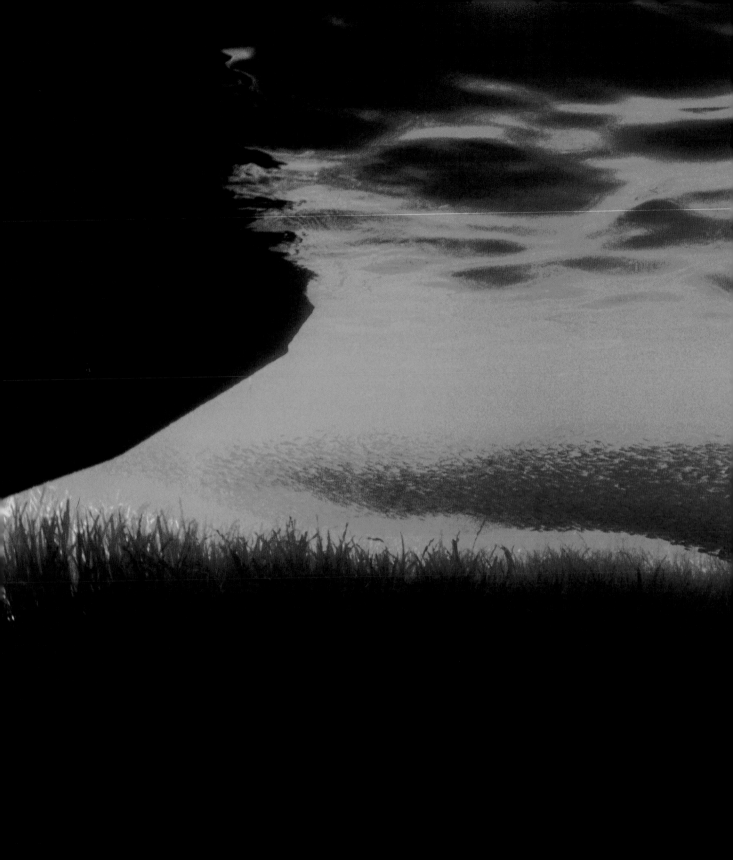

⬆ A SCHOOL OF SILVERSIDES TAKES SHELTER IN THIS CAVERN IN THE CAYMAN ISLANDS.

➲ SPONGES IN A CORAL CAVERN AT BABYLON, GRAND CAYMAN.

she recalls. "I had been wanting to do it for years and I had expected to be disappointed, but in fact it was unbelievable, absolutely stunning." Her recollections are vivid:

It's so clear and the ice is just so beautiful, and there's so much life down there. You get these 'life booms' in very cold areas and this was very evident in the White Sea because it was teeming with different kinds of creatures – and very odd things! People say normal diving is like being weightless in space and seeing this weird and wonderful world with mad creatures, but I found even crazier stuff.

The cold didn't bother Phoebe, even though her toes and camera froze. "It was minus two degrees, but I'm a cold water baby!" she says.

Cave diving is something which divers tend either to love or loathe. To some people there's nothing more exciting than the challenge of squeezing through narrow gaps

and penetrating long passages into the heart of the subterranean world. For others, the thought of all that rock over their heads is enough to send them groping for the sunlight. One of the most famous cave divers in recent times was the late Rob Palmer. He led many expeditions to the Blue Holes of the Bahamas, and here he describes the appeal of these unusual formations on a dive into a hole they christened Stargate:

It was like falling down an immense well, skydiving through clear green waters into nightfall. [We emerged] into a chasm of awesome clarity and stunning dimensions. Floating in mid-water, at a depth approaching 40 metres, we hung in dreamlike suspension, looking down an endless tunnel, unable to move. In dreams, this might be accompanied by a sensation of unease, or outright fear, the ingredients of nightmare. The feeling here was completely different, one of awe, of immensity, of staggering delight. [11]

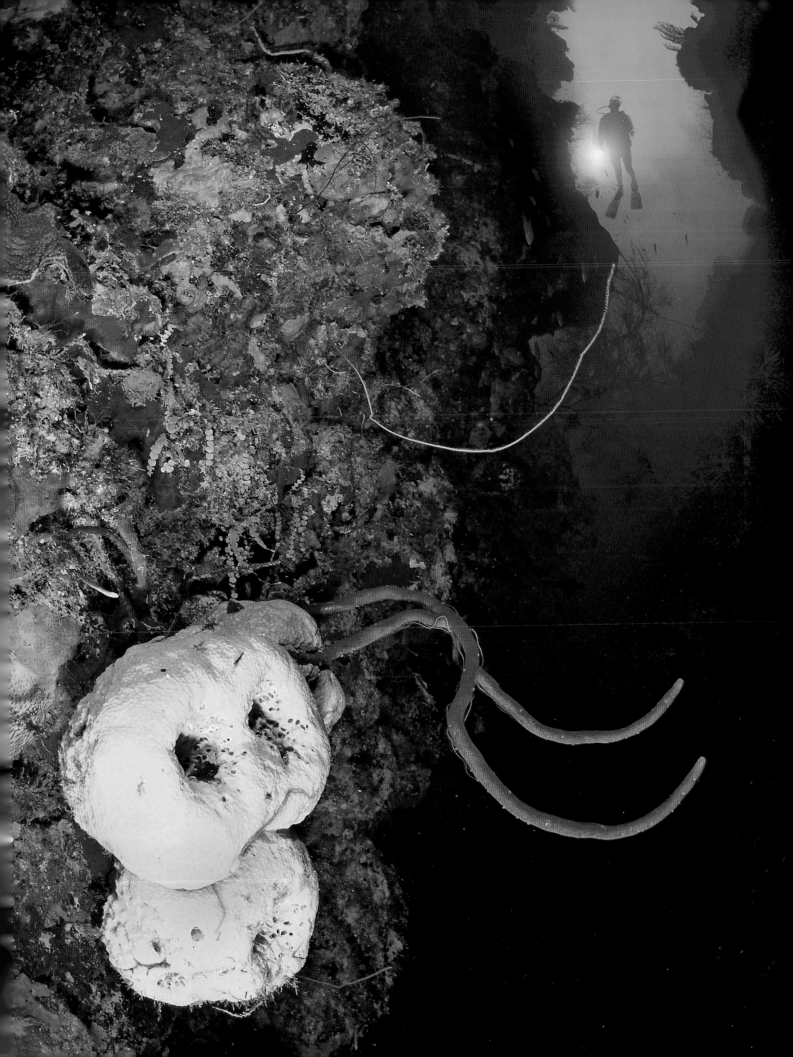

Not all cave diving requires special training. Caves that are technically 'open' to the sea are classed as caverns, and these are generally safe to enter with an experienced guide. Whether cave or cavern, each has its own unique ecosystem. Jade Berman, a young diver who was the 2003 Rolex European Scholar for the Our World-Underwater Scholarship Society, told me that one of her most interesting dives was in a series of caves in southern France, where she was captivated by the carnivorous sponges:

These carnivorous sponges, which look a little like hydroids, have developed tentacles covered with microscopic, Velcro-like hooks. With the hooks, they snag shrimp-like crustaceans (mysids) as they swim by. Within a day after capture, the cells of the sponge migrate to envelop the crustacean, which slowly suffocates. Digestion then begins!

Kelp forests can also offer amazing diving. Samantha Fanshawe, Director of Conservation at the UK's Marine Conservation Society, got hooked on kelp diving when she gained a Fellowship to the University of California at Santa Cruz. "When the conditions are good, diving in kelp forests is out of this world," she explains. "Because it looks like a forest, it's the closest thing to a terrestrial environment that there is underwater." She describes the experience vividly:

You get this feeling of almost not being underwater, but instead of floating through a forest. There's so much to see at almost every single level, and the variety of fish is enormous. You're looking up at these massive 80–100ft kelp strands and in among are all these different fish, all of them with their own particular niches at different levels.

At the bottom levels of the kelp forest are the bigger fish, such as Rock Cod and Sheephead Wrasse. Then further up there are massive shoals of Blue Rockfish hanging beneath the canopy, with schools of damselfish and wrasse passing among the stems. Trevor Norton also enjoys diving among this 'super-seaweed': "The best way to be overwhelmed underwater is to sink lazily into the tall forests of giant kelp," he explains. "This forest is every bit as imposing as any jungle on land and far easier to penetrate. You can glide beneath the luxuriance of the fronds, slide between the stems and hide among the shadows below." [12]

The lure of wrecks

Shipwrecks hold an enduring fascination for divers. Countless vessels have come to grief on coral reefs, where the sharp edges lurking just beneath the surface are notoriously hazardous for navigation. Colder waters, too, are littered with wrecks: there are tens of thousands around the British Isles alone.

Each shipwreck is a ghostly memorial to a moment in history – often one of great drama or tragedy. But once sunk, the ship gains a new lease of life as a home for marine species, as the holds, cabins, decks and superstructures are

"The surrounding haze creates mystery and a feeling of discovery. Sometimes snagged nets wreathe hulks in aquatic cobwebs that add an air of witchery. But it is the gloom inside that generates unease. It is impossible to enter into the black heart of a hulk without feeling that below in the darkness something awaits you..."

Professor Trevor Norton

A COLOURFUL SEAFAN GROWING INSIDE THE WRECK OF THE *ULYSSES* AT GUBAL ISLAND IN THE RED SEA.
BOW OF THE *GIANNIS D.* (ABU NUHAS, EGYPT)

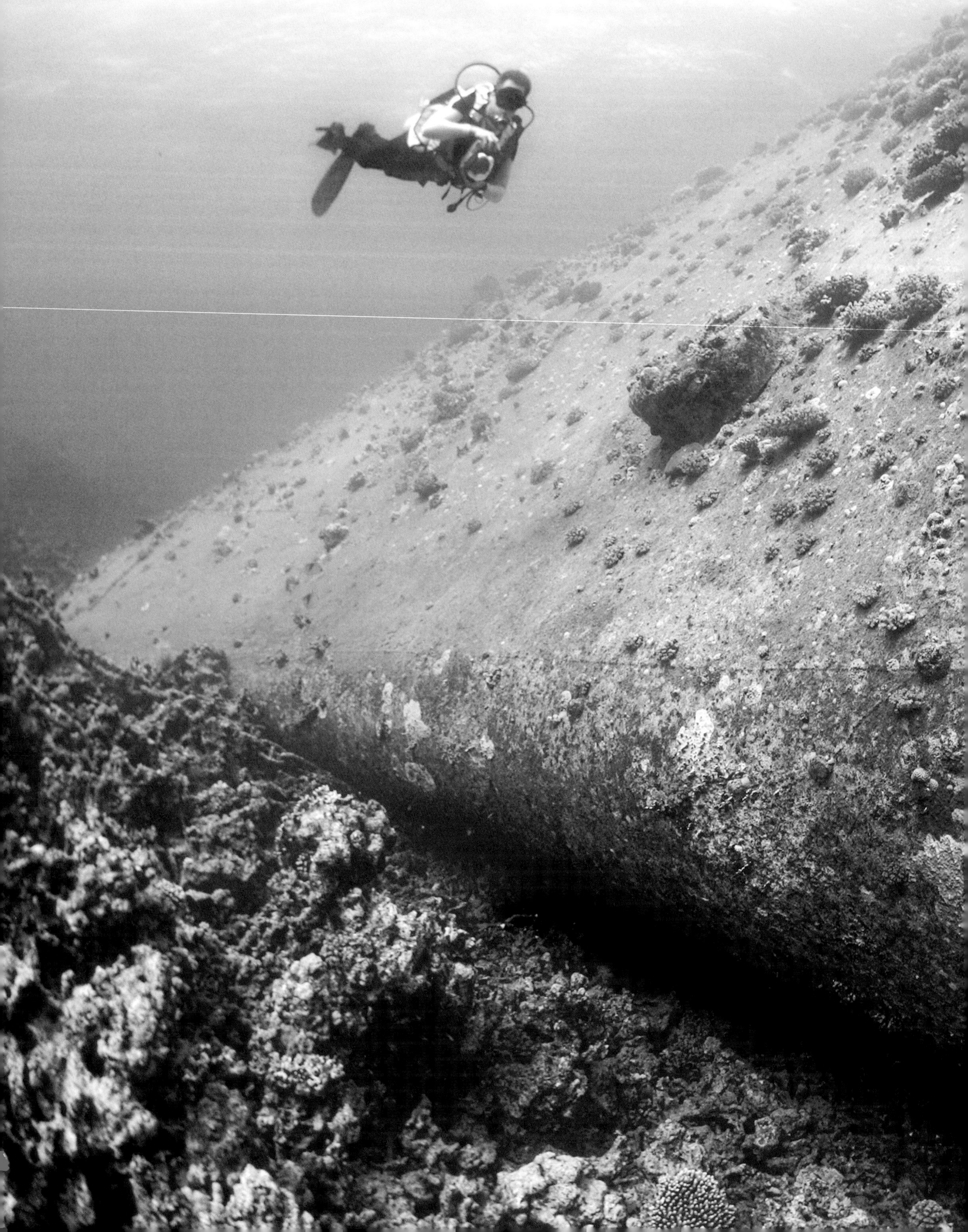

"I am always moved by the sight of a hull lying at the bottom of the sea. To me, it seems that a ship in that situation has entered the 'great beyond', into another existence, a world of shadows."

Jacques Cousteau

EXPLORING THE WRECK OF THE *CARNATIC*. (ABU NUHAS, EGYPT)
DIVERS EXPLORE THE WRECK OF THE *GIANNIS D*. (ABU NUHAS, EGYPT)
ISRAELI ARMY TRUCKS AND TANKS MAKE AN EERIE DIVE SITE. (SHARM EL SHEIKH, EGYPT)

colonised by corals, sponges, molluscs and fishes. "I am always moved by the sight of a hull lying at the bottom of the sea," said Jacques Cousteau. "To me, it seems that a ship in that situation has entered the 'great beyond', into another existence, a world of shadows." [13]

This sense of tragedy, of human loss, often permeates a wrecked ship. "They ooze atmosphere and are the eeriest places on earth," wrote Professor Trevor Norton in his marine memoirs, *Under Water To Get Out Of The Rain*:

The surrounding haze creates mystery and a feeling of discovery. Sometimes snagged nets wreathe hulks in aquatic cobwebs that add an air of witchery. But it is the gloom inside that generates unease. It is impossible to enter into the black heart of a hulk without feeling that below in the darkness something awaits you...Wrecks are the result of a catastrophe and sometimes the victims remain within. The divers' nervous excitement is fed by the suspicion that the very next cabin they enter may contain the remains of a hapless mariner. [14]

The fact that many wrecks might also be mass graves poses a moral dilemma for the diver. If the wreck is relatively recent, it is considered distasteful, as well as disrespectful, to dive it. The *Salem Express*, for instance, is the wreck of a ferry that sank offshore from Hurghada in the Egyptian Red Sea in 1991; nearly five hundred Muslim pilgrims, on their way back from Mecca, were drowned. Some dive guides refuse to go near it; some will refuse to go inside; and yet others ignore the whole controversy and dive it anyway. In Britain many wartime wrecks are protected as war graves, and diving them is banned. It's a dilemma: how old does the wreck have to be before you can dive it?

One of the most famous wreck diving locations in the world is Truk (Chuuk) lagoon, in Micronesia, where some sixty Japanese warships were sunk by American warplanes on February 17th, 1944. Sylvia Earle is one of thousands of divers who have explored these ships and discovered "submerged guns wreathed with garlands of feathery coral, the masts of ships shaggy with sponges and lacy hydroids, the doorways and passages havens for thousands of small fish." The ships are a beautiful monument, she says:

Some resemble cathedrals, tall masts and arches framed with shafts of sunlight and hung with living masterpieces; others are reminiscent of colourful gardens, alive with blue, green, silver, and gold flashes from fish that flit like flocks of birds among trees of coral, shrubs of sponges. [15]

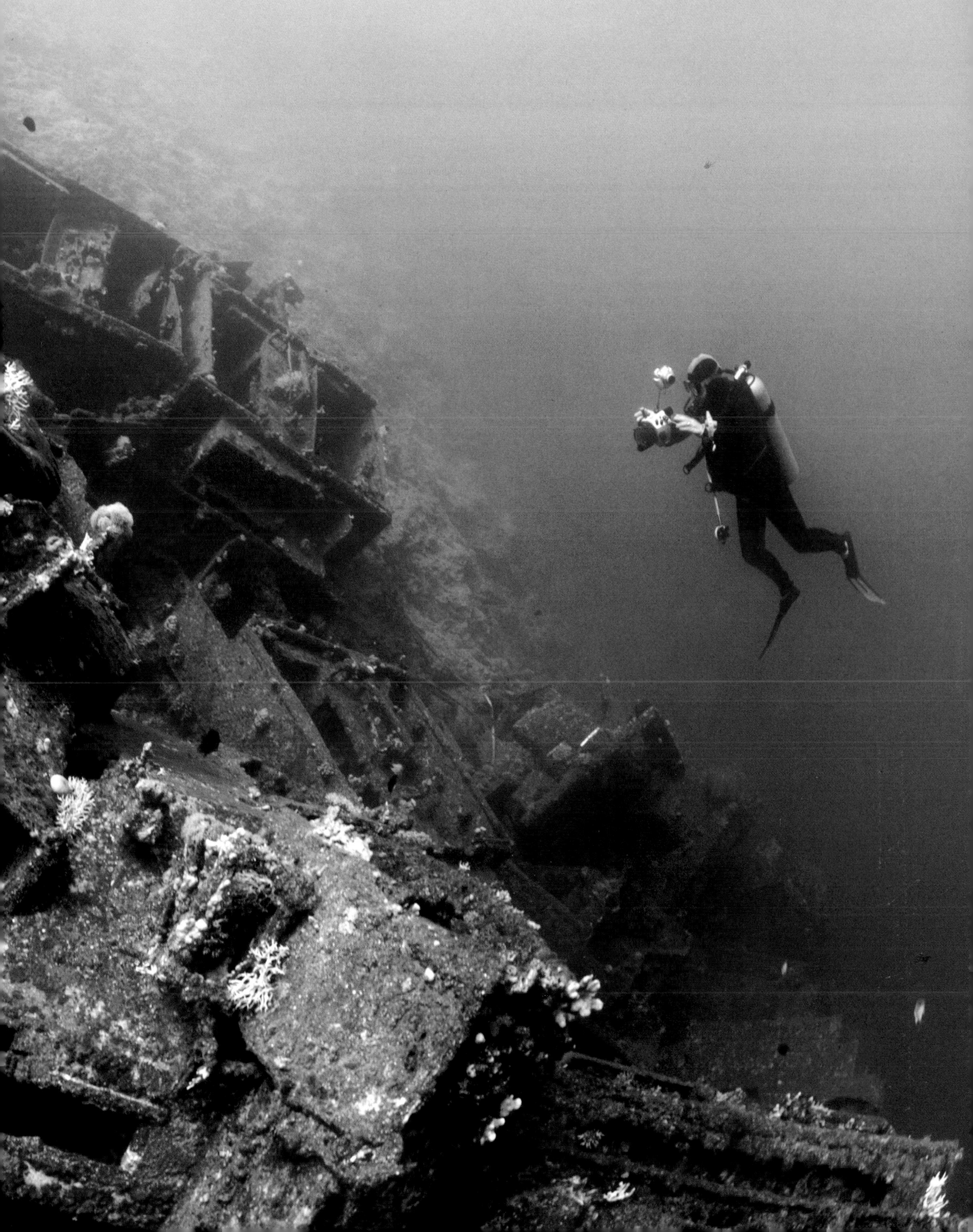

Shipwrecks provide a wide variety of habitats for marine life, adding surface areas to the true reef and increasing the productivity of the seabed. Decks and other flat surfaces provide a substrate for the planktonic larvae of corals and sponges to settle on; cabins become caves where shrimps, silversides, and other small creatures can hide; and encrusting plants take what space they can. As the fish life blossoms, predators such as jacks, grouper, barracuda and sharks start to make regular visits, as though word has spread that there's a new take-away restaurant in town.

"You're seeing how the sea just reclaims anything that goes down in it," says Lizzie Bird, a former BSAC National Diving Officer. "Recently I was on the Isle of Man diving a scallop dredger which went down a couple of years ago. You couldn't see the wreck because it was totally covered in primrose sea anemones. The whole wreck was just outlined in marine life, rather than metal – for me, that's what's exciting about wreck diving."

Britain's most famous wreck diving is at Scapa Flow in the Orkney Islands, where the German High Sea Fleet was scuttled in June 1919. The Red Sea and the Mediterranean have scores of fantastic wrecks, as does Australia's Great Barrier Reef.

Technical divers love deep wrecks, where they can test their kit – and themselves – to the limits. Starfish Enterprise, for instance, is a British technical diving team that has explored a number of historically significant wreck sites including the *Lusitania* at 93 metres (304 feet), the *Brittanic* (sister ship to the *Titanic*) at 119 metres (389 feet), and the P&O liner *Egypt*, which lies in 120 metres (393 feet) in the Bay of Biscay. These expeditions can take years of planning, says team member Christina Campbell. At the time of the *Brittanic* dive, Christina became the deepest female wreck diver in the world. "You do get a huge sense of achievement," she says, "if you've swum around the whole wreck and had a really good look at everything and maybe challenged yourself but felt safe the whole time." Having the correct mental approach, she adds, is also vital to a successful deep wreck dive.

Wreck diving doesn't have to be quite so difficult: exploring a shallow wreck is easy enough for a beginner, but those who want to venture into deeper, darker depths should make sure they have the appropriate training or the guidance of experienced professionals.

Treasure troves

On ancient wrecks the possibility of sunken treasure gives the diver an extra, exciting incentive. "Nothing, except perhaps the landing of a flying saucer in one's backyard, is quite so disruptive of everyday life as the discovery of sunken treasure," wrote Arthur C. Clarke in *The Treasure of the Great Reef,* [16] while Prince Charles has described his experiences of wreck diving while serving in the Caribbean for the Royal Navy:

> I have had ample opportunity to explore the sea in many different places – diving on a wreck of 1867 in the British Virgin Islands, for instance, and experiencing the extra-ordinary sensation of swimming inside the hull of the old schooner as if it was some vast green cathedral filled with shoals of silver fish. Or diving on a 17th-century Spanish wreck off Cartagena in Colombia, doubtless sunk by some predatory predecessor in the Royal Navy, and coming up with 'Pieces of Eight' and musket balls. [17]

Not many of us, of course, can claim that our ancestors were responsible for sinking whole fleets, which no doubt helped when it came to claiming the 'Pieces of Eight' salvaged from the wreck (and I can almost hear Prince Charles articulating that hyphenated 'extra-ordinary').

Underwater photographer Zena Holloway recalls a shoot for *National Geographic* in the River Plate in Uruguay, where the wreck of the *San Salvador* yielded slightly more than she had planned for:

↩ WORLD WAR II MOTORBIKES IN THE HOLD OF THE *THISTLEGORM* IN THE RED SEA.

I was standing on the bottom looking around me and there were skeletons, skulls, buttons, leather shoes and things like that all over the place. It had sunk with everybody except the captain on board – the sails had come down and caught all the women in their skirts, and all the men were in their fighting uniforms, which were heavy. At one point our guide disappeared into the gloom and came back with a bucketload of melded-together silver coins – it was one of those incredible dives where you just sucked the tank dry, it was so interesting! Quite sad, but fascinating.

Artificial reefs

Wreck diving has become so popular that ships are often sunk deliberately in order to create artificial reefs. The boats used are generally decommissioned naval vessels, confiscated smugglers' boats and the like. But anything, really, can make an artificial reef and people have sunk aircraft, tanks, tugboats, freighters, bits of discarded oilrigs and much more besides. The vessels must first be made safe for divers and cleaned of toxins and pollutants.

One of those to kick off the trend was a former Russian Navy destroyer, which was sunk in the Cayman Islands in 1996. Re-named *Captain Keith Tibbetts* in honour of a local diving personality, the 95-metre (310 feet) ship was sunk in 20–30 metres (65–98 feet) of water off the West End of Cayman Brac. Unusually for a ship that was deliberately being scuttled, it went down with someone on board – in this case, Jean-Michel Cousteau. In full scuba gear, Cousteau clung to the railing as the ship disappeared beneath the waves because, he says, he had wanted to know since he was a child what happens to the skipper when the boat goes down. "It was a fabulous experience," he says. "Now I know what captains go through when they sink with their ship. Not only am I the world's expert, but I am the only one who has come back!"

Many more artificial reefs have since followed. The biggest ever ship put down purely for the pleasure of scuba divers is the *Spiegel Grove*, a former ex-US Navy vessel, which is located ten kilometres (six miles) off-shore from Key Largo, Florida. The total project cost for sinking this massive, 155-metre (507-feet) ship in June 2002 was US$1.25 million. The ship actually sunk upside down, but was righted by Hurricane Dennis in summer 2005. Britain acquired its first ever artificial shipwreck in 2004, when the former Navy frigate *HMS Scylla* was sunk off Whitsand Bay,

⊕ GLASSFISH INSIDE THE ENGINE ROOM OF THE *GIANNIS D.*
(ABU NUHAS, EGYPT)

Cornwall, under the supervision of Plymouth's National Marine Aquarium. Canada is also big on artificial reefs, with British Columbia in particular boasting an armada of wrecks, including four 111-metre (366-foot) Canadian destroyer escorts.

Shipwrecks like these not only provide a wide range of habitats for marine life; they also relieve the pressure on other dive sites, helping to disperse people from nearby reefs or wrecks. Some purists, however, prefer the real thing, and there are divers who devote their lives to tracking down virgin wrecks so that they can be the first to explore them on scuba. Others question whether spending millions of dollars on artificial reefs is a sensible use of resources, given that money is badly needed to protect real reefs.

Archaeology and Atlantis

Artificial reefs are now fairly commonplace. The latest developments are shipwreck parks, shipwreck trails, and underwater shipwreck museums. The lead has come, surprisingly, from land-locked Indiana University, which has established shipwreck parks in California, Florida and the Caribbean. The university helped create the world's first shipwreck park in 2002, with the 1742 Underwater Archaeological Preserve offshore from Bayahibe, in the Dominican Republic. The underwater museum consists of 18th-century cannons, ballast stones, cannonballs, ceramic pieces and an anchor from the wreck of two Spanish galleons. Lying in three to five metres (10–16 feet) of water, the park is easily accessible by snorkellers as well as divers. A second underwater museum, the Guaraguao Reef Cannons Reserve, was created nearby in 2004. At 12 metres (40 feet) it is slightly deeper, and covers around 180 square metres (600 square feet) of reef.

"Our ethic is to put things back in the sea rather than bring them up," says Charles Beeker, director of the programme. "Go to any museum and there are plenty of cannons and the like on display – why go to a wreck site and bring up more? What we're doing is not only protecting a resource but also interpreting it for the public," he explains. "It's a combination of underwater archaeology, marine biology and history." The underwater parks have proved so popular that Beeker is now planning an underwater museum of Taino history, with artefacts created by the earliest inhabitants of Hispaniola set in a freshwater spring. You will literally be able to dive into early Caribbean history. "Bringing things up from the seabed is such a 1960s mentality," says Beeker. "We're in the 21th century now – we can go and look at it all underwater."

Similar parks have started to spring up elsewhere: in 2005 the first divers were allowed to visit what is believed to be Blackbeard's pirate ship, *Queen Anne's Revenge*, which sank off North Carolina in 1718. Marine archaeologists said that the supervised dives, which are part of a two-day marine archaeology programme, will boost tourism and increase our knowledge of the shipwreck.

It's risky to speculate on what might happen next in the world of diving (remember, Cousteau and Hass were confident we would all be living in underwater suburbia by now). But it's a safe bet that imaginative underwater attractions such as shipwreck parks and sculpture parks will continue to spring up. One such enterprise, the 'Lost City of Atlantis', is already underway just offshore from

Cayman Brac in the Caribbean. Designed and built by the Caymanian artist known as Foots, the project incorporates a series of sculptures placed on the seabed in around 12–15 metres (40–50 feet) of water. The sculptures, which have been colonised by a wide variety of marine life, are set on a huge sandy plain that features plenty of stingrays and eagle rays. They are easily reached as a shore dive and are set to become a major dive attraction. Gigantic columns, a massive pyramid, a sundial and over a hundred other artefacts are all part of Foots' ambitious dream:

Ⓚ A STINGRAY PASSES BENEATH A DIVE BOAT AT STINGRAY CITY, GRAND CAYMAN.

I've always been fascinated with ancient ruins and mythology ever since I was a child, and what I'm creating here is one massive sculpture, a work of art. But once it goes into the sea and nature starts taking hold then it becomes a masterpiece. No artist in the world can do what nature is doing to these structures.

Atlantis is set to become a major dive attraction for the Caymans, a 'must-see' for anyone visiting the islands.

Foots' vision isn't hard to imagine: a nice little shark swims around an underwater column; an eagle ray flaps past a tumbled-down temple; and your buddy glides through an elegant archway draped in soft corals. Everyone will be down there snapping away with their digital cameras, plugging into that cultural meme of lost cities, blue water and exotic tropical fish. In doing so, they we will be creating a mythological landscape from our past, a romanticised underwater Eden that we had once only dreamed of.

going underwater:
how we dive

"Be healthy by eliminating all earthly concerns from your dive plans to fully savor the joy of diving." **Lou Fead**

IF FLYING UNDERWATER IS YOUR DESIRE, THERE ARE THOUSANDS OF DIVE SCHOOLS ALL OVER THE WORLD THAT CAN TEACH YOU HOW. TODAY SCUBA TRAINING IS A SOPHISTICATED GLOBAL INDUSTRY THAT WILL TAKE YOU ALL THE WAY FROM LEARNING TO PLAY WITH THE FISHES AS AN EIGHT-YEAR-OLD, TO MASTERING THE COMPLEXITIES OF TECHNICAL MIXED-GAS DIVING AND MUCH MORE. MOST OF US START WITH AN OPENWATER COURSE, WHERE YOU LEARN TO DIVE SAFELY IN THE SEA, BUT FROM THAT POINT YOU CAN MOVE ON TO EXPLORE AS MANY DIFFERENT TYPES OF DIVING AS YOU CHOOSE. THE GREAT THING ABOUT DIVING IS THAT IT OFFERS SOMETHING TO EVERYONE – FROM THOSE WHO WANT TO SNAP MINISCULE BEASTIES ON THE SEABED, TO THOSE WHO ARE ITCHING TO PLUNGE UNDER THE ICE.

This variety keeps diving growing, embracing everybody from the techno whiz-kid who can't wait to debate the pros and cons of different kit configurations, to the holiday diver who's happy simply floating around in ten metres looking at pretty fish. And whatever their level, all divers have benefited from those who've pushed the envelope over the years: specialist equipment originally designed for use in hazardous environments such as caves and deep wrecks now makes ordinary diving safer and more enjoyable for everybody – the octopus regulator and inflatable surface marker buoy ('safety sausage') being just two examples.

When Jacques took Simone and the little Cousteaus down to the seaside in Sanary-sur-Mer for their 'usual Sunday afternoon underwater excursions', none of them had anything except mask, snorkel, fins and a tank. They wore just swimming costumes, not wetsuits, and breathed through cumbersome twin tubes, rather than a single hose regulator. In Cousteau's time there was no such thing as a flotation jacket, or what we now call a buoyancy control device (BCD), so for buoyancy control they simply used their lungs. Jean-Michel Cousteau confesses that he still sometimes dives without a BCD. "If you get your weight right," he told me, "you're perfectly neutral and you go up by inflating your lungs and down by exhaling. It works very well."

Diving for all

Cathy Church is just one of thousands of divers of her generation who learned to dive simply by experience, only later gaining proper qualifications. "I remember my first

dive was in the kelp forests of California," she recalls. "No-one was certified in the 1960s – we just strapped on the tanks and away we went. When we came back up I asked the guy 'How deep do you think we were?' and he said, 'Well, we threw out about 100 feet of line so I guess we were pretty deep'."

Today diving is a much safer sport than it was when Cathy Church, Helmut Debelius, Ned DeLoach and many others gleefully plunged to over 30 metres (100 feet) on their first dive. Professional training is widely available and we can buy or rent reliable, well-engineered equipment almost anywhere we want to go diving.

These developments have opened up the sport to a wider range of people. It is no longer such a male-dominated activity, and has become something we do with our friends or family on holiday. There's a huge amount of pleasure to be had from sharing the diving experience with your nearest and dearest, and today it's not unusual to see two or even three generations from the same family on a dive boat. Organisations such as the Handicapped Scuba Association have also opened up diving for the disabled, who often find that the weightlessness of water offers a sense of freedom that they are denied on land.

As diving has grown, it has also attracted a growing band of celebrities. Well-known divers include writers and journalists such as Anthony Horowitz, Mariella Frostrup, Frederick Forsyth, Tony Parsons and Wilbur Smith; actors such as Josie Lawrence, Jack Davenport, David Jason, Richard E. Grant and Amanda Holden; musicians including pop diva Charlotte Church, conductor Simone Young and Pink Floyd's Nick Mason; and broadcasters as diverse as Ruby Wax, Anneka Rice and Dom Joly.

Despite pioneers such as Simone Cousteau (possibly the world's first female scuba diver), Lotte Hass, Sylvia Earle, Eugenie Clark and others, mainstream

A DIVER RIDES AN UNDERWATER SCOOTER. (TURTLE FARM REEF, GRAND CAYMAN)

"The untroubled soul gains the greatest benefits from the adventure of exploring underwater" **Lou Fead**

diving remained broadly male-oriented for many decades. Particularly in Britain, it was steeped in a culture of machismo that was a barrier to women taking up diving. "In the old days it was very much a chaps' world, because to start with diving grew out of the Navy," says Lizzie Bird, who in 1999 became British Sub Aqua Club's (BSAC) first female National Diving Officer, responsible for national training programmes. Club diving revolved around guys bragging in the pub afterwards about how deep they'd been (and their wet dreams usually involved a brass porthole or two they'd jemmied off a shipwreck). Furthermore, training used to be very militaristic in style and attitude, says Louise Trewavas, who founded *Dive Girl* magazine and is now a columnist on *Diver* magazine.

That kind of approach kept women away from the sport for a long time. The way it's taught now is more egalitarian, focused around what you do underwater rather than trying to become some superhuman secret-mission type diver or something. Women are turned off by that whole 'action man' thing: they want to go down there and enjoy the underwater scenery, not bomb someone's submarine!

The irony is that women are often better divers than men. Male divers are like male drivers, says Tim Ecott in *Neutral Buoyancy*, preoccupied with comparing their equipment as though discussing engine size and torque in a sports car. Women tend to be less interested in the technicalities of the gear, just as long as it does the job. They also tend to take more care in preparing for a dive, and to be less frenetic underwater. According to Tim, this more relaxed approach means that women normally consume less air underwater, allowing them to stay down longer and see more, which – after all – is the whole point of diving.

The best divers are reflective, methodical individuals who do all the right things calmly, believed Cousteau. Problems underwater require a cool head, not brute force. Mark Caney, of PADI International, believes this also gives women an advantage:

That's why most of the best divers are women rather than men, because it's to do with attitude rather than muscle. If you watch someone who really knows what they're doing they plan everything out, their movements are very economical, and they're part of the ocean rather than fighting with it.

Surprisingly, many of the world's top underwater photographers aren't that keen on equipment technicalities. "You don't need the latest high-tech gadgets or to go deeper and longer than everybody else to have an absolutely fabulous experience underwater," says author and underwater photographer Lawson Wood. "Some of our best experiences have been swimming along the surface with just a mask and snorkel anyway. Like most sports, if you do it regularly you're going to get confident and comfortable and that's what makes your diving safe and interesting," he adds. Charles Hood agrees: "I'm one of those divers who just want to put on a perfectly bog standard set of equipment and get in the water," he says. "The thought of sitting there for hours discussing D-rings is enough to make me want to scream quietly into my regulator." Similarly, for underwater photographer Zena Holloway, diving has become second nature: "I'm not interested in the gear, it's just like – throw the tank on your back and get in the water," she says. "It's part of the process of getting underwater, it gets me to where I want to be to get the pictures. Technical discussions about equipment bore me senseless."

⊙ A SLOW AND CONSIDERED APPROACH GIVES YOU THE BEST CHANCE TO SEE CREATURES OTHERS MISS, SUCH AS THIS PYGMY SEAHORSE. (BALI, INDONESIA)

↑ A PHOTOGRAPHER INSIDE A SCHOOL OF SILVERSIDES. (DEVIL'S GROTTO, GRAND CAYMAN)
→ → A REEF HOOK ALLOWS A DIVER TO STAY IN ONE PLACE WITHOUT STRUGGLING AGAINST THE CURRENT. (RASDHOO ATOLL, MALDIVES)

Diving is not a competitive sport, despite the efforts of a few retrograde types to make it one. So those who are not technically minded need not feel intimidated, just as long as they know the basics of their equipment and can dive safely – which is what counts. The diver festooned with accessories like a Christmas tree will probably not have a relaxing time underwater. The diver who is streamlined, with the minimum kit needed for diving safely in that particular environment, will get more out of it. And, with less gear to worry about, there are many ways of learning how to dive *better*, in order to maximize the benefits of being underwater.

Use your brains, not your back

The untroubled soul gains the greatest benefits from the adventure of exploring underwater. Each aspect of the dive... achieves its greatest effect on the uncluttered, receptive human soul. Be healthy by eliminating all earthly concerns from your dive plans to fully savor the joy of diving. Be healthy in mind, body and soul for diving![1]

This advice to leave your anxieties and troubles behind when you go diving comes from a legendary American diving coach, Lou Fead. He was a deep submersible pilot before becoming a NAUI instructor in 1969, and went on to become a leading light in American national diver education while teaching at the Diving Locker in San Diego, California.

Lou's legacy to diving was a training manual called *Easy Diver*, published in 1983. Many of the techniques were designed for abalone hunters braving the California surf, but much of it is as valid today as it was then. Lou's motto was 'dive with your brains, not your back', and he demonstrated how to do this. Sticking to your dive plan, your limits and your buddy were all key factors.

Lou Fead claimed that kitting up was one of the most stressful parts of diving, and one which people enjoyed the least. His solution was to 'fun pack' your dive bag. This he likened to 'combat loading' an attack cargo ship, in that you put in first what you want to come out last. So your fins, mask and snorkel go in first, followed by wetsuit, regulator and BCD. When getting ready to dive, you start by preparing your tank, then put on your wetsuit and finally take out your mask, fins and snorkel and so on.

"If you watch someone who really knows what they're doing they plan everything out, their movements are very economical, and they're part of the ocean rather than fighting with it." **Mark Caney**

This all makes good sense, but you'd be amazed by how many divers find themselves searching for a lost fin when they're already kitted up with a heavy tank on their backs. So, work backwards: rinse out your mask and make sure that your mask, snorkel and fins are handy, at the right level, before doing anything else. Ditto accessories, cameras and so forth. Make sure your weightbelt is also where you want it. If you've just struggled into your wetsuit and are already feeling hot and stressed, get in the sea or step under an outdoor shower to cool off before tackling the next stage. And finally, use whatever is handy – be it quayside bollard, tree stump, or nearby table or bench – to make sure that your tank is propped up at the right height before getting strapped in.

The key to stress-free kitting up is to ensure that all your gear is well placed for easy access, without bending down, once you start the process. Imagine there's a diver shape, with the gear laid out around it, and all you have to do is step in and put it on with the minimum of effort. "The lazy way is best!" said Lou, wisely.

The diving business has grown so sophisticated in recent years that there are plenty of dive centres now which offer 'full service' diving: willing staff are on hand to help you kit up and you never even have to think about moving a tank around or lifting anything heavy. So if that's your way of being lazy, that's also great – diving isn't a weightlifting contest. Strength isn't the key to being a good diver.

The art of neutral buoyancy

One of the most important skills for any diver is the ability to master neutral buoyancy. That sense of effortless floating grace doesn't happen by accident: it's a matter of practice and technique.

Some divers seem to flounder around underwater like badly adjusted hippos, while others move through the ocean with the fluid grace of dolphins. The hippos are a nightmare to be around: they bump into everything, kicking up clouds of sediment and damaging corals; they use more air and get tired more quickly: in a confined space, they can be a serious risk. But the dolphins glide smoothly through the water and emerge feeling fresher than when they began. Most of us lie somewhere on a spectrum between these two types, usually depending on how much diving time we've had lately. But how can we become more dolphin than hippo? It all comes down to buoyancy skills.

First, always do a buoyancy check if you haven't dived for a while, if you're diving in a new environment (i.e. salt rather than fresh water), if you've got new equipment (especially a wetsuit or buoyancy jacket), or if any other factors have changed. Floating at the surface, with an empty buoyancy jacket and a medium breath of air, your eyes should be level with the surface of the water.

Second, learn to fine-tune buoyancy by using your breathing: deeper breaths and exhalations will make you rise or sink more; shallower breaths and exhalations will allow you to make smaller adjustments.

Third, use only short bursts to inflate and deflate your BCD. "Overestimating buoyancy control, either by adding or removing too much air at once from the BCD, is a common mistake," says Robert Rossier, author of Dive Like a Pro. If you squeeze too much air into your BCD to stop yourself from sinking, you can find yourself heading back up again before you know it. You have been 'overcontrolling' your buoyancy. The same thing can happen on an ascent: you think you're going up too fast, so you dump all the air from your BCD – which leaves you too heavy, and on the way back down. "The trick is to make small adjustments," says Rossier, "and to make them more often."[2]

Buoyancy is affected by a number of factors, including your equipment, the environment (the Red Sea, for instance, is saltier than most, so you'll need more weight) and the cylinder you're using. This is one good reason to keep a dive log, noting all these variables and how much weight you used. "It takes practice and attention to detail to master buoyancy control," says Rossier, "but understanding the subtleties is the first step to mastering the skill. Follow these tips, and before you know it, you'll be gliding above the reefs with grace of a dolphin."

> "Buoyancy control is something that you're doing 100 per cent of the time that you're in the water!"
>
> **Marcus Allen**

⬆ USE WHATEVER IS AVAILABLE TO EASE THE LOAD. HERE A DIVER KITS UP RESTING HER TANK AND FINS AGAINST A TREE STUMP. (FELIDHOO ATOLL, MALDIVES)

Perfecting buoyancy skills

Buoyancy control is an art that only comes with practice, says Marcus Allen, chairman of BSAC. He points out that, unlike many other diving skills, it is "something that you're doing 100 per cent of the time that you're in the water, one way or another." Thus he advises practising for each different environment, making sure that your weight belt is well balanced, and that you have weights on your ankles, tank or whatever else it takes to get the configuration correct. "It's worth fiddling around until you get it right," he concludes.

There are also special training programmes for buoyancy control. These include the Diamond Reef system, designed by Pete Wallingford of Buoyancy Training Systems in Seattle. This consists of seven diamond shaped structures arranged like an underwater obstacle course through which you have to swim. The aim is to increase your awareness, and to improve skills such as ascending, hovering, breathing and body movements by practising things that you would normally do during a real dive rather than in a mere pool exercise.

Steve Warren of Mavericks Diving in London was the first instructor to incorporate buoyancy skills into dive courses in the UK. His interest began when several studies of diving accidents concluded that more than half of diving accidents or fatalities involved loss of buoyancy control. "It's an interesting concept that there should be such a thing as an optional buoyancy control course," he explains. "To me that's a bit like offering a driving course with an optional course on braking." Buoyancy control receives little attention in open water courses, simply because there isn't time. "The vast majority of recreational divers haven't been trained in buoyancy control to any kind of standard," he says. He also emphasizes the important distinction here between neutral buoyancy and 'neutral trim' – which is the art of adopting the optimum profile in the water:

If you're neutrally trimmed, you're perfectly horizontal and more streamlined. So you have to make far less effort to swim, breathing less heavily and therefore using less air, and you will have a more comfortable and a longer dive. If you're purely horizontal you're also going to do far less damage to the surrounding environment. Remember: fins do not have nervous systems! You can kick something with your fin, or damage something with the downdraft, and not be aware of it. Same thing when you go inside a wreck: it's very easy to start kicking up silt, unless you're neutrally trimmed as well as neutrally buoyant.

Divers should also practice remaining neutrally buoyant while carrying out skills such as mask clearing. "During the Diamond Reef training we get divers multi-tasking, so we'll get them to swim through as they clear their mask," explains Steve. "Usually, when clearing their mask most people over-exhale, with the result that they sink into the diamond and get caught on it again. Do that inside a wreck, and you're going to land on something sharp or silt up the bottom," he says.

The aim is to acquire very precise buoyancy skills. "Say you're a photographer and you want to drop down into a small bit of reef without touching anything," says Steve. "You've got to learn to work like a helicopter, so that you exhale gently to drop down into the position you want to be in, and then you inhale to come up because you don't want to start kicking until your fins are well clear. Again, this is where being neutrally trimmed helps."

"My air consumption is horrible. Every time I take a break from my rebreather and put on a scuba tank I feel like a novice diver and I go through air like crazy. It's all a matter of practice – after I've been on open circuit for a couple of days it all comes back."

Howard Hall

Relax, use less air

Your buoyancy skills will improve with practice. The same applies to air consumption. It's embarrassing to be an air-guzzler, always the first back from a dive because your tank's running low, but you might be surprised to learn that even very experienced divers use more air on their first few dives.

"The more diving you do, the better your air consumption becomes," says Jack Jackson, who ran a dive centre in the Sudanese Red Sea for 12 years and has since written 17 books on diving or dive destinations. "But when you haven't dived for a while, you're almost as bad as everybody else – until you've been in the water for three or four dives and got it all going again," he adds.

Award-winning filmmaker Howard Hall spends around 400 hours per year underwater using a rebreather or closed circuit diving system. Rebreathers give you a virtually unlimited supply of air, since they recycle what you breathe out. Using them requires different skills, and Howard admits that when he goes back to diving on compressed air (open circuit) he has to start from the beginning: "My air consumption is horrible. Every time I take a break from my rebreather and put on a scuba tank I feel like a novice diver and I go through air like crazy," he says. "It's all a matter of practice – after I've been on open circuit for a couple of days it all comes back." Even people with thousands of dives in their logbooks take time to re-adjust to scuba.

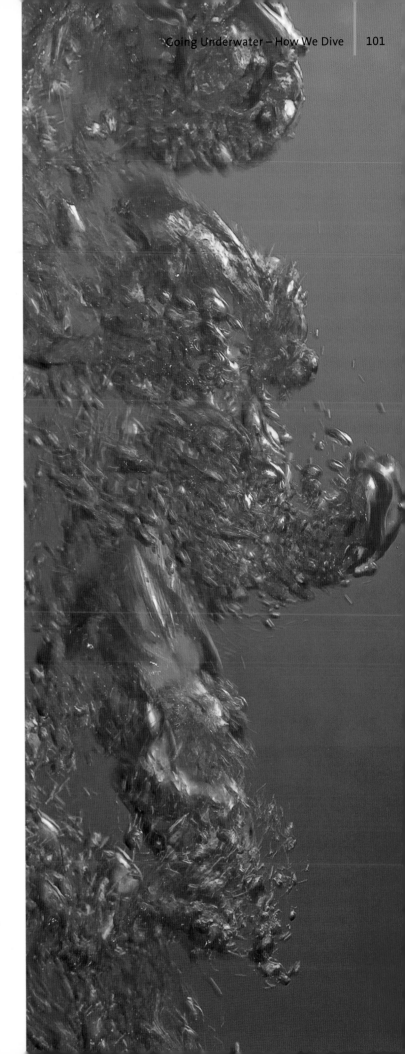

↑ A FLYING GURNARD SOARS ACROSS THE SEABED AT LEMBEH STRAIT, INDONESIA.

"If you're neutrally trimmed you're perfectly horizontal and more streamlined. So you have to make far less effort to swim, breathing less heavily, therefore using less air, and have a more comfortable and a longer dive. If you're purely horizontal you're also going to do far less damage to the surrounding environment."

Steve Warren

Using less air comes down to diving more often, and being relaxed. Photographer Linda Pitkin once made a celebrated dive where she squeezed enough air from her tank to last two hours and fifty minutes underwater. It took place beneath Swanage pier, a popular dive site on the south coast of England. "I was spending a long time watching a dragonet that was blowing plumes of very fine sediment out from the top of its head," she recalls. "I was really enjoying watching this creature." Linda was in just three to five metres (10 to 16 feet) of water, which helped reduce her rate of air consumption, but the trick to making it last, she says, is slowing down:

I have managed some very long dives underwater, and I do it by more or less switching off. I don't do a lot: as a photographer, I stay in one spot and I observe things for a long time before I photograph them. Because of that, I slow my breathing rate right down. I've always had a sense of not wanting to rush in at creatures blowing vast quantities of bubbles all over them, so I don't breathe a lot.

↑ DIVERS GOING ON A TRY DIVE IN CALM SHALLOW WATERS OF GRAND CAYMAN. BUILD YOUR DIVING EXPERIENCE IN SMALL STEPS.

Slowing down means being economical with your movements and thinking through what you're going to do right from the beginning. Take your time kitting up: hurrying can lead to oversights, and what seems trivial at this point can easily become disastrous an hour or so later. If you start in a relaxed state while gearing up, you can carry that state of mind through your dive. Take it easy, don't rush.

Jeff Rotman, who has worked for top publications from *Life* to *Le Figaro* and travelled with his cameras to almost every ocean in the world, says that the right level of comfort underwater is one where you're practically falling asleep – which actually happened to him once. "I've fallen asleep before just waiting to decompress, lying on a sandy bottom at three metres," he confesses. "That's the level of comfort you want to be aiming for," he adds. "You should be as relaxed as possible and that only comes with a lot of hours in the water." In other words, just spend more time diving. Who could argue with that?

Comfort zones

The best way to feel comfortable underwater is to stick within the range of your abilities. Many different variables can affect a dive, including water temperature, surface currents and visibility. You should always be aware of these, and never dive when the conditions are beyond your experience. Saying 'no' to a dive is one of the hardest skills to learn.

Assessing your own physical, mental and emotional fitness is also an important step in judging whether or not to dive. Too often there's pressure to go ahead, when in reality (because of a cold, fatigue, a hangover or other reasons) we know we shouldn't. Ignoring stress is potentially hazardous: stress can distract you, and limit your ability to focus on problems and sort them out. Of course many people go underwater to escape stress: this is fine, just as long as they don't take it down with them.

"Divers have to be honest with themselves and not be pushed into something which is beyond their capabilities," says Lizzie Bird. Peer pressure, for instance, can make people undertake dives that they wouldn't normally, which

means that they may not be totally prepared. "If anything does go wrong – it could be kit you haven't practised with, it could be diving in conditions you haven't experienced before – you need a first and automatic reaction to be able to deal with it," says Lizzie. "If that's missing, when something goes wrong it can then get out of control," she warns. "I think the main cause of accidents is probably people doing things that they are not quite prepared for or not quite ready for."

Professional diver Richard Bull, a technical consultant to the television and film industries, says that being comfortable underwater starts when he's gearing up. "The moment I get tucked into my diving suit," he says, "I think 'hang on, this is why I'm here', which is a good feeling." Bull has dived in some of the most challenging conditions on the planet, from the Antarctic to the Amazon. His advice to those contemplating a difficult dive is to always listen to their instincts if it doesn't feel right:

People should know the difference between their stomach turning over because it's an adventurous dive and they're looking forward to it, and apprehension, because they know they really shouldn't be doing the dive. One of my favourite sayings is that it's better to be on the boat wishing you were in the water than being in the water at 40 metres and wishing you were on the boat.

"I have managed some very long dives underwater, and I do it by more or less switching off. I don't do a lot: I stay in one spot and I observe things for a long time before I photograph them."

Linda Pitkin

⊖ A *RISBECIA TRYONI* NUDIBRANCH GLIDES ACROSS THE SEABED. (LEMBEH STRAIT, INDONESIA)

DIVERS RETURNING TO THE BOAT AFTER THEIR DIVE. (VALLEY OF THE DOLLS, GRAND CAYMAN)

Bull has the accumulated wisdom of thousands of hours underwater to back up his instincts about doing the right thing, even if this means aborting the dive. "Never be afraid to walk away from a dive," he advises. "Interestingly, it's usually only the really experienced divers who will walk away from the dive," he adds, "because they've got nothing to prove."

Bull is referring to advanced dives here, but the same principle applies to any diving – which is to know your limits and stick to them. Mark Caney believes that most diving accidents are due to a mismatch between the diver's abilities and the situation they find themselves in,

and that divers can reduce the risk of accidents by more training. He also believes that a diver must be able to visualise in advance each particular dive in order to work out a strategy for dealing with any problems that might arise: "Imagine what would happen: If I notice my gauge is down to a certain level, if I find I've swum by mistake into some fishing net, if I can't see my buddy – what would I do?" Imagination is thus a vital part of a diver's preparation: "Most potential accidents or incidents can be envisaged, and if you develop a set of responses in your head, then you are far more likely to actually do the right thing when the stress is there."

sport. "In probably 98 per cent of accidents one of the fundamental rules of diving has been broken," comments Mark Caney, "typically more than one." Although there is always some degree of risk to scuba diving, there aren't a great many unknowns. Provided you follow the rules, it is a relatively safe sport.

Best of buddies

The buddy system is one of the cornerstones of modern recreational diving: it means you dive in pairs, checking each other's equipment before the dive and keeping an eye on each other throughout.

Jacques Cousteau insisted on the buddy system from as early as 1943, after Dumas had a particularly harrowing wreck dive where his air hose had got caught on a barnacle-encrusted pipe. Dumas, wrote Cousteau, had found himself "a hundred feet down, cut off from his comrades by a wild surf, and knowing that none of us intended to join him."[4] He eventually managed to inch his way painfully back down the pipe and free his air hose. "After Dumas's ordeal on the pipe, we made a rule never to go down alone," wrote Cousteau. "It was the beginning of team diving, the essence of aqualung work," he pronounced.

Being a good buddy means understanding your partner's abilities, and making sure that you're both clear about what you want from the dive. If you're buddied up with a diver you don't know and you're not comfortable with their attitude, you can politely decline to dive with them. (Reckless or gung-ho attitudes to deep diving are particularly risky.) Once underwater, keep in touch with your buddy; always stay within arm's length so that you can reach out to communicate something. Think ahead for both yourself and your buddy: monitor your buddy's contents gauges as well as your own, and check continually for any signs of distress, discomfort, equipment snags and so forth.

The best buddies are usually regular partners or friends that we get to know well enough to understand their capabilities and diving style. For Louise Trewavas, diving with her long-term partner Mark Brill means that they can read each other's minds underwater. "He knows exactly what I'm thinking about without me even having to explain it," she says. "All I have to do is to look at him and he can tell if I'm having a fantastic time, or if something's going wrong he'll usually come over and sort it out before I've even realised I've got a problem. And vice-versa."

A significant number of diving accidents are caused by panic. "It is not sharks and octopus that threaten the diver," noted Hans Hass. "The greatest danger lies within him, in his own head, in his own spinal cord, there lies the real enemy."[3] Calm and composure are the diver's most important defences, observed Hass. In training today, this is often expressed as the mantra 'stop...breathe...think... act'.

There are 700,000 active divers in Britain, making 1.75 million dives a year, with a fatality rate of between 10 to 15 divers per year. *Diver* magazine comments that this death rate seems 'modest' for what is considered a risk

"Diving with someone you trust as a diver is a very good idea. But diving with someone you love brings a shared joy and dependency which is a reinforcement of the closeness you feel above water."

Tim Ecott

Holding hands underwater is a great way for couples to go diving: not only can you communicate instantly with just a gentle squeeze but it's also very reassuring in cases where one diver is more experienced than the other. "There is great intimacy in diving with another human being," says Tim Ecott. "Diving with someone you trust as a diver is a very good idea. But diving with someone you love brings a shared joy and dependency which is a reinforcement of the closeness you feel above water."[5]

Not all couples make great buddies, though. Some partners are disaster areas once they get underwater together. Underwater tussles over shared cameras, arguments over who is leading the dive, over-dependence on the more competent partner, and an inability to act in a detached manner if a problem arises are just a few of the pitfalls.

Photographers can make terrible buddies – they'll spend thirty minutes waiting for some obscure marine worm to poke its head out of a hole and, in the process, forget about you entirely. And some have no qualms about placing you in a slightly dodgy position in order to get that much sought-after shot. The anonymous buddy who picked John Bantin to go diving with some years ago in the Sea of Cortez probably still regrets it to this day. John was having a frustrating trip, and was halfway through the week with nothing in the bag when he discovered an elephant seal with amorous inclinations towards divers. This presented the perfect photographic opportunity. "I would go in with an unsuspecting buddy, because I knew exactly what was going to happen and what a great picture it would be," he recalls. "The elephant seal would hover above the diver, then wrap its flippers around and shag 'em. And what do you do if an elephant seal shags you? Nothing – you let it." But then it all went horribly wrong:

I was all ready to get this marvellous picture, and everything was lined up for the shot. The guy's swimming along, oblivious to what's happening, the elephant seal is hovering above him getting ready to grab him and do his best, I'm ready with my camera – and then, to my amazement, the elephant seal opens its mouth. I'm watching, mesmerised, as it then proceeds to swallow my buddy's head. I attacked the elephant seal to get him to let go – it was a bit like attacking a sofa, but the elephant seal got the idea and swam off. My buddy said to me afterwards 'what happened down there? I was swimming along and it suddenly went dark'. I was at a loss to explain...and the worst thing was, I didn't get the picture either.

With a buddy like John, who needs enemies? Some people prefer diving alone, particularly experienced photographers who simply want to get on with the job without having to think about their diving companion. "I'm a great believer in solo diving," says Jack Jackson. "Obviously you've got to be very experienced, you've got to be very good with your equipment – and you've got to be able to rescue yourself. And you musn't be scared to say, 'I shouldn't do this dive'," he adds. Charles Hood agrees that solo diving definitely has a place in shallow, controlled conditions, but warns that; "deep diving solo isn't right."

PADI finally accepted the case for solo diving in 2001, although hedged around with numerous conditions. But they stress that the buddy system is still best: it has provided tangible benefits to millions of divers, and the safety record has improved dramatically over the past few decades as a result. There is no substitute underwater for another set of eyes and hands.

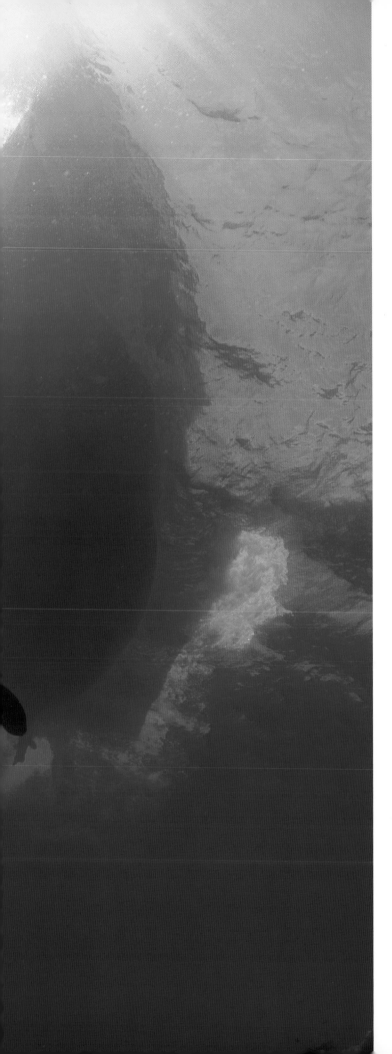

"People should know the difference between their stomach turning over because it's an adventurous dive and they're looking forward to it, and apprehension, because they know they really shouldn't be doing the dive. One of my favourite sayings is that it's better to be on the boat wishing you were in the water than being in the water at 40 metres and wishing you were on the boat."

Richard Bull

← BOATS ARE A MAJOR HAZARD FOR DIVERS.
(FELIDHOO ATOLL, MALDIVES)

Slow down, see more

Divers spend huge amounts of energy just moving through the sea, finning endlessly along, looking around the next rock or reef for a bigger or more colourful fish. And on guided dives we often use up most of our air charging around in a big, noisy, bubble-blowing mass, just like a group of package tourists being shepherded hurriedly around the sights of Rome or Paris.

This non-stop whizzing about means that dive guides are constantly moving on to new sites, often allowing only the most superficial look at each one. As Tim Ecott discovered when he worked as a dive guide in the Seychelles, clients were often reluctant to visit the same dive site twice in one week:

'We've been there already', they would say. This is as illogical as saying that you have seen a sunset on a particular beach once, and don't need to see it from the same place again. The point is that we spend only a brief period underwater, usually barely an hour at a time, and the probability that we will see everything in that moment is nonsensical. Could you stand in a forest and see all the birds that visit a tree in one hour of one day in the year and say that you know that tree?[6]

Sylvia Earle draws a similar analogy when comparing guided dives with her experience living in the Tektite habitat for extended periods. "It is comparable to taking a walk in the woods for half an hour versus camping there, day and night, for a couple of weeks," she says. "Patterns come into focus, shy creatures reveal themselves... stay underwater long enough and individual fish become recognisable, not just as gray angelfish or filefish or barracuda, but as very specific characters whose habits become as familiar as those of our neighbors."[7]

Photographers, like scientists, also need an in-depth understanding of reef behaviour in order to get results.

⊕ → A RELAXED DIVER GETS A MUCH MORE COMPLETE EXPERIENCE FROM THE UNDERWATER WORLD. (MALDIVES)

"I was once on a rebreather shooting some small creature when I heard what sounded like a storm coming. All the fish went into hiding, and as the storm came closer I realised it was a group of divers passing by"

Guy Chaumette

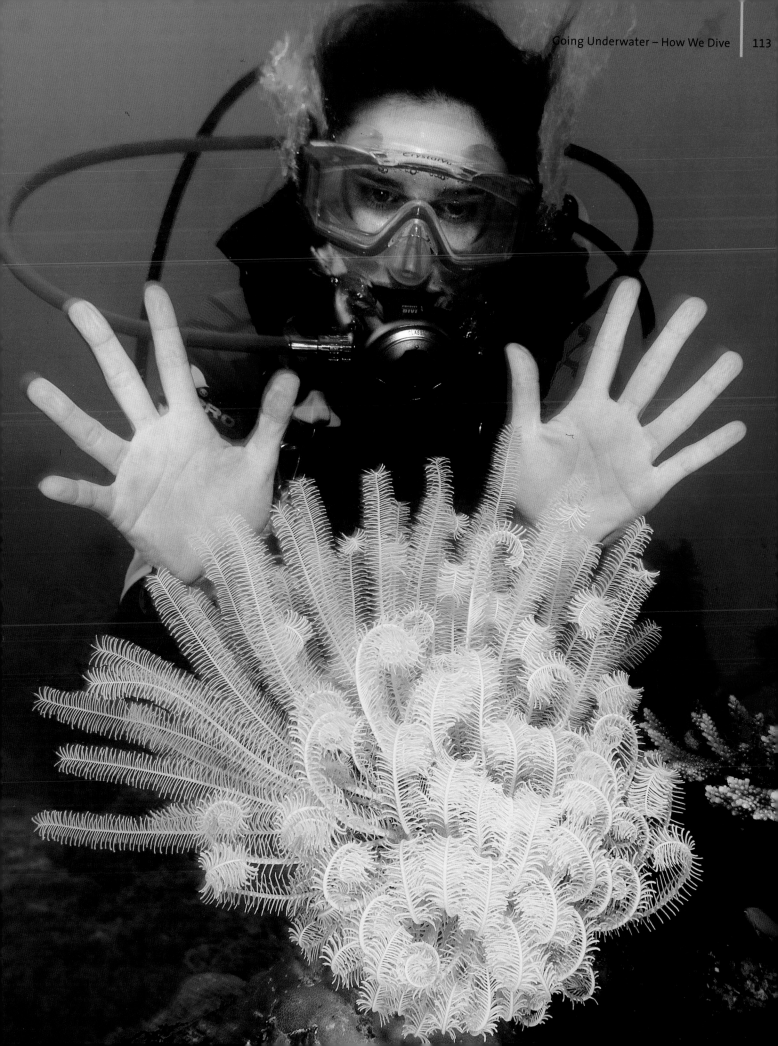

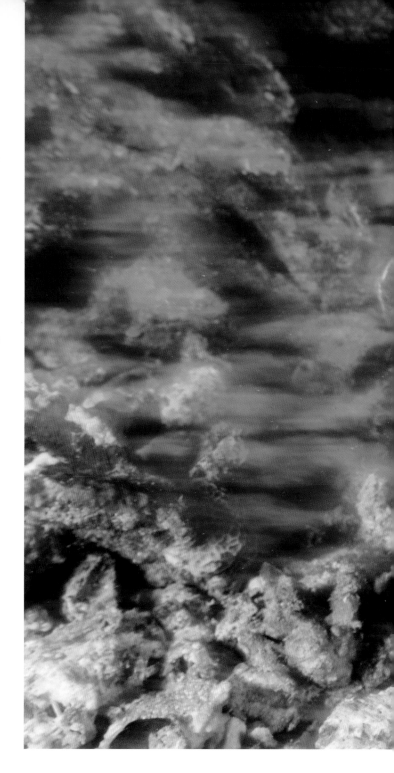

"Shy creatures reveal themselves... stay underwater long enough and individual fish become recognisable as very specific characters whose habits become as familiar as those of our neighbors."

Sylvia Earle

"I'm happiest on a reef when I get the chance to dive on the same dive site repeatedly," says Alex. "In Thailand, for instance, I once dived the same site over 30 times in a period of six days. The reef is not just a mish-mash of animals; it is divided up for many species into well-defined territories," he explains. "Only by repeatedly diving on the reef do I learn where these territorial boundaries lie."

As you become more aware of the general layout and workings of the reef, you'll begin to get more of an idea of the different levels of habitation, the many-layered strata of this underwater community. The habits of reef creatures will start to reveal themselves: who lives where, which neighbours get along, who is doing what to whom – and why. It soon becomes one big underwater soap opera.

Divers are often wide-eyed with astonishment when films reveal animal behaviour they hadn't even guessed at. But it is simply by slowing down that filmmakers manage to produce this amazing material. "Most people don't see the things that I see... because they swim right past them," says Howard Hall. In the Cocos Islands Hall was filming a giant mantis shrimp, about 12 inches (30cm) long, which ate passing fish. "Nobody, including the dive guides, knew that this thing was there, because nobody had bothered to get down in the sand and spend time looking," says Howard. Real observation of animal behaviour takes time and patience, he advises, and it also helps to do some research, so that you know what to look out for: "In the process of looking for something you expect," he adds, "you're very likely to see something unexpected as well."

Not many of us, admittedly, will be able to devote quite so much time looking for interesting creatures. On average Hall and his team spend around seven to eight hours per day in the water, and on his most recent film once recorded 10.5 hours in a single day. A typical animal behaviour sequence for an Imax film takes him four days to film. "This is a great deal of time to spend watching a shrimp!" he says. "People say I must have lots of patience but in reality I just find it very interesting, and I never get tired of watching subtle behaviours. Even after four days you are still learning new things."

Howard and his team use closed-circuit rebreathers (hence their long bottom times), which minimises their impact on the environment they're filming. A rebreather gives you a startling insight into just how noisy and disruptive normal scuba divers are, as filmmaker Guy Chaumette recounts:

I was once on a rebreather shooting some small creature when I heard what sounded like a storm coming. All the fish went into hiding, and as the storm came closer I realised it was a group of divers passing by. All the fish hid as the group passed, then when they had gone the fish came out again. It was very intriguing to watch all these divers just carry on finning – and missing all these creatures.

It's a theme we hear again and again from professional divers – we're missing so much of what is there. We don't all have the opportunity to use rebreathers, or to stay for days at a time on a single dive site, but we can start to be more aware of how our own presence is affecting the fish.

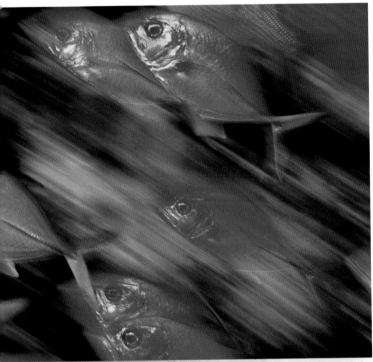

"Charge past at high speed and you will miss them. Slowing down is how filmmakers manage to produce such amazing material."

Being relaxed and breathing calmly are an important part of developing this mindset. Once fish perceive that you aren't a threat, they quickly go about their normal business.

As well as working in Florida and the Caribbean, fish behaviour specialist Ned DeLoach spends around three months of the year around the Lembeh Straits in Indonesia, one of the most biologically rich regions on the planet. With three other marine life specialists, DeLoach has published a reef fish identification book for the Tropical Pacific and is currently working on a similar title covering invertebrates. "We're always trying to get divers to slow down," he says. "We don't move around a lot and when people come diving with us from time to time what we consistently hear afterwards is 'Wow, I never even thought of kneeling down and waiting by a patch reef for ten minutes!'" DeLoach draws a comparison with hunting, noting how you're much more likely to see game by sitting quietly inside a hide than by walking through the woods. "It's the same thing underwater," he says. "It's just hard getting this across to divers sometimes."

Guy Chaumette agrees, pointing out that many divers find it difficult to stay still for any length of time. "People want a tour of the reef as if they're in a museum," he observes. In fact, like in a museum, it's often better just to go and sit in front of one painting and appreciate everything that's in it rather than trying to see every work of art in the whole building. "If you keep doing the tour, you will only ever see the tip of the iceberg," he says.

So, try finding somewhere to sit down, kneel or otherwise stay static for a while. It could be over rubble, or maybe on the sand – checking to make sure you're not

Ⓡ HORSE-EYE JACKS (MALDIVES)
Ⓛ TIME TO RELAX AND WATCH THE MARINE WORLD. (GRAND CAYMAN)

landing like a clumsy invading alien on top of someone's burrow. The important thing is to take some time out and stay still. This lies at the heart of the art of diving. It's a more subtle approach that puts the focus on marine wildlife. And just because you're staying still and concentrating on what's happening in front of your face doesn't mean you're going to miss out on the big fish action, either. Simply remember to keep one eye out on the blue for whatever is passing by.

Local knowledge

The guided dive and the reef tour still have their place: a knowledgeable guide should know his or her local reef intimately, and will be able to point out the regular inhabitants of the reef to their clients. "The dive guide who is doing the same route time after time is actually going to impart a lot of knowledge, and those people are going to get a lot out of the dive," says Lawson Wood. "The clients don't have enough confidence to go off by themselves or understand what they're looking at. Seventy-five per cent of the people who we see every week in the Caymans like to go with a dive guide for those reasons," he adds.

Although there are undoubtedly plenty of people who will continue to prefer the mass guided dive, for others it's hard to change the pattern – and indeed in some destinations only guided dives are permitted. There's no reason these shouldn't also involve a reef-watching stop, as long as there's a suitable location. But the priority of many dive guides is the fast tour. I once asked a dive guide in the Red Sea if I could spend some time just watching the reef, and not rush around the dive site. He thought it was a great idea and readily agreed. But what happened during the dive? We did a thorough figure-of-eight pattern around the site, covering just about every bit of reef there was to see – and the guide just kept going, finning continuously and failing to slow down at any point. I could have asked him to slow down – if I'd been able to catch up at all. (If you ever find yourself in a similar situation, I suggest you just stop and wait: your guide will have to come back and find you eventually.)

Usually at the end of a dive there is a period toodling around in the shallows de-gassing. This can be an excellent opportunity to sit down for five or ten minutes near a shallow reef and watch fish (another benefit is that your remaining air will last longer). But it's better to try and build a more substantial chunk of time into your dive in which to

⊕ THIS SMALL CORAL HEAD IS A HOTBED OF BIODIVERSITY, BURSTING WITH COLOUR AND LIFE. (RAS MUHAMMED, EGYPT)

"Could you stand in a forest and see all the birds that visit a tree in one hour of one day and say that you know that tree?"

Tim Ecott

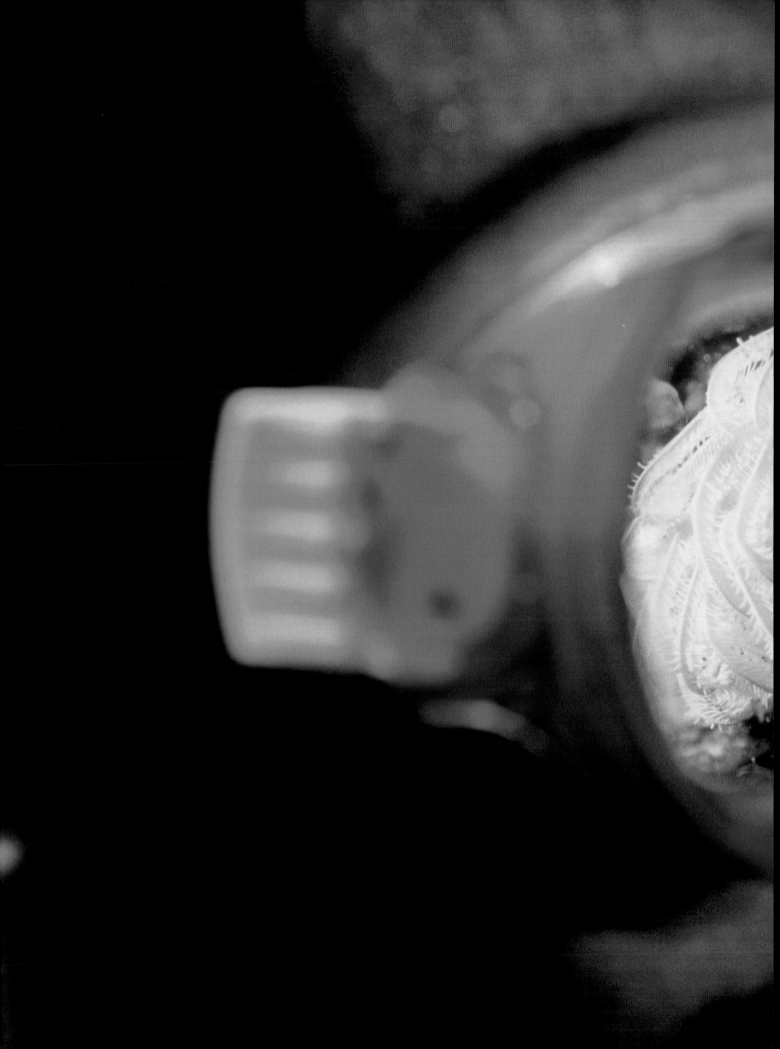

"People say I must have lots of patience but in reality I just find it very interesting, and I never get tired of watching subtle behaviours" **Howard Hall**

↑ MOST DIVES INVOLVE CONSTANT SWIMMING. SLOW DOWN! (FELIDHOO ATOLL, MALDIVES)

→ CHAIN MORAY (MAGGIE'S MAZE, GRAND CAYMAN)

find a safe, sheltered spot from where to watch what's happening. It's shifting the balance to let the marine life come to you, rather than chasing around after it. Sometimes this isn't possible – there's no sandy patch, or it's a drift dive, or a deep wall with no seabed – but when you can, try and relax by sitting on the seabed, slowing down your breathing, and observe what's going on.

Doing your own thing in this way is obviously much easier if you're in buddy pairs. In some cases it's not going to be appropriate to strike off on your own, or even to stay still for any length of time. It might be impossible on a drift dive where you're floating along in the current, for instance, or a deep wall, or on a dive involving tricky navigation that requires in-depth local knowledge. But if you can find a quiet spot and settle down just to watch what's going on it can be incredibly rewarding. Cleaning stations are always a good bet (*see Chapter four,* 'The art of fish watching'). "When I was working as a dive guide I always encouraged people to go off in buddy pairs and spread out over the reef rather than being a group of ten divers with so many bubbles and so much noise," says Guy Chaumette. "Unfortunately not many dive resorts encourage people to dive in buddy pairs – it's all about group diving. It's like you have to fight with the resort and the dive guide for them to leave you alone and to accept that you can survive in the water," he says, "which is ridiculous, because you passed your diving licence for one thing and one thing only, and that is to be able to go underwater unsupervised."

Guy believes that we should start every dive with a break. "People may have just arrived at the resort after a stressful journey, they've had all the hassle of sorting out their paperwork and gear, trying to remember how many weights they need and so forth," he says. "Then they jump in the water and the stress makes them fly over the reef like rockets." Guy personally prefers people to settle down right under the boat and take a few minutes to relax, breathe slowly, and start to feel comfortable before moving off. Many liveaboard trips will start with a similar 'check-out' dive.

If you're diving with a group, you'll have to persuade the dive guide that you want at least one or more breaks from finning around. These breaks also help divers become more relaxed and comfortable in the water, allowing an opportunity to sort out minor problems, re-adjust equipment, and deal with anything that can't be tackled properly while trying to keep up with the group.

However you go about it, the key to gaining a deeper understanding of the marine world is to stop rushing around. "The temptation is to continue swimming, in a greedy effort to see more and more," says Osha Gray Davidson. "But this is a foolish notion – a habit based on terrestrial experience," he says. "The secret of diving in the heart of biodiversity is to stay in one place, to hover and focus on what's directly in front of you. You'd run through your entire tank of air before seeing all the different organisms in one spot." The art of diving is also the art of staying still, and of being able to see the underwater world with fresh eyes.

the art of
fish watching

"The best way to observe a fish is to become a fish."

Jacques Cousteau

A DIVER IS TREATED TO THE
SIGHT OF BARRED HAMLETS
SPAWNING AT DUSK.
(SUNSET HOUSE REEF,
GRAND CAYMAN)

AS THE GLOWING SUN SINKS TOWARDS THE OCEAN HORIZON, THERE IS A CHANGE OF SHIFT ON THE REEF. ANGELFISH, BUTTERFLYFISH, WRASSE AND OTHER DAYTIME CREATURES RETREAT INTO SMALL CRACKS AND CREVICES, WHILE SQUIRRELFISH AND SOLDIERFISH START TO EMERGE FROM UNDER THE CORAL OVERHANGS WHERE THEY HAVE BEEN LURKING ALL DAY. CORAL POLYPS STRETCH OUT THEIR TENTACLES FOR A NIGHT-TIME FEED AND SEA URCHINS, NORMALLY SEDENTARY DURING DAYTIME, MOVE SLOWLY UP THE REEF WITH THEIR SPINES WAVING, ON THE HUNT FOR FOOD. FEATHER STARS AND BASKET STARS ARE ALSO ON THE MOVE, WHILE THE GORGEOUS SPANISH DANCER VENTURES OUT TO DINE ON ANEMONES AND SPONGES, AND SCHOOLS OF SNAPPERS AND GRUNTS MOVE OFF TOWARDS THE SEAGRASS BEDS TO GRAZE UNDER THE COVER OF DARKNESS.

But before the reef switches fully into night-time mode, when there is still just enough light to see without a torch, something else is taking place that is even more crucial to the cycle of life.

On the reef's edge, a male parrotfish is dashing around trying to court a female – showing off his prowess by spreading his fins and raising his tail. Each time he approaches her, his movements become more frenetic, until gradually she succumbs to his advances – rising off the reef as she does so. As I watch, the male circles her until suddenly they both make a dash up for the open water. At the peak of their climb, the pair rapidly release their eggs and sperm together, before speeding back down separately to the safety of the reef.

As I fin slowly along, the same parrotfish – clearly not yet ready to bed down for the night – is trying his luck with another female. Above us, the gametes (the eggs and sperm of the fish) join the plankton-rich surface currents that will carry them away from the reef and its predators.

I continue my dive and the gametes drift oceanwards in the gloom. Within a day or two, the fertilized eggs will begin to develop into miniature parrotfish, each one complete with a bulging yolk sac to give it nourishment. These will join the great swirling mass of organisms we call plankton – the word being derived from the Greek *planktos*, meaning wandering.

Each little parrotfish larva, drifting in the open ocean, is at the mercy of the currents and wind, with no power to alter its course. It is now part of a huge community of plants and animals in the great marine food web. At the base of the web are the microscopic, single-celled algae called phytoplankton. These are grazed by herbivorous zooplankton, a collection of tiny animals that include the larvae of crustaceans, worms and fishes. Then come the macrozooplankton, larger fish and invertebrates such as jellyfish that eat their carnivorous way through the web along their respective food chains. And so on, up to larger predators such as mackerel and squid – which in turn are prey for even larger predators such as tuna and sharks.

A parrotfish larva, whose chances of survival in this oceanic soup are millions to one, must eat or be eaten. As it chomps on the surrounding plankton, its body mass grows by a third each day and its defining features start to emerge. Typically, it will spend anywhere from two to four weeks drifting with the currents before it is ready to find a permanent home. (There are some exceptions, such as Moorish Idols, that can survive in the floating plankton for up to one hundred days – a record for reef fish). Once its senses have developed enough, the juvenile fish seeks out a safe new habitat in which to lie low. Mangroves and seagrass beds make popular nursery grounds for many species, allowing them to settle for a while before relocating to their adult habitat.

Our young parrotfish begins its settled life hiding among algae, only venturing forth to forage for small crustaceans and passing plankton. It hasn't yet acquired the bright mantle that makes it one of the most easily recognisable fish on the reef, and has to make do with drab greys, reds and browns until it matures. But so far, so good.

Sex on the reef

Fish watching is an acquired skill – and few aspects of fish behaviour are harder to watch than spawning, particularly since it mostly takes place at dusk, when many divers are already engaged in their own mating rituals, sipping sundowners on a tropical seashore.

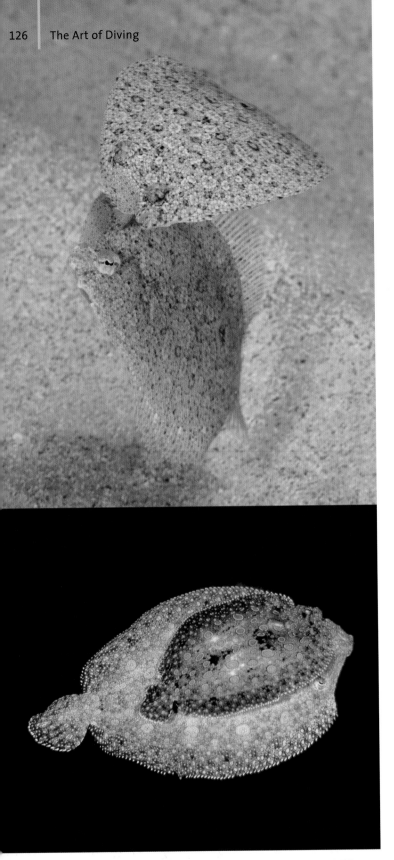

⬆ ⬆ TWO MALE EYED FLOUNDER FIGHTING OVER MATING RIGHTS

⬆ A SMALL FEMALE PEACOCK FLOUNDER POSITIONS HERSELF ABOVE A LARGER MALE DURING A SPAWNING RISE.

⬀ A MALE YELLOWHEAD WRASSE PERFORMS HIS COURTSHIP DANCE TO ENTICE FEMALES...

➡ ...AND IT IS SUCCESSFUL: A SMALL, DRAB FEMALE RISES UP FROM THE REEF AND JOINS HIM ON A SPAWNING RISE.

(ALL IMAGES, GRAND CAYMAN)

Although most dive resorts offer night diving, very few schedule dusk dives. Late afternoon is usually the time that boats are moored up at the quay, being rinsed down for the day. And on a live-aboard, most people have finished their quota of dives and are ready for a hot shower and cold drink – or they're thinking ahead to a night dive. But if you're familiar with the location and are suitably qualified, there's no reason why you shouldn't go off with a buddy and have a gentle look around at dusk to see what you can spot. It doesn't need to be a deep dive. But do take a torch, since it *will* get dark.

Timing is crucial: the optimum time for watching spawning is the last forty-five minutes before sunset and the first thirty minutes afterwards. "Watching these forms of fish behaviour is a key element of dusk diving," says Alex, who has made a speciality of shooting spawning behaviour. "And it's all the more amazing because so few divers have seen it. This isn't because it's difficult to see," he adds, "but because divers just aren't in the water at the right time."

So, you've managed to get your buddy and yourself underwater in good time. What should you be looking for? "Once you get your eye in, you will know spawning every time that you see it," explains Alex. "It's very easy when divers first start looking to think that every behaviour they're seeing is spawning behaviour – parrotfish voiding themselves for instance, or two fish fighting." What you're really looking for is two fish pairing up and swimming quickly off the reef into the open water, releasing a small cloud of eggs and sperm as they reach the top of their upward flight, and then returning to the safety of the reef. The fish are trying to maximise the chances of their offspring surviving by releasing their gametes into the great planktonic soup as far away as possible from their hungry neighbours. It makes addictive viewing, he claims:

Once you start watching for them you'll realise that courtship patterns are very elaborate and it can be the most fantastic time of day to dive. It gives you such a huge insight into the reef, because all these fish that seem to have been swimming around pretty aimlessly all day are suddenly doing things with a purpose, and you begin to understand what it's all about.

Understanding fish behaviour enriches the diving experience a hundredfold. But how *do* we know what's going on down there? Luckily for us, ichthyologists have spent thou-

sperm, but the females need more time for their eggs to hydrate before they're ready to release them. The courtship allows time for egg preparation; as the female gets ready, she becomes more receptive to the male's advances and often initiates spawning by rising up and hovering off the bottom.

Once you know what spawning looks like you may be able to spot up to a dozen or more species at it. Because reef fish live in warm water and have fast metabolic rates, they often spawn every day. Some species do it during daytime, but most prefer dusk: in the Caribbean and Indo-Pacific, about 80 per cent of species that spawn by broadcasting their eggs and sperm do so at sunset. Tangs, wrasses and parrotfish are among the more obvious species to look out for. Some destinations schedule dusk dives specifically to watch spawning events: in Indonesia, Malaysia, Yap and Fiji, for instance, you can join mandarinfish dives to watch these gaudy creatures emerge from the reef, fight and spawn.

sands of hours underwater trying to put the pieces together. A lot of their knowledge has been brought together in the indispensible *Reef Fish Behavior*, by Ned DeLoach and Paul Humann, which focuses on the reefs of the tropical western Atlantic. For author Ned DeLoach, there's no question that dusk diving is the best opportunity to find out what's really happening on the reef: "That is *the* greatest time to be underwater," he told me, "because that's when all the reproductive activity is taking place." As well as spawning, there are the extended courtship displays that precede it and which, according to DeLoach, are often "entertaining, passion-packed melodramas":

> *Courtship behavior varies but always revolves around a basic theme: a revved boy fish relentlessly chases, cajoles, corners, nudges and shows-off to a seemingly indifferent girl fish. To an untrained eye courtship often appears as nothing more than fish milling near the bottom. But after observing one or two fish trysts, the signs become unmistakable.*[1]

Telltale clues to courtship behaviour include colour and pattern changes, body twitches, fin displays, swollen abdomens, females hovering in mid-water and males swimming quickly in and out of the area and chasing away competing suitors. The males come to the party ready to shed their

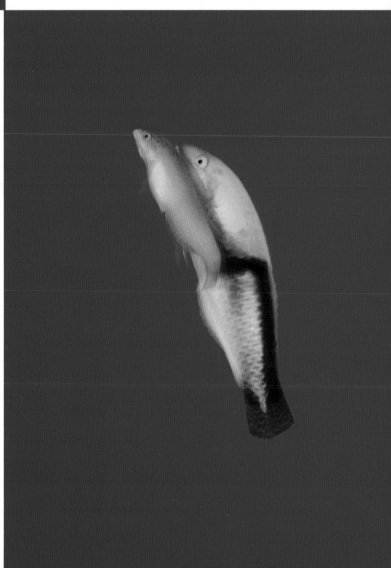

⦉ A MALE LIONFISH COURTS A FEMALE AT DUSK. (ABU NUHAS, EGYPT)
⦉ LIONFISH ON A SPAWNING RISE IN THE RED SEA. (ABU NUHAS, EGYPT)

"Gone is the image of fish as drudging and dim-witted pea brains, driven largely by 'instinct', with what little behavioural flexibility they possess being severely hampered by an infamous 'three-second' memory. Now, fish are regarded as steeped in social intelligence, pursuing Machiavellian strategies of manipulation, punishment and reconciliation; exhibiting stable cultural traditions and co-operating to inspect predators and catch food."

Laland, Brown and Krause, Fish and Fisheries

Spawning is usually triggered by sea temperature: in the Red Sea, May to September tends to be peak season; in the Caribbean it varies from the southern islands, where many species spawn during the northern hemisphere's winter season, to the northern islands, where the very same species will spawn during the 'summer' season. But temperature is not the only factor: in the Maldives, for instance, it is the relative strength of the tides that acts as the main catalyst for spawning. There are still great gaps in our knowledge, especially since observations tend to be limited to particular reefs or islands where researchers have been working. "Trying to figure out when fish spawn can often be a challenge," says DeLoach. "Some species in the Caribbean – although we've dived with them hundreds and hundreds of times, we've never actually seen them spawn."

Other kinds of spawning

Among the most spectacular marine events are mass spawnings, when countless fish release millions of gametes into the water column. Large species such as snapper or grouper tend to spawn only once or twice a year and may travel hundreds of kilometers to join in. At Ras Muhammad at the tip of Egypt's Sinai peninsula, for instance, huge spawning aggregations of Bohar Snapper gather in early summer. At Gladden Spit in Belize, Dog and Cubera Snapper form massive spawning schools in the spring (drawing Whalesharks as if from nowhere to feast on their eggs). In Puerto Rico, up to seven thousand Blue Tang have been observed in spawning aggregations.

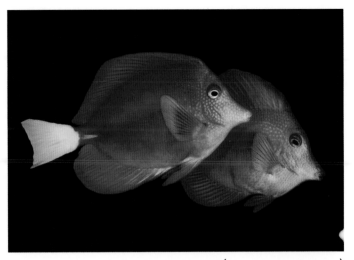

↑ A MALE EMPEROR TANG COURTS A FEMALE. (RAS MUHAMMED, EGYPT)
↗ A CLOWNFISH TENDS TO EGGS IN ITS NEST BENEATH AN ANEMONE. (SIMILAN ISLANDS, THAILAND)
→ A LARGE MALE ROCK BEAUTY CIRCLES A SMALLER FEMALE AS HE COURTS HER. (EDEN ROCK, GRAND CAYMAN)
→ → A DIVER WATCHES CLARK'S ANEMONEFISH. (ARI ATOLL, MALDIVES)

All around the world's oceans different species perform similar mass spawning aggregations.

Some species go for mass spawning in one location, but change strategy elsewhere: in the Red Sea, Brown Surgeonfish often spawn *en masse* near the edge of the reef, while in Malaysia they've been known to spawn as lone pairs.

Another phenomenon is 'harem spawning', in which one male fertilises the eggs from several females. In the Caribbean you can observe this behaviour in the Rock Beauty, in which the larger male develops a dark face and courts several females in his harem at once. He first selects one and circles around her, displaying his fins and nuzzling her belly as she rises up to spawn; he then repeats the performance for other females. In the Red Sea, one of the easiest harem spawners to spot is the ubiquitous Anthias, which swims up above its harem to perform a courting dance with an exaggerated wiggling of its tail and pectoral fins. As the females succumb to the male's advances, they rise up to join him, before making a mad dash to release their eggs and sperm in the water column. Sneaky bachelor fish, with no harems of their own, will try and cut in on the action by rushing to spawn with females while the dominant male is busy elsewhere. If a large colony is spawning, there will be no shortage of hungry fish downcurrent – often fusiliers – dashing in for a twilight snack on the nutritious eggs.

Fish also spawn by laying eggs on the reef itself. This is known as benthic egg laying. Although you might not catch the fish actually at it, you can certainly find them looking after their eggs, which gives a clue to the spawning location. "One of the easiest ways to find fish spawning is to look out for easily recognisable species such as damselfish or clownfish," explains Alex. "Not only do they spawn during daytime but you can quite often see them guarding their eggs on the reef, which gives you a good idea of where to look." Clownfish will peel back a little bit of their host anemone to clean a tiny patch of rock where they lay their eggs, leaving them protected under a fold of

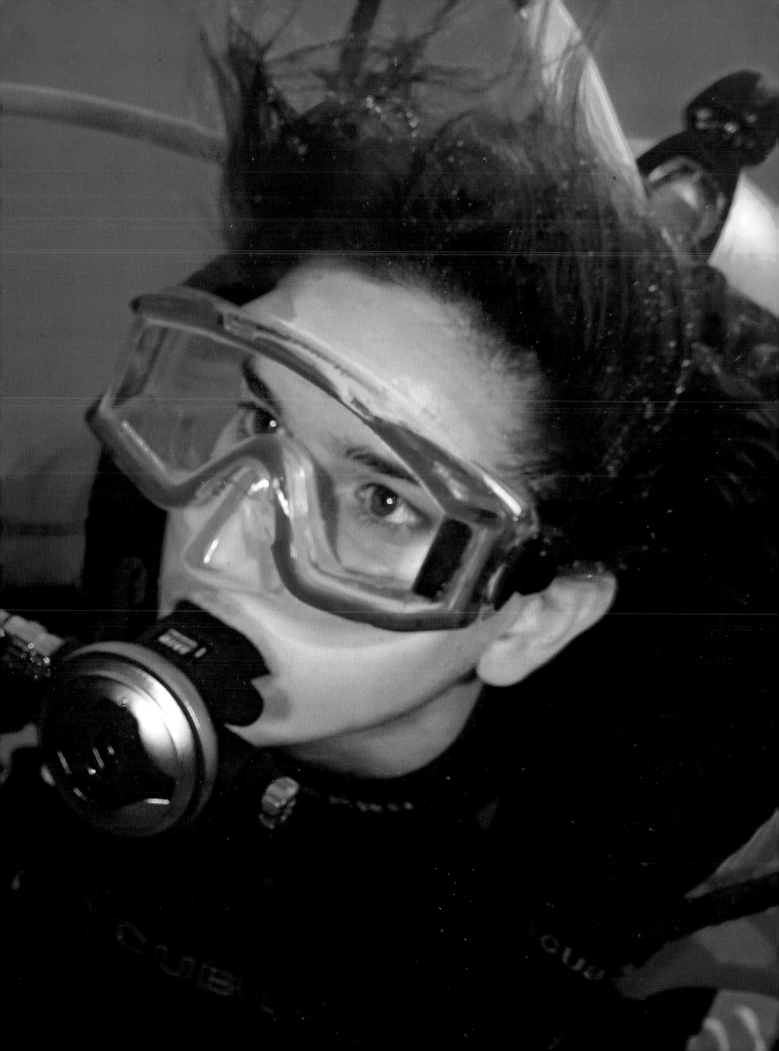

⬆ THREE FEMALES SPAWN IN THE NEST OF A MALE WHITEBELLY DAMSELFISH. (SHARM EL SHEIKH, EGYPT)

tentacles. Check the edges of anemones, and you'll see the egg patches with the clownfish guarding them.

Wreck sites also offer good opportunities to watch fish mating behaviour: the clean, flat surfaces of sunken ships are popular for egg deposits (the wreck of the *Ulysses* in the northern Red Sea, for instance, is home to a massive colony of Sergeant Majors). Most benthic egg-laying of this kind takes place at dawn, which is another reason we don't see it happening.

Meet the parents

Most divers are familiar with the highly aggressive behaviour of Titan Triggerfish. During the spawning season the male will defend a nest of eggs on the seabed with frightening ferocity: these large fish have no hesitation in attacking divers and driving them out of their territory. (They're considered one of the most dangerous fish in the sea under these circumstances, far more aggressive than sharks, and

"Courtship behavior varies but always revolves around a basic theme: a revved boy fish relentlessly chases, cajoles, corners, nudges and shows-off to a seemingly indifferent girl fish. To an untrained eye courtship often appears as nothing more than fish milling near the bottom. But after observing one or two fish trysts, the signs become unmistakable."

Ned DeLoach

One novel way in which some fish protect their eggs is by incubating them in their mouth. This is known as mouth brooding. Fish from six families worldwide use this technique. These include the Yellowhead Jawfish, in which the male takes on nursery duty for about a week before the young hatch out. In the Caribbean, where this fish is found, you can usually spot this behaviour between spring and autumn.

These methods are just a few of the numerous ways in which marine creatures reproduce. Alex finds the number of permutations mind-boggling:

What really makes this type of fish watching so intriguing is that fish employ such a great variety of reproductive strategies and tactics. There is external fertilization, internal fertilization, egg laying, broadcast spawning and even mouth brooding. Species form pairs, or spawn in groups, there are harems, sex

personally I always give them a wide berth, just in case it's spawning season.)

Leaving eggs lying around on the seabed, even when heavily guarded, is a risky strategy. Many crustaceans overcome this problem by carrying their eggs around with them. "Whenever you see a shrimp, lobster or crab in the ocean it is always worth checking for eggs," says Alex, pointing out that on average around 25 per cent of adult crustaceans on the reef are carrying eggs at any one time.

changes, deceptions concerning sexual identity and even some fish, like hamlets, that switch sexual roles several times in an evening. If fish used the internet there would certainly be some weird websites!

Hamlets are among the few vertebrates that are true simultaneous hermaphrodites, meaning that each fish has fully functional male and female reproductive organs. So when hamlets spawn they alternate sex roles on each spawning rise, taking it in turns to both release eggs and to fertilise them. This strategy is called egg trading.

Seaslugs – often flamboyantly attractive, despite their unappealing moniker – are also hermaphrodites. Individuals seldom encounter each other on reefs, being fairly uncommon, so when they do actually meet it makes sense to make the most of it. Since each seaslug is both male and female, both can go away after mating and lay eggs, thus maximising their reproductive output.

Herbivores

As our parrotfish matures it will develop the bright, gaudy colours that make it so distinctive. It will also develop a set of fused teeth, which will allow it to chew algae off the hard surface of the reef and to bite through calcareous algae. Bony teeth plates in its throat work like a grinding mill, allowing it to crunch up the gritty calcium carbonate and get at the nutrients.

Somewhere between a quarter and a half of all fish on the reef are herbivores – or plant eaters. Without their constant nibbling, coral reefs wouldn't exist in their present form. Their daily feeding routine also makes them among the easiest fish to spot: since algae is not very nutritious, they must ingest large quantities of it to meet their energy needs, so spend nearly all their time eating – face down, tails in the air. Alongside parrotfish, surgeonfish are among the main consumers; they tend to browse more selectively,

⊕ A PAIR OF ANTHIAS DASH AWAY FROM REEF TO SPAWN AT DUSK. (RAS MUHAMMED, EGYPT)

⊗ A PAIR OF LEOPARD HEADSHIELD SEASLUGS MATING AT NIGHT. (LEMBEH STRAIT, INDONESIA)

⊕ SOHAL SURGEONFISH IN A HIGH-SPEED TERRITORIAL DISPUTE OVER THEIR GARDENS. (ABU NUHAS, EGYPT)

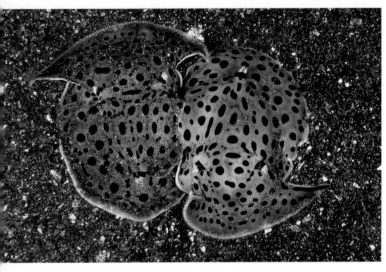

taking quick bites here and there. Other herbivores include damselfish, rabbitfish, chub, some butterflyfish and some angelfish. Invertebrates such as sea urchins are also important grazers, helping to keep surfaces free of weed so that new corals and other attached invertebrates can find space to settle and grow. A single urchin keeps around one square metre (three square feet) of reef or rock free of algae.

Competition for food among all these herbivores is intense. Some fish farm their own plants in order to safeguard a personal supply: damselfish, for instance, defend territories where they farm their own algae by pecking back the corals and weeding out unwanted plants to leave a luxuriant growth for their personal consumption. They are very effective farmers: the algae in their undersea gardens grows up to seven times faster and is generally much taller and more abundant than algae in surrounding areas. Larger and more aggressive fish, such as the Sohal Surgeonfish, will vigorously defend their algal lawns from rivals and other herbivores. Tiny damselfish will even have a go at visiting divers and snorkellers who wander too close to their precious gardens. Smaller and less aggressive herbivores manage to grab a share by getting together in schools and raiding the algae farms *en masse*.

In shallow water the competition for plant food tends to be at its most intense, which is why you'll notice sandy zones around inshore patch reefs or coral heads. These plant-free areas, known as halos, usually extend for around ten metres (33 feet), since this is about as far as herbivores dare to swim from the protection of the reef.

Carnivores

Although our parrotfish began life as a plankton eater, it went through a phase of eating small crustaceans before settling into its adult diet of algae and ending up as a herbivore. In other words, it briefly became a carnivore. This is a normal pattern for reef fish, which may go through several different phases as they mature. Their diet may also change in order to take advantage of temporary food supplies – the parrotfish, for instance, will dine on certain sponges when they're available. This strategy, known as optimal foraging, ensures that fish can gain the most energy with the least effort.

Most fish that you see on the reef are primarily carnivores, and will eat almost any other kind of animal,

⊕ A FROGFISH SETS ITS AMBUSH AND WAITS, CAMOUFLAGED AMONG SOFT CORALS. (RAS MUHAMMED, EGYPT)

⊖ A RAINBOW MANTIS SHRIMP CARRIES A LARGE CLUTCH OF RED EGGS. (LEMBEH STRAIT, INDONESIA)

including such apparently unappetising fare as hydroids and fire corals. The ubiquitous Sergeant Major, for instance, has a highly successful strategy of eating anything from plankton and algae to seaslugs and shrimp larvae.

Fish eaters can be divided into two broad categories: those, such as barracuda, that live in open water and hunt their prey by active pursuit; and those, such as lizardfish, that lie motionless on the reef waiting to ambush whatever they can. Among the latter are some real masters of disguise, including frogfish, scorpionfish and stonefish.

With so many fish dependent on eating other fish, you may wonder why we don't see them in action more often. "It's partly because it all happens so quickly," explains Ned DeLoach. If a hunter can't swallow its prey all at once, another fish may take advantage of the situation and pounce on it to grab a free lunch of its own. "Especially when it's a fish eating a fish, they will usually try and get it down in a very quick gulp. It's only when they catch something that they

⊙ THE BOXER CRAB IS UNUSUAL BECAUSE IT HOLDS STINGING
ANEMONES IN ITS CLAWS FOR ITS DEFENCE. THIS BOXER CRAB HAS
BEEN INFECTED BY A PARASITIC BARNACLE, WHICH IS GROWING INSIDE
THE CRAB AND HAS PRODUCED A CREAM COLOURED CLUTCH OF EGGS
ON THE CRAB'S UNDERSIDE. THE CRAB WILL CARRY AND DEFEND THE
PARASITE'S EGGS AS IF THEY WERE ITS OWN. (BALI, INDONESIA)
⊙ A DEVIL SCORPIONFISH HIDES IN THE SAND READY TO POUNCE.
(LEMBEH STRAIT, INDONESIA)

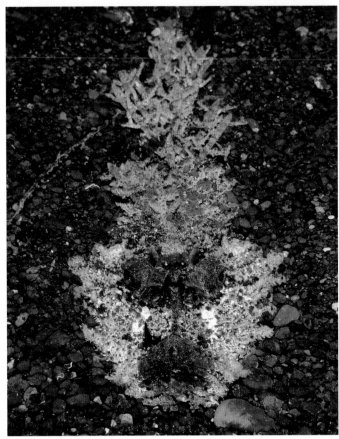

can't immediately swallow that we're afforded a chance to
photograph or observe it," says DeLoach.

The Giant Frogfish, for instance, is a "leading candi-
date for the 'Fastest Gun on the Reef'," according to Helen
Buttfield in *The Secret Life of Fishes*. This well-camouflaged
carnivore has its first dorsal spine modified into a long
fishing pole with a wormlike lure on the end, which it jig-
gles to tempt prey closer. "Any hungry little fish moving in
to investigate is instantly inhaled by the suction created
when the frogfish opens his great mouth," she explains.
"This vanishing act, invisible to the human eye, has been
timed at one one-hundredth of a second!"[2]

A diver visiting a coral reef packed with schools of fish
lazing around in the shallows and predators swimming past

heedless of their prey may get the impression that there's not much going on, and that fish seldom eat. "Nothing could be further from the truth," says Ned DeLoach. "The majority of fish spend their time locating, stalking, capturing and digesting prey."[3] If a shoal of fish looks inactive, it's because they're resting after having been out hunting all night. The predators, meanwhile, are waiting until twilight, when their chances of success are much better.

During normal daylight hours the survival odds are balanced in a fish's favour, as long as it remains within reach of a hiding place and stays on the lookout. But once daylight begins to fade, the odds swing towards the predators. "During the last twenty minutes before complete darkness, the low-light conditions are so favorable to the big predators that the water above the reef is virtually devoid of reef life,"[4] says DeLoach. The smaller and more vulnerable fish retreat into their hiding holes first, followed by larger fish such, as the parrotfish, getting ready to settle for the night.

Cleaning stations

Something else that often puzzles divers is why they never see sick fish. One reason is that weak or dying fish are eaten almost immediately, but another is that infections or wounds can heal up rapidly because most fish regularly visit cleaning stations.

Cleaning stations are fixed locations on the reef where cleaner fish and shrimps tidy up their 'client' fish by picking off irritants such as mucus, bits of dead skin and the parasites that burrow into the flesh around their eyes, gills, nostrils and mouths. In return, these nutritious tit-bits make a good meal for the cleaners. Thus a cleaning station combines the roles of health clinic and beauty salon. And studies have shown that perhaps half the reef fish in the Caribbean, for instance, visit one at least once a day. Some fish make repeated daily visits – particularly wounded fish, which may spend half their day being serviced.

A cleaning station is generally located high up on the reef, its services being advertised by the little fluttering dance of the cleaner fish or the waving of the shrimps' antennae. In the Indo-Pacific the most widespread cleaners are wrasse, whereas in the Caribbean this role is usually performed by various species of goby. Quite a few other fish act as part-time cleaners and the juveniles of some species perform cleaning duties before they mature. There are also cleaner crabs and six species of cleaner shrimp.

A client fish usually hovers just off the reef as the cleaners get to work, picking parasites off its sides and fins or occasionally darting inside its mouths or under its gill covers. Once the cleaning starts, the client fish tend to go into an immobile, trance-like state. A truce is in operation while cleaning is in progress, enabling small fish to enter the mouths of giant predators without fear. Different species adopt different postures while being cleaned: goatfishes hang with their heads down; grunts and surgeonfishes stay horizontal; others hang with their heads pointing upwards; and some stay on the seabed. And a queue often forms for the cleaner's services, with fish hanging off the reef awaiting their turn.

Many fish change colour while being cleaned, possibly to make it easier for the cleaner to spot the parasites, or perhaps simply to inform the cleaner that they're ready. Tiger Grouper and goatfish turn different shades of red; Yellowmouth Grouper go very dark; and Black Surgeonfish turn blue and white, or grey and white.

Many bottom-dwelling species, such as groupers, flounders, morays, and lizardfish, are cleaned in situ by gobies and shrimps. The two often work in tandem, with the gobies cleaning flanks, fins and the larger surfaces, and the shrimps performing the more delicate work around the eyes, gills and mouth. Some groupers and morays have one or more cleaner shrimps that live alongside them in their lairs – their own personal valets, so to speak.

Mutual benefits

This type of inter-relationship between two species is known as symbiosis – or 'living together'. It's thought that the symbiotic relationship between cleaner fish and their clients is vital to overall reef health. In a famous study published in 1961, marine biologist Conrad Limbaugh removed all the cleaning organisms from two small, isolated reefs in the Bahamas; within two weeks all except the territorial fishes had disappeared from the reefs. Many of the fish that remained soon developed swellings, ulcerated fins and sores. Limbaugh concluded from this that cooperative behaviour was more important in nature than the tooth-and-claw struggle for existence. "Almost overnight, this glowing portrayal of cooperative behaviour captured

⊕ A CLEANER WRASSE ATTENDS TO A FEMALE ANTHIAS IN THE RED SEA.
(GULF OF SUEZ, EGYPT)
⊕ ⊕ A ROVING GROUPER AND CLEANER WRASSE.
(RAS MUHAMMED, EGYPT)

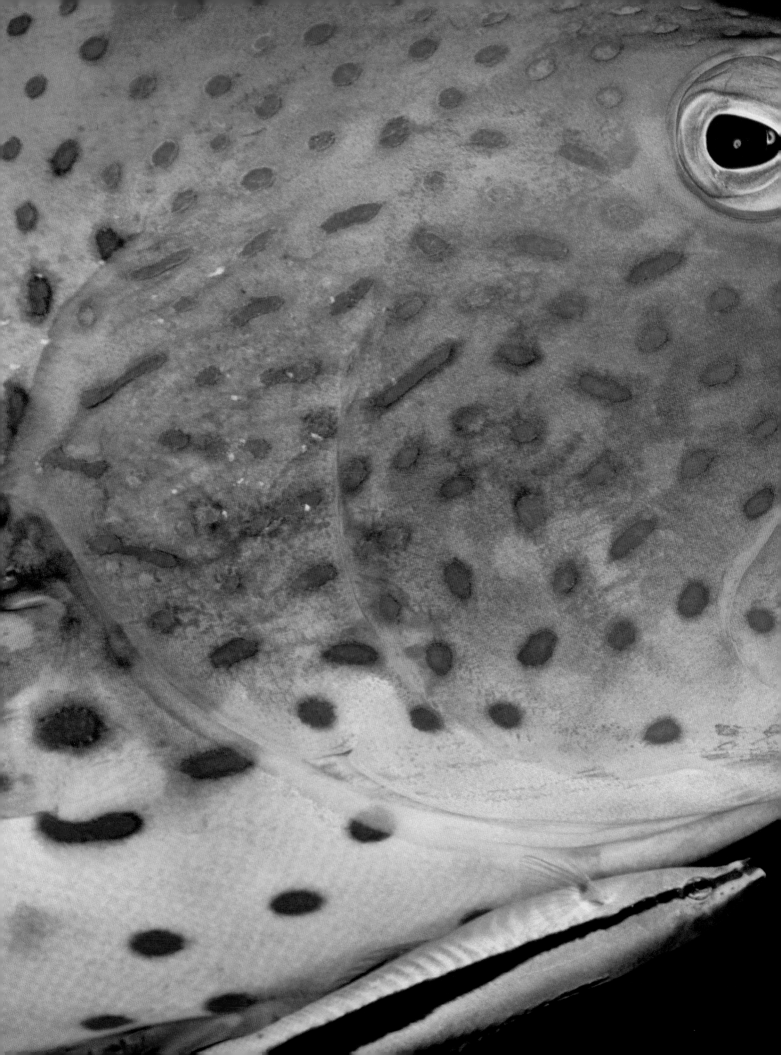

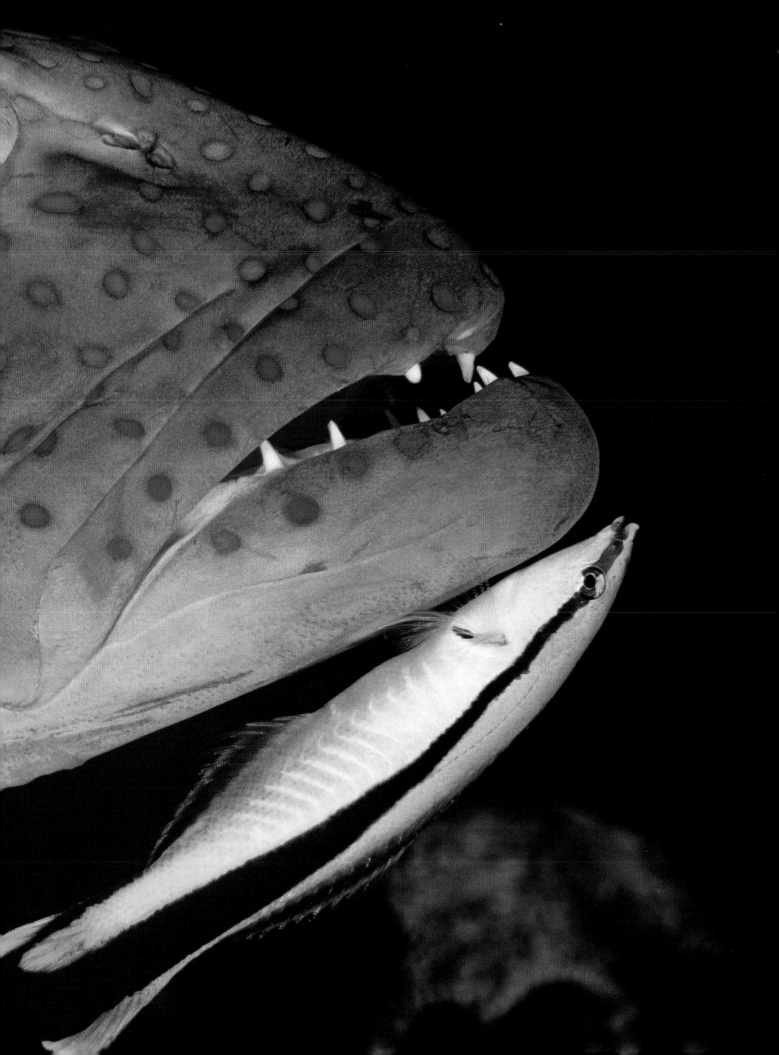

the hearts and minds of both the public and scientific community,"[5] notes DeLoach.

It wasn't until a decade later that someone tried to replicate Limbaugh's experiment, and they found that cleaning symbiosis wasn't as straightforward as depicted. The new studies, which removed cleaners on Pacific reefs, showed very little change in the abundance of fishes and no increase in disease rates. Biologist George Losey suggested, intriguingly, that cleaner fish might be better understood as parasites that have taken advantage of bigger fishes' desire for tactile stimulation and conditioned their clients to visit them. In other words, they are offering a massage in exchange for dinner. Other forms of behaviour seem to support this idea: some parrotfish, for example, hang around in the 'head-up' cleaning pose inside sea plumes, where no cleaners are present. Are they being stimulated by the caress of the soft gorgonian branches? Possibly tickling and stroking of this kind and parasite control aren't mutually exclusive: fish come in for a touch-up, and end up with a clean-up too.

Of course, fish being fish, there's always going to be one freeloader trying to exploit the system. In this case the culprit is the Sabretooth Blenny. This devious fish looks very similar to a cleaner wrasse, and advertises its services with a similar dance. But as soon as a client approaches, the blenny dashes in and takes out a big chunk of flesh with its teeth.

Whatever the truth behind cleaning stations, they make great places for fish watching, allowing the diver to observe some of the more complex interactions in the marine world. Although most fish are in a trance-like state while being cleaned, they're still alert to what's going on around them and may move off if you approach too quickly. Ned DeLoach advises that "to get a closer view, pause at least ten feet away for a few minutes before making a cautious approach." The patient diver, he suggests, may even receive a manicure from a shrimp or goby:

> *Your best bet is to look for shrimps advertising their business by waving their antennae. Slowly extend the back of your hand with the palm angled slightly away. The shrimps usually make tentative contact before hopping aboard, picking around the nails or at rough or broken skin. The gobies are quite cautious and only smaller individuals fall for the ruse, but at times we have had several of the tiny fish scampering over our hands.*[6]

Cleaning stations can also produce some surprises, as Howard Hall found while filming a sequence of ocean sunfish or Molas being cleaned by a half-moon perch. "While we were filming that, a whole school of baby Molas, maybe thirty or forty of them, came in", he recalls. "I'd never seen baby Molas before and I didn't know that they schooled, so that was really spectacular." It's possible, believes Hall, that the baby Molas were also coming in to be cleaned.

Smart as a fish

Fish may be smarter than we think. According to Dr Phil Gee of the Department of Psychology at the University of Plymouth in the UK, who carried out a series of studies on learning in fish, they can even be taught to tell the time. Dr Gee made his findings by training fish to collect food at certain times of day. Initially, the fish were taught to press a lever to get food. When they had mastered this, researchers restricted the availability of food to certain times. The fish soon worked out that if they hit the lever at the right time, food was sure to arrive. "Their activity around the lever increased enormously just before the set hour when food was dispensed," said Gee. "It shows us that they are able to learn."[7]

Another series of studies explodes the stereotype of fish as less intelligent than other vertebrates. According to a special issue of the academic journal *Fish and Fisheries*, fish are cultured, clever and have good long-term memories – more like three months than the three-seconds with which they are often caricatured. And although they might have small brains, we shouldn't be judging intelligence on the basis of brain volume; in some cognitive domains (such as memory), fish even compare favourably with non-human primates. Biologists Laland, Brown and Krause claim that there has been a 'sea change' in our perception of the psychological and cognitive abilities of fish:

> *Gone (or at least obsolete) is the image of fish as drudging and dim-witted pea brains, driven largely by 'instinct', with what little behavioural flexibility they possess being severely hampered by an infamous*

⊕ FISH WITH INJURIES OR PARASITES TEND TO BE REGULAR CLIENTS OF CLEANING STATIONS: A BLACKBAR SOLDIERFISH CARRIES A PARASITIC ISOPOD ON ITS HEAD. (BULWINKLE 3, GRAND CAYMAN)

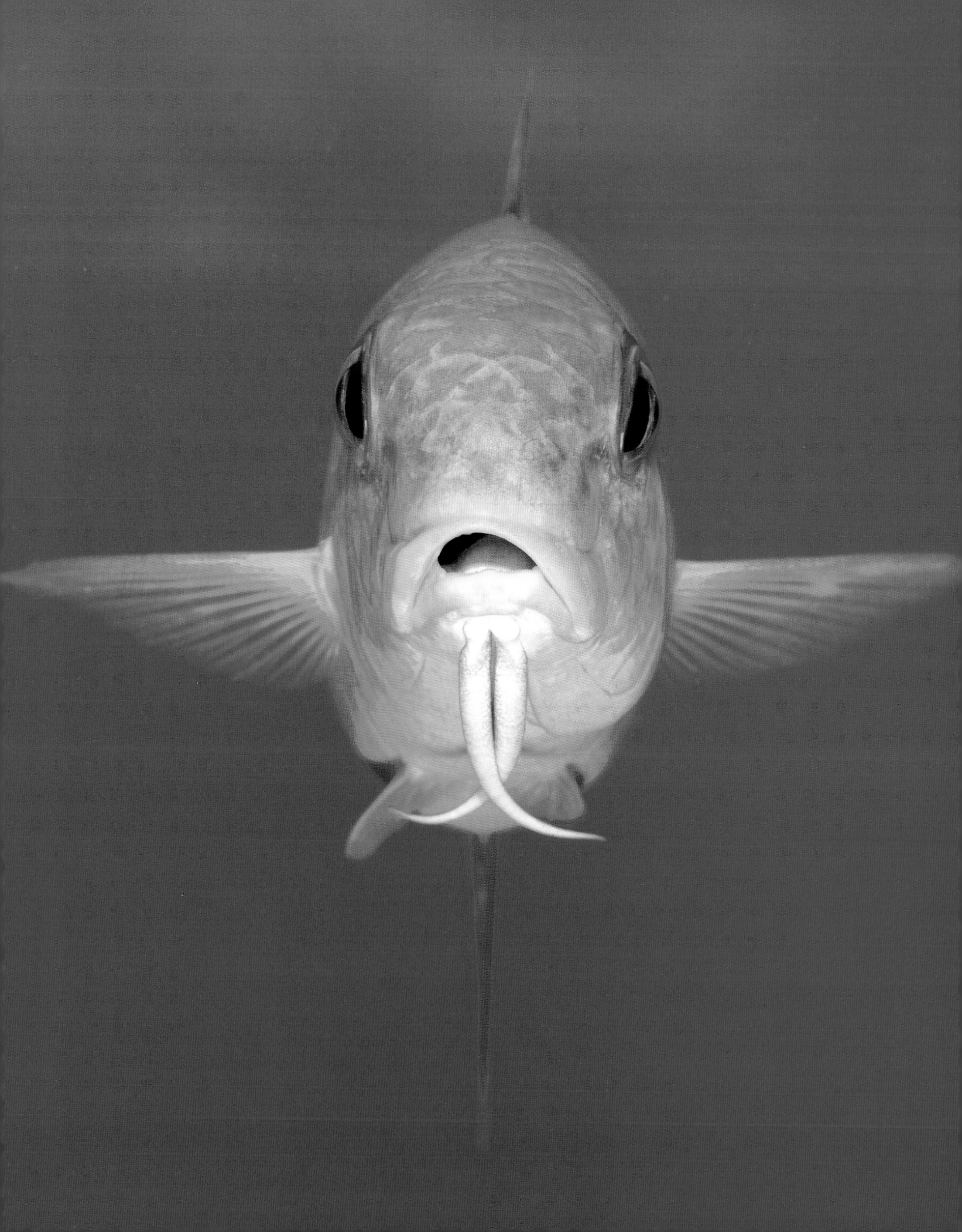

three-second "memory". Now, fish are regarded as steeped in social intelligence, pursuing Machiavellian strategies of manipulation, punishment and reconciliation; exhibiting stable cultural traditions and cooperating to inspect predators and catch food.[8]

Fish can identify shoal-mates, monitor the social status of others and track the relationships of third parties. They can also use tools, build complex nests and bowers and navigate mazes. Many of these abilities will come as no surprise to divers who have watched fish in the complex, eat-or-be-eaten world of coral reefs rather than simply observed them in a goldfish bowl.

Getting closer to fishes

Film-makers Guy and Anita Chaumette believe that we don't give enough credit to fishes. Their films explore the possibilities of interacting with marine life in a non-threatening manner to gain new insights into their behaviour. If fish enjoy visits to the cleaning station, they argue, perhaps they will also enjoy being caressed by a human. In their award-winning film *Talking with Fishes,* Guy sets out to prove this by gently approaching a Nassau Grouper, which allows itself to be stroked under the chin and, eventually, all over its body. He then repeats the performance with first a small Spotted Moray and then a large Green Moray. After initial hostility, the large moray eventually accepts him: "She appears to be really enjoying herself," he says. He even manages to tickle a venomous scorpionfish under its chin, and beguile a nurse shark into having its back stroked.

Guy's amazing success in approaching marine life is partly down to patience while filming, but also because he has learned the value of imitating the animal's behaviour. This is a trick he first learned in the Maldives, while working as a dive guide and escorting groups to the cleaning station at Manta Point on Lankanfinolhu reef. Guy would move away from the group and began to act like a manta: "I was mimicking the manta with my arms, not moving that fast but just gliding with my arms outstretched," he tells me. "Very soon the mantas were going over me, under

me, and even touching the end of my hand with the tips of their wings."

This 'dance with mantas' was the first time Guy used this technique, and it is one he has since employed to good effect with many other animals:

If you cross your arms sideways over your chest and put your hands out to your sides like paddles, pretending to be a turtle, you can get extremely close. It takes between two to five minutes and then they begin to accept you. With the Caribbean squid, we mimic them by extending our hands and using our fingers like they use their arms and tentacles. Rather than the animals running away from you, they are tricked into coming back – and they even come and touch you.

Not many of us would want to risk our fingers with a sharp-toothed, short-sighted moray eel, or indeed a deadly scorpionfish, but divers have been 'talking with fishes' almost since the invention of scuba. Groupers, in particular, have always seemed amenable to touch. In *The World Underwater Book*, Peter Dick described making friends with a grouper in Kenya whom he christened Rip: "Only a few pounds in weight, he let me tickle him under the chin and usually followed me around," he wrote. "Like most groupers he had a character similar to a puppy dog, darting here and there and generally getting in the way."[9] A grouper called Ulysses became a scene-stealer in Cousteau's film *The Silent World*, allowing the divers to stroke his sides and rolling over with pleasure 'like a dog'. Cousteau wonders what the fish is thinking: "What idea can a grouper have of a human being? That question has troubled me for years since I first began to dive."[10]

Divers are always proud when they manage to hand-feed a grouper, Cousteau noted, and imagine that they have somehow created a bond of affection between themselves and the animal. "One of the favourite subjects of debate aboard the *Calypso* was the level of intelligence among groupers," he wrote, in *Life and Death in a Coral Sea.* "Some of the divers believed that these fish were capable of a certain kind of affection [while] some of the men aboard were more skeptical." Cousteau and his companions performed an experiment in which they placed several mirrors on the seabed to test the aggressiveness of the grouper in defending its territory against a perceived invader (in fact, its own reflection). Sure enough

YELLOW GOATFISH (TURTLE FARM REEF, GRAND CAYMAN,)

SERGEANT MAJORS ARE ONE OF THE FIRST FISH DIVERS LEARN.

'intruder'; one of them even died after eating the broken fragments. "We found the grouper floating belly-up on the surface," said Cousteau, who arrived at the conclusion that "unfortunately, even a grouper cannot digest glass."[11] So much for learning about grouper behaviour.

To touch or not to touch?

But how much *can* we interact with marine life? Is it safe? Is it desirable? Should we just stick to fish-watching? Clearly, plenty of creatures enjoy the attention. "You can stand a lobster on its nose and stroke it from its tail to its head," says Professor Trevor Norton, "and it will go into a trance and stay in a headstand until you take it out – it's most peculiar!" You can do the same thing with an octopus, which, if stroked in the right place, just glazes over and stays there. On the other hand you certainly wouldn't want to tickle a triggerfish, or even pander to a pufferfish – as dive instructor Randy Jordan of Jupiter, South Florida, discovered to his cost in 2003 when he wiggled his fingers in front of one to entice it out to play: the puffer promptly bit off his finger and ate it.[12]

Divers now are taught not to touch anything, and we've certainly come a long way since it was considered acceptable to hitch a ride on a Whaleshark or turtle. Hanging on to a turtle causes it considerable stress and may prevent it from surfacing to breathe. Also, touching marine life while wearing gloves can damage protective mucus; some dive destinations now enforce a 'no gloves' rule in order to discourage divers from touching anything at all.

Climbing into giant barrel sponges was once a popular pose for underwater models until we realised the damage that was being caused. Jeff Rotman is just one of many photographers who has archive material of girls inside barrel sponges and divers riding Whalesharks. "You just can't do that stuff anymore," he says. "The number one rule now is 'don't touch', and I think that's what we should abide by." Yet at the same time he also worries that we may have moved too far in the other direction: "I think it's gone overboard because some of these animals enjoy the interaction."

Among those who agree with Rotman is Lawson Wood, whose environmental credentials are beyond question: a founding member of the Marine Conservation Society, he also helped create Scotland's first marine nature reserve at St Abbs and Eyemouth. "Fish like being touched," says Lawson. "As long as you're not wearing gloves, then it's fine." More controversially, he suggests that Whalesharks might enjoy it too:

Give its head a good scritch-scratch. If a Whaleshark wants interaction with you, it will stay there. If it doesn't like it, it will swim away. OK, don't swim up behind it and hang on to a fin – the Whaleshark can't see you and will feel threatened. But if you approach it with hands open, nice and slow from the front, it can see you aren't a threat and will let you scratch its head. What's the problem?

The problem is that many less experienced divers don't know what they can and can't touch, and there are so many poisonous creatures in the sea that it's best to be on the safe side. If something moves slowly enough to allow you to touch it, there's usually a good reason not too. "Some animals can be touched," comments Alex, "but it requires a certain level of knowledge as to exactly what and when, to make sure you're not damaging anything. People might watch a dive guide doing something and feel that they can replicate it," he adds, "without quite understanding the amount of thought and experience that's gone into that action. Without that knowledge," he concludes, "it remains risky – for both the animal and you."

Feeding fish

Feeding marine animals is another controversial area, and most marine conservation organisations advise against it. However, there are those who argue that, given the huge amount of damage humanity inflicts on the world's oceans, introducing small amounts of food – or extra biomass – into the water isn't the worst of our sins.

Stingray City in Grand Cayman is a prime example of where feeding animals artificially has created an underwater encounter of considerable value not just to the island's economy but also to the public's appreciation of marine life. Stingrays swarm in to be fed when the diving and snorkelling boats arrive, and then just as quickly revert to rooting around in the sand again for their normal food immediately afterwards. "They don't just hover around

⊕ A DIVER AND STINGRAY BOTH ENJOY A CLOSE
ENCOUNTER, AT STINGRAY CITY, GRAND CAYMAN.

↑ SETTLE DOWN ON THE SEABED AND LET THE FISH GET USED TO YOUR PRESENCE. (DAHAB, EGYPT)

waiting for the next boat to show up," says Lawson Wood. Ned DeLoach also argues that artificial feeding activities do not generally affect fish behaviour:

Being close to so many wild creatures is exhilarating. Reef visitors generally enjoy the experience, and the fishes certainly aren't complaining. However, some ecologists argue that these free lunches might permanently alter the fishes' ability to search for more traditional foods. This seems unlikely. Remember, these are opportunistic feeders; if their free meals suddenly come to a halt, they are certainly not going to starve.[13]

There can be problems when animals have been fed at a particular location and come out expecting food from the next batch of divers who come along. One logical solution is for a feeding location never to be used for anything other than a feeding dive, although this is impossible to enforce on a busy dive site used by more than one dive centre. Shark feeding also presents its own particular set of issues (discussed further in *Chapter five*.)

There's no doubt that fish feeding can get out of control, and the frenzies that can ensue are certainly undesirable. Nobody wants to return to the days when you got into the water somewhere like Hanuama Bay on Oahu, Hawaii, only to find yourself snorkelling through a sort of paste soup and being mobbed by aggressive Sergeant Majors. Similarly, feeding boiled eggs to Napoleon Wrasse in Red Sea resorts has now, thankfully, stopped. But some professionals, keen conservationists even, still feed fish. Cathy Church admits that they use processed cheese in aerosol cans at Sunset House in Grand Cayman. "We do feed them on occasion. Not very often, but just enough to keep them around," she says. "I think it's important that people get close to these fish and understand them better so that they can enjoy them more and protect them better," she says.

The feeding of fish snacks to turtles in Barbados means that as many as 20 turtles sometimes swamp dive groups, looking for hand-outs, as soon as the boats moor up. Some people find this distressing. But it could be argued that since we've slaughtered millions of turtles over the past centuries, hand-feeding a couple of dozen off one beach doesn't even begin to redress the balance. In the bigger scheme, it's neither here nor there. But it's not diving in a natural wilderness, either.

The underwater orchestra

On scuba, our constant exhaust bubbles obscure what's really going on underwater. But once you've heard a pistol shrimp do its stuff when you're on a rebreather, you'll never again call it the 'silent world' down there. If you can manage to coax one of these extraordinary crustaceans out of its lair, it will snap at you with an explosive 'crack!' – just like a pistol shot – which resounds through the water.

Scientists do not entirely know how much fish communicate through sound, and what intricacies of social behaviour are served by their constant underwater chatter. But there's no doubt that the fish world is a noisy place. Sylvia Earle found that by using a rebreather she could hear "the crunch of parrotfish teeth on coral, the sizzle and pop of snapping shrimp, the grunts of groupers, the chattering staccato of squirrelfish." She describes how this opens up a new underwater world of sound: "The 'silent underseas world' hums, trills, drums and crackles with a symphony of vital signals sent and received. I was thrilled to be able to tune in."[14]

Sound is also incredibly important to marine mammals. Dolphins and other toothed whales use sound to communicate with each other, and hunt mostly by echolocation (sending out short bursts of sound waves that bounce off objects and return to them, giving a detailed 'picture' of objects in the water.) Larger baleen whales use different kinds of calls, songs and whistles to communicate with each other and socialise. Humpbacks, for instance, sing long, complicated songs during the mating season; the songs can last from a few minutes to half-an-hour and can be heard from up to 160 kilometres (100 miles) away through the water.

Once the sun has gone down, according to Trevor Norton, this undersea cacophony gets turned up a notch: "When night falls, massed fishy choruses raise the sound level by as much as thirty-five decibels – the difference between a quiet street and rush-hour traffic," he says. "Fish listeners believe that these choruses reverberate over the entire 2,000 kilometres (1,250 miles) of the Great Barrier Reef and chorusing keeps loose shoals together."[15] A night-dive with spawning toadfishes is an unforgettable experience, according to DeLoach: "The amorous males send forth a cacophony of whistling calls, measured to be up to 30 to 40 decibels louder than any other known sound produced by fishes."[16] Squirrelfish also get very noisy at dawn and dusk, routinely challenging any other fish that approach their territories.

"Fish can identify shoal-mates, monitor the social status of others and track the relationships of third parties. They can also use tools, build complex nests and bowers and navigate mazes. Many of these abilities will come as no surprise to divers who have watched fish in the complex, eat-or-be-eaten world of coral reefs rather than simply observed them in a goldfish bowl."

◉ SHY HAMLETS SPAWNING IN THE CAYMAN ISLANDS.

BLUELINE SNAPPERS (ARI ATOLL, MALDIVES) ⊕

The most sophisticated vocalists on the reef are damselfishes, particularly the Bicolour Damselfish. These tiny plankton-eaters use a wide range of calls to communicate with other members of their hierarchies, says Ned DeLoach:

Territorial males constantly challenge similar-sized rivals for social position. Hovering head down an inch or so off the bottom, the contestants face one another and emit a series of combative pops. During courtship, inspired males wearing black masks perform a series of eye-catching dips, each accompanied by a chirp. Females respond to these acoustical overtures from as far as 20 feet away. Interested females are not only able to distinguish between the locations of the callers but also to differentiate between suitors and to assess their relative size.[17]

Life on the reef is an amazingly complex mosaic, a four-dimensional puzzle for fish behaviourists and biologists. There are many forms of fish behaviour that we are only just beginning to unravel, from the intricacies of mating and spawning to grooming, cleaning, and communication. But you don't have to be an ichthyologist to appreciate the art of fish watching: sometimes it's enough simply to enjoy looking at these weird and wonderful creatures in all their myriad shapes and colours.

Up close and personal

One way to get more intimate with marine wildlife is to stop for a while. Another way is simply to get closer to the reef, since we're often just too far away to see anything. "Most people I see diving around Cayman Brac on a daily basis are basically just going underwater to have a swim," says Lawson Wood. "They're usually 15 to 20 feet off the reef. I understand that we don't want people handling the reef, but you're not going to see anything from that distance," he adds. "I take great delight in having less experienced people come with me and showing some of the things that I'm taking pictures of – the little shrimps and so on – pulling them in closer and closer until they really start to appreciate what they're looking at." If you're lucky enough to have Lawson as your personal guide, this is a good strategy. A group of people crowding in on the reef, however, is going to cause damage.

Guy Chaumette agrees that we need to look at what's under our noses more carefully. "I recommend that you go into a stationery shop before you leave and buy a magnifying lens," he suggests. "They are excellent for watching little creatures such as Pedersen's Shrimps, nudibranchs or even coral polyps," he says. "Most people don't even know what a coral polyp looks like," he adds, "because they are very small and you don't normally look at them." A submersible torch is also a good idea, even during the day. Water progressively filters out colours as we descend (starting with red then orange, yellow, green, blue and indigo) and a torch will help restore them. Eels and lionfish also seem

drawn towards lights, even by day.

As with almost everything we do underwater, the greatest rewards come from simply slowing down. "Blend in, breathe slowly, approach animals gradually and use slow, controlled movements," says Douglas David Seifert, contributing editor with *Dive* magazine. "Remember, most animals in the ocean have no idea what we are, other than large and noisy. Their main concern is trying not to be eaten, so they approach any confrontation with a freeze, flight or fight response." Make certain they freeze rather than take flight, suggests Douglas, and then they will either lose interest in you or may even become curious enough to approach closer. After all, the best kind of fish watching is when it's the fish that are watching you.

"Most animals in the ocean have no idea what we are, other than large and noisy. Their main concern is trying not to be eaten."

Douglas David Seifert

meetings with
remarkable
creatures

"The villains of undersea myth are sharks, octopi, congers, morays, stingrays, Mantas, squids, and barracudas. We have met all ... and the monsters we have met seem a thoroughly harmless lot."

Jacques Cousteau

I'M ON BOARD A BRIGHTLY COLOURED *DHONI* IN THE MALDIVES, CRUISING SLOWLY DOWN THE WESTERN SIDE OF ARI ATOLL ALONG THE OUTER REEF EDGE. THE CREW IS POSTED IN THE BOW AND ON THE ROOF, SCANNING THE DEEP BLUE WATER AROUND US. A DOZEN OR SO PEOPLE ARE ALSO LOOKING OUT TO SEA, THEIR FINS ALREADY ON THEIR FEET AND THEIR MASKS PUSHED BACK ON THEIR FOREHEADS. SUDDENLY, ONE OF THE LOOKOUTS SHOUTS "GO, GO!" AND WE ALL LEAP OVERBOARD INTO THE WATER.

Afloat in the ocean, I look down and around me through my mask, but can see nothing except empty blue water. I'm wondering how on earth you can predict an encounter of this type, and preparing myself for disappointment, when something truly amazing comes slowly into view: a big, beautiful Whaleshark, swimming calmly along just a short distance off the reef and no more than three metres below the surface. I fin alongside this wonderful creature until, with a languid sweep of its huge tail, it powers its massive bulk beyond me and disappears into the depths.

We clamber back on board, jabbering animatedly. Even Alex – a seasoned pro – loses his poise: "Wow!" he exclaims, "It was so big and spotty!" And he waves his arms about in imitation of the great creature.

Small wonder that we were excited. The Whaleshark is the biggest fish on earth, reaching up to 12 metres (40 feet)

in length and weighing up to 15 tonnes – about three times the weight of an average African elephant. Like the great whales, it is a filter feeder, using its enormous mouth to scoop up huge volumes of water, which it passes through sieve-like structures inside the gill slits on either side of the head in order to filter out the plankton, squid and small fish that make up its diet. It feeds mainly at night, and during the day cruises slowly along the reef accompanied by its remoras and pilot fish.

There are good reasons why we were using just basic snorkelling gear for these encounters: there's no way that a dozen or so people would be able to clamber in and out of the *dhoni* so quickly carrying heavy scuba equipment, and once in the water the noise of exhaled bubbles can drive the Whaleshark away. Besides, there's something entirely appropriate about it being just you, wearing nothing

"Third Fisherman: Master, I marvel how the fishes live in the Sea. First Fisherman: Why as men do a-land; the great ones eat up the little ones."

William Shakespeare, *Pericles,* **Act 2, Scene 1**

but swimsuit, fins and mask, down there with this huge animal: not only do you feel closer to it, but in the silence of the sea its presence seems all the more majestic.

After our first encounter with the Whaleshark, the boat moved forward so that we could jump in again for another try. On our third sortie it stayed with us for ten minutes or so, allowing me a good look at its broad head, tapering to a powerful tail and caudal fin, and the large, creamy spots, chalky stripes and beautiful grey whorls that covered its body. Remoras hung from either side of its pectoral fins like engines under the wings of a jet. I looked right into the dark, primal depths of its eye, but this enigmatic giant was giving nothing away.

We still have much to learn about Whalesharks, which adds to the sense of adventure and discovery when diving with them. What we do know is that they bear live young – a pregnant female caught off Taiwan had 307 embryos inside her – and are slow to develop, reaching sexual maturity at around 30 years and going on to reach an age of 60, or per-haps even more. Whalesharks are also thought to migrate between feeding areas, although it's not clear whether they form separate populations in major oceans. Some certainly travel huge distances: one covered 13,000 km (8,000 miles) during the three years in which it was tracked.

Beasts of the sea

Our Whaleshark experience once belonged to the realms of divers' fantasy, but encounters with these great beasts of the ocean have become increasingly possible as we learn more about them.

Rob Bryning of Maldives Scuba Tours, who operate Whaleshark safaris from their live-aboard dive boat MV *Sea Spirit*, now sees these huge fish on 80 percent of his trips: "For a while we thought they were seasonal," he says. "But

Ⓚ → WHALESHARKS IN THE MALDIVES.

⊕ THESE GIANT FILTER FEEDERS CAN WEIGH UP TO 15 TONNES.
(ARI ATOLL, MALDIVES)

tion (on which they sailed by raft from Peru to Tahiti in order to investigate the feasibility of early navigation):

Knut had been squatting there, washing his pants in the swell, and when he looked up for a moment he was staring straight into the biggest and ugliest face any of us had ever seen in the whole of our lives. It was the head of a veritable sea monster, so huge and hideous that if the Old Man of the Sea himself had come up he would not have made such an impression on us. The head was broad and flat like a frog's, with two small eyes right at the sides, and a toadlike jaw which was four or five feet wide [...]. The monster came quietly, lazily swimming after us from the stern. It grinned like a bulldog and lashed gently with its tail.[1]

when we put time into searching for them, we realised that they're here more or less all year round – and we're confident that we can find them most of the time."

It helps, of course, that Whalesharks seem to be comfortable with people. As long as they don't feel threatened by anyone diving down in front of them or trying to touch them, then they'll often swim alongside snorkellers for no obvious reason other than curiosity.

The growth in tourism could be good news for Whalesharks. Sadly these remarkable creatures are highly threatened by fishing, their meat still fetching a high price in Taiwan and elsewhere in Asia, even though the International Union for the Conservation of Nature and Natural Resources (IUCN) classifies the Whaleshark as 'vulnerable' on its red data list. However, Taiwan has recently dropped its annual quota from 120 to 65 animals, and in April 2005 it hosted a conference to investigate the alternatives to hunting offered by Whaleshark ecotourism. Certainly there is an economic incentive for protecting the species: today it is estimated that the annual income from watching Whalesharks is worth US$1.45 million in Belize, $US5 million in the Seychelles and US$6.5 million in Western Australia.

Like many other denizens of the deep, Whalesharks have long been demonised by folklore. For centuries, descriptions of these harmless fish were based on fear and ignorance, and sought to feed the popular appetite for tales of sea monsters. This was perhaps not surprising in Victorian times and earlier. Yet even in the middle of the 20th century, the Norwegian explorer Thor Heyerdahl mined the same rich seam in describing his crew's meeting with a Whaleshark during the celebrated *Kon Tiki* expedi-

Heyerdahl and his companions watched, fascinated, as the Whaleshark rubbed against the raft. The fish was so big that when it swam in circles around them its head was visible on one side while its tail stuck out from the other. "So grotesque, inert and stupid did it appear when seen full-faced," wrote Heyerdahl, "that we could not help shouting with laughter, although we realised it had enough strength in its tail to smash [us] to pieces if it attacked us." The excitement soon went to the Norwegians' heads: "It became too exciting for Erik," wrote Heyerdahl, and he described how his companion plunged a harpoon "deep into the Whaleshark's gristly head."

Such brutal 'sport' seems inconceivable today, when people are prepared to fly halfway around the world just for the privilege of spending a few minutes in the company of these creatures. For many, these precious moments will be among their lifetime's highlights underwater. Divemaster Patrick Weir, for instance, describes his meeting with a Whaleshark in the Cayman Islands as: "easily the most memorable encounter I've had in ten years diving." On this occasion, having just finished leading the second dive of the day, he discovered a Whaleshark right next to the boat:

Immediately everybody grabbed their masks and cameras and jumped in, and we played with this Whaleshark for about 45 minutes. I looked right down his mouth into his stomach, that's how close I was. I put my eye to his and I could see my reflection in his eye! There was as a remora or suckerfish as big as me stuck to the side of him. Quite an amazing experience!

① WHALESHARKS SEEM TO BE COMFORTABLE WITH PEOPLE. (ARI ATOLL, MALDIVES)

Devil fish

Another animal that has suffered from an image problem is the Manta Ray, which is referred to as 'devil fish' in many countries and is the subject of endless fishermen's folklore. Cousteau, however, was quite clear that this demonisation was all nonsense: "We were warned that mantas killed divers by wrapping their wings around the man and smothering him, or by enveloping the diver and crushing him against the floor. But far from inspiring fear, they arouse admiration in any man lucky enough to see them in flight."[2]

Mantas can weigh up to 1350kg (2,970lb) and have an estimated life span of around 20 years. Despite their great size, they are – just like Whalesharks – harmless filter feeders. Their 300 or so tiny teeth are not used for feeding, but may play a role in courtship when the male grasps the tip of the female's wingtip in his mouth before inserting his clasper (a penis-like organ) into her vent to copulate. The eggs develop for somewhere between nine to twelve months inside the female, but where or when she gives birth is still a mystery. It's likely that Mantas migrate across the oceans, but little is known about where they travel. Several tagging and sonic telemetry programmes are currently trying to answer these questions.

Whatever the secrets of a Manta's life cycle, it's certainly a beautiful beast to observe underwater – and the firm favourite of thriller writer Frederick Forsyth. "They're the most awesome things to watch," he says. "They're giants but they're gentle, they're timid but also incredibly elegant and they don't seem to swim but to fly, with these great fins which are basically wings. Definitely the most amazing thing I've seen underwater," he concludes.

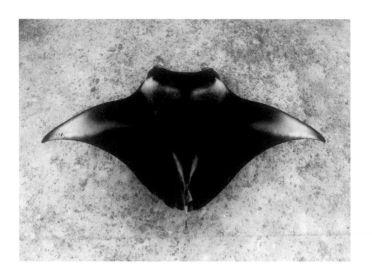

Mantas have few predators apart from large sharks, but they sometimes become accidentally ensnared in nets or fishing lines. Filmmaker John Boyle had a remarkable experience while on location in the Cocos Islands, when he was approached by a huge Manta that had become entangled in fishing line and appeared to be hanging around in the hope of assistance. "It was intriguing, because the Manta was hovering in the water," he says. "It wasn't moving so it was gradually sinking in a circle – then it would come back, and again it almost hovered." Boyle attempted to free the Manta, but ran short of air and had to return to the boat, leaving the poor creature to an unhappy end – or so he thought. He was subsequently astonished to see a picture of the same Manta taken by Howard Hall in the same place just one week later, and to learn that Hall and his wife had managed to cut the ray free. "It was amazing that we had both had the feeling that it was saying 'come on guys, get me out of this'," recalls Boyle.

This outlandish suggestion may not be so far from the truth: Mantas commonly frequent cleaning stations, where they usually hover while the little critters do their work – often gliding off a little way before turning back for more. Perhaps this distressed individual had cast the divers in the role of cleaner fish.

The best way to watch Mantas at feeding stations is to settle down quietly behind a rock down-current, so your bubbles don't disturb them. I've seen tourists in the Maldives, laden down with expensive camera equipment, sitting on the cleaning station – and no doubt wondering why they weren't getting any pictures. Mantas often feed near the surface too, at which point snorkelling becomes the better option.

The Manta's evil reputation among fisherfolk may be attributable to reports of outsized individuals leaping out of the water and landing on small vessels, smashing the boats and their occupants. Such stories are probably apocryphal, although Mantas certainly do jump out of the water. Exactly why, nobody knows: it could be to escape predators, to rid themselves of parasites or to communicate with each other (the impact of a big Manta hitting the surface can be heard for several kilometres underwater). Or perhaps the 'devilfish' is simply playing.

⬅ A MANTA RAY EFFORTLESSLY FLOATS LIKE AN ALIEN SPACECRAFT.
➡ FOUR REMORAS HANG ON FOR THE RIDE.
(BOTH IMAGES, MALE ATOLL, MALDIVES.)

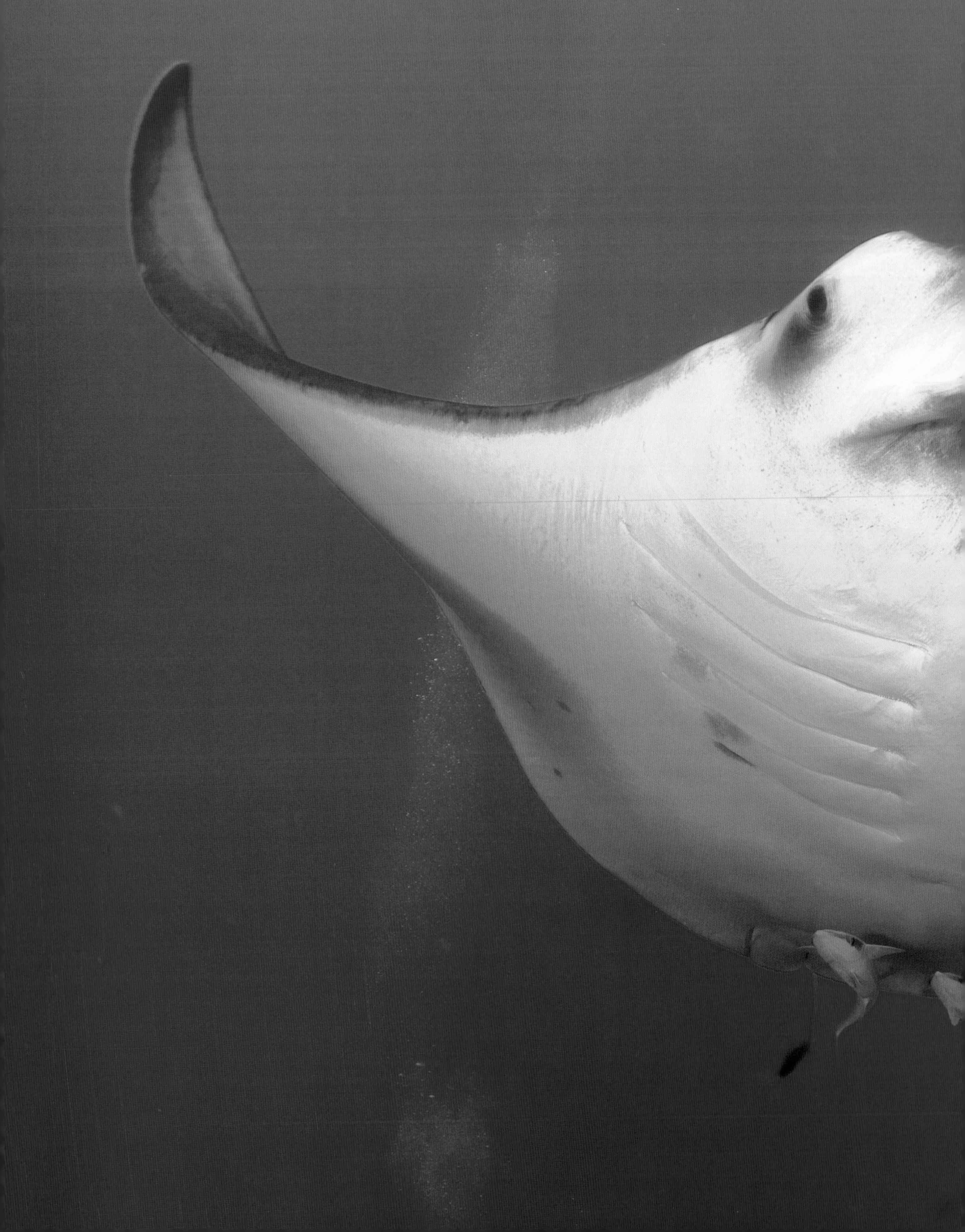

"They're the most awesome things to watch, they're giants but they're gentle, they're timid but also incredibly elegant and they don't seem to swim but to fly, with these great fins which are basically wings."

Frederick Forsyth

Sharks: monsters or myth?

Sharks, it hardly needs saying, have a fearsome reputation. By now, it should also hardly need saying that this reputation is undeserved – based as it is upon centuries of ignorance and prejudice. Meeting these elegant predators underwater can make for a thrilling diving experience and, once over the initial apprehension, most divers actively seek sharks out. While knowledge and experience tell us that attacks on divers are incredibly rare, most of us still get a bit of an adrenaline buzz from observing these apex predators on their home territory.

Shark attacks are, of course, extremely rare. According to the ISAF (International Shark Attack File) there are on average around three or four human fatalities worldwide from unprovoked attacks, and rarely more than ten. When attacks do happen, they are usually directed towards surfers or swimmers. It is almost unheard of for a shark to bite a scuba diver – partly, perhaps, because sharks are very wary of bubbles, which do not naturally occur in their world, except in the defensive threat displays of whales and dolphins.

The rare attacks that do happen usually result from a case of mistaken identity: the shark has confused the outline of a swimmer or surfer with that of its normal prey such as, for instance, a seal. "When you think how many hundreds of millions of people there are bathing in the world's oceans and how few shark attacks there are every year," says Fabien Cousteau, "it's clear that they're not mindless at all and they do everything in their power to *avoid* us."

So the shark question really needs to be turned on its head. The real issue is not how many sharks kill people, but rather how many *are killed by* people. At a conservative estimate, over 100 million sharks are slaughtered annually in order to supply the Asian shark fin soup industry. Shark 'finning' is a particularly brutal practice, which involves cutting off the fins before throwing back the shark, leaving it to bleed to death or drown. "The scale of shark finning worldwide is horrendous," says Jeremy Stafford-Deitsch, founder of the Shark Trust. "And poaching is epidemic, even in places where sharks should be protected such as the Galapagos and Cocos Islands."

Shark tourism – divers paying to see sharks – is one way of protecting shark populations, effectively giving them a higher economic value when alive than when dead. In many areas shark feeds are now common and can guarantee divers an encounter with several different species. Some environmentalists argue that we shouldn't be 'upsetting the natural balance' in this way, but Stafford-Deitsch believes that this is missing the point:

My position is that if it's done appropriately, then feeding can be immensely valuable for sharks. It provides local economies with a sustainable income from the resource, and they tend to be more protective of the environment in which it's taking place if they're deriving some benefit from it. Obviously there are some issues around how the feeds are conducted: I'm in favour of those places where the divers and sharks are kept separate. There are some operators who 'wrangle' with the sharks, grabbing them and turning them upside down and so forth. I don't think this is a particularly positive way of treating the animals. People get very hot under the collar about shark feeds but in reality they should be worrying about shark finning, or sport fishermen who regularly kill sharks. Most of the concerns people have around shark feeding are easily addressed by using common sense, or following the Shark Trust's code of practice.

The sharks most commonly encountered by divers are reef sharks, with the bigger oceanic sharks (such as Whitetip, Silky, Thresher, Blue and Scalloped Hammerhead) usually seen – by definition – further out in the deep, or around isolated seamounts. Most sharks are wary of divers, although when they're in large schooling aggregations you can sometimes get closer: in the Galapagos, for instance, huge schools of female Scalloped Hammerheads come together prior to mating, and visit cleaning stations on the reef where butterflyfish and King Angelfish remove their parasites.

Up close with Great Whites

To look out into the blue and see a mass of hammerheads (a much-coveted sight, known to divers as 'shark wallpaper') is exciting enough. But for a shark to swim so close that you can actually count its teeth is a quite unforgettable experience – especially if the shark in question is that ultimate predator, the Great White.

⊕ SOME SHARKS LOOK VERY DIFFERENT FROM THEIR POPULAR IMAGE. THIS TINY CORAL CAT SHARK RESTS ON THE SEABED. (INDONESIA)

Mike Rutzen, a quietly spoken South African, runs a shark viewing operation off the Cape coast that has produced some extraordinary insights into the behaviour of Great Whites. He can, for instance, persuade the sharks to open their mouths and just hang in the water behind the boat – simply by rubbing their noses. He has also made a speciality of freediving and interacting with them in open water, which has helped put paid to a few myths. "People used to say to me that if you put your toe in the water the Great White would just bite it off," he says, "but that just isn't true." In Mike's experience, Great Whites are far from the savage killing machines of the popular imagination: "The thing that impresses me is that these animals are

⬆ ➡ DESPITE THE GREAT WHITE'S FEARSOME APPEARANCE, ITS BAD REPUTATION IS LARGELY UNDESERVED. (BOTH IMAGES BY ERIC CHENG; GUADALUPE ISLAND, MEXICO)

intelligent enough to accept you in the water, read your body language as non-threatening and then interact with you in a very calm manner."

Rutzen only freedives with Great Whites if the conditions are absolutely right: the visibility has to be at least eight to ten metres (26 to 33 feet), with calm seas and clear skies so that the boat crew can also keep tabs on what's happening in the water. "We only ever work with sharks we call players – that is, they're really relaxed around the boat," he says. "And we do everything very slowly. You've got to watch them and know what they are doing: every animal is watching every other animal, and they're also watching you, so you have to find a place to fit into this without disturbing the equilibrium." Rutzen and his dive buddies video all their encounters, replaying them again and again in search of subtle clues that reveal what the sharks are up to.

The Great White has always had a bad press. Even Hans Hass, whose great experience underwater generally produced fairly accurate observations, fell for the myth. He believed that this shark possessed an entirely different set of 'innate reactions' to others, and that this explained why it "behaves so mechanically, and automatically swims up to attack even a being that is strange to it – a human being."[3] The film *Jaws* fuelled this myth and created worldwide shark hysteria by portraying Great Whites as savage and vindictive man-eaters – a fact now regretfully acknowledged by author Peter Benchley himself, who has since become an advocate of shark conservation. But Mike Rutzen believes that the negative publicity has also produced a positive side-effect by raising the profile of the species: "Fortunately for us Great Whites are extremely good ambassadors for all sharks," says Rutzen, "because everyone is interested in them."

"Great Whites are extremely good ambassadors for all sharks because everyone is interested in them."

Mike Rutzen

Fabien Cousteau is another diver who believes that Great Whites are both misunderstood and have a role as champion for all the 400 or so other shark species out there. His most recent project has involved filming Great Whites from inside a mini-submarine, nicknamed Troy, built as a perfect replica of the sharks themselves. The anatomically-correct, four-metre (14-foot) long 'wet' sub (Cousteau is in full diving gear inside it) can travel at five knots, fast enough to keep pace with a shark.

"I chose Great Whites, firstly because they're very intelligent and have a very large brain mass," he told me, "and secondly because they're very visual creatures." He also explained how he had always wanted to live out a childhood fantasy inspired by the Tintin book *Le Trésor de Rackam le Rouge*, in which the hero and his dog Snowy drive a shark-shaped submarine: "I thought that was the neatest thing!" he confesses. Of course it helps to be a Cousteau if you want to live out your childhood underwater dreams in quite such a spectacular fashion, especially if you need to call on the film industry's top engineers to help you build a hi-tech replica, complete with prosthetic skin, that is good enough to fool the sharks themselves.

"There have been far too many shark films," says Fabien, "but my idea was to take a more Diane Fossey/Jane Goodall-type approach; to try and *become* one of them." The real sharks, filmed in Mexico and Australia, responded to his creation with gaping, gill puffing and other characteristic communicative behaviour. Fabien found the whole experience to be pretty illuminating: "Being able to study them up close, and to observe them when there was no artificial stimulation, such as bait, affecting their behaviour, was a real treasure trove." He even played with the idea of introducing shark pheromones into the water to test their reaction to his creature, but unfortunately these can't be manufactured. "So no Great White humping!" he concedes, "Not that I would have wanted to be in there anyway, because if you know anything about shark mating behaviour, it's not a particularly gentle event."

The shark behaviour recorded with Troy was, nonetheless, "phenomenal", insists Cousteau. His resulting film, *In The Mind of A Demon*, is about his attempt to set the record straight:

> *Great Whites are one of the flag-bearers of the ocean, or they happen to be the one that gets the most attention, so we need to be able to use that in a*
> *on, and hopefully have them at least gain a little bit of respect for what these animals do and the essential role they play in our marine ecosystem.*

Taking a ride inside a fake shark is one thing, but taking one *on* a real-life Great White is something else altogether. The competitive Cousteaus, it seems, are vying to outdo each other – and this time it was Jean-Michel who took the plunge in South African waters alongside renowned Great White expert Andre Hartman. "To cut a long story short," explains Jean-Michel, "I ended up snorkelling and then grabbing the dorsal fin of a 13-foot Great White and taking a ride. It was a very special moment."

Apex predators

Another shark with a fearsome reputation is the Bull Shark and, again, conventional wisdom warns that you should stay well away. I once joined Jeremy Stafford-Deitsch for an encounter with a group of Bull Sharks at Walker's Cay in the Bahamas, where they had been living off scraps discarded by sports fishermen. Snorkelling in just a few feet of water with these formidable creatures (the biggest of which, dubbed 'Bahama Mama', was three metres [ten feet] long) was an incredible experience, and left me overwhelmed by their extraordinary grace and power. "They don't have the mindset that people attribute to them," says Stafford-Deitsch. "They have a very specific repertoire of prey items, which you don't fit into. If anything, they think you're another predator." I was glad to hear it.

Walker's Cay was thrown into the media spotlight sometime later when a shark chomped on the leg of Erich Ritter, a self-proclaimed shark 'expert' who was being filmed for the Discovery Channel's 'Shark Week' at the time. Ritter, a passionate advocate of interacting with free-swimming sharks, claimed that he could protect himself from attacks by modifying his heart rate and that he had never been bitten thanks to his expert knowledge of their behaviour.

When I swam with these sharks, Stafford-Deitsch had warned me to wear a full-length black wetsuit, and gloves. I'd even put away my underwater notebook when it seemed that the sharks were becoming curious about its white flesh-like pages. Ritter, on the other hand, was wading barelegged in murky, chest-deep water when the accident happened. A remora had grabbed a piece of bait thrown to lure the sharks away, and had swum with it between

SHARKS HAVE BEEN AROUND FOR 380 MILLION YEARS. (IMAGE BY ERIC CHENG; TIGER BEACH, BAHAMAS)

A CARIBBEAN REEF SHARK (GRAND CAYMAN)

Ritter's legs. A female Bull shark had then snatched the bait, unfortunately taking a piece out of his calf at the same time. The resulting film, *Anatomy of a Shark Bite*, only further served to demonise the species: "This is the staggering discovery that Eric presents us with," notes Cyber Divers News Network. "If you stand among hungry, macro-predatory, chummed-in sharks that are searching for food, sooner or later you will be bitten."

Ritter's accident added to the already controversial debate on shark feeding which had been taking place in Florida (just a shark's swim away from Walker's Cay) since the late 1990s, and which culminated in a state-wide ban on marine wildlife feeding by divers in January, 2002.

Meanwhile the decline continues, and sharks – which have been around for 380 million years – are today being slaughtered at an unprecedented rate. A recent report showed that populations of the Great White, Scalloped Hammerhead and Thresher Shark in the Atlantic fell by up to 90 per cent over the past 15 years, and all other species, with the exception of the Mako, have declined by more than 50 per cent. The Shark Trust estimates that some previously abundant species may now have been reduced to a mere two per cent of their original population. Removing these apex predators could have a devastating knock-on effect on the whole marine ecosystem. All divers therefore have a responsibility to do their bit in promoting the conservation and understanding of these fascinating animals.

Those big, bad barracuda

Barracuda can look intimidating when you meet them underwater, and over-imaginative divers like to describe these elegant predators as 'menacing', 'mean-looking' or 'sporting an evil grin'. Certainly new divers can find the barracuda's habit of following close behind and lurking in your blind spot rather unnerving. But, despite the unfriendly appearance of those big, glinting eyes, and the open mouth lined with two rows of razor-sharp teeth, barracuda are usually harmless to people.

Although barracuda may try and steal fish from spearfishermen and have sometimes been known to attack shiny objects (such as dive knives) that resemble silvery fish, they virtually never attack divers. The last recorded death from a barracuda attack was in 1957, off the coast of North Carolina, USA.[4] The fish owes its bad reputation to fishermen, who sometimes get bitten when the barracuda is fighting for its life in their boats.

⊕ A GREAT BARRACUDA LOOMS FROM THE SHADOWS.
(CHUB HOLE, GRAND CAYMAN)

There are around 20 different species of barracuda, widely distributed throughout tropical and sub-tropical waters. The largest of them, the Great Barracuda, can reach a size of 1.5 metres (five feet) and weigh up to 40kg (88lb). It has few predators except possibly shark and tuna. Some species are usually solitary; others occur in quite large aggregations over reefs. They rest by day and hunt by night, striking with lightening bursts of speed and slashing so vigorously with their teeth that sometimes their prey is sliced in two. But don't worry about the one that's following you: it's just curious.

'Murderous' morays

Like barracuda, moray eels have a fearsome reputation. Their open mouths and gruesome-looking teeth can certainly appear threatening, and divers often misinterpret the constantly opening and closing mouth as evidence of a moray's willingness to bite. In fact the eel is simply breathing, this action serving to pump water over its small

⌝ THE HONEYCOMB
MORAY IS ONE OF **200**
SPECIES OF MORAY
WORLDWIDE.
(NORTH MALE ATOLL,
MALDIVES)

↑ A PAIR OF MORAY EELS ENTWINED ON THE SEAFLOOR AT RAS MUHAMMED IN THE RED SEA.

gill openings. Cousteau quickly discovered the harmless reality behind the reputation. "The moray disseminates propaganda with its evil eyes and bared fangs," he wrote. "Alas, it is as prosaic as you and I and the cat. It is a confirmed home lover, and wishes to be unmolested in the routine of life."[5]

There are around 200 species of moray worldwide, easily identifiable by their long, muscular bodies. They lack scales, caudal, pelvic and pectoral fins, and instead move around by using their long, continuous dorsal and anal fins. Normally reclusive, they spend daytime mostly sheltering under a ledge or in a crevice, and come out to hunt by night.

It's always worth following a moray if you see one emerge during a night dive. They ambush their prey, clamping it between their powerful jaws before swallowing the victim whole. Their three rows of razor-sharp teeth (two in the lower jaw; one in the upper) need constant cleaning, so there are nearly always cleaner fish or shrimp in attendance.

The beautiful patterns of morays make them a favourite subject for underwater photographers. South African photographers Annemarie and Danja Köhler believe that the eels have distinct individual personalities and can actively recognise regular visitors by their appearance or behaviour. "We cannot doubt this," says Annemarie, "because all too often we have been picked out selectively by favourite 'pet' creatures from underwater groups in which other members were strangers." In *The Diver's Universe* they describe their encounter with a large moray on a reef in Mauritius:

For some reason or other, without any specific encouragement or enticement, the eel started following us on the reef. We never made a fuss, instinctively deciding to wait for the eel to call the tune. We did not know whether it had perhaps been fed by others, yet it never engaged in the sniffing and nudging antics that such hand-fed creatures tend to display. Day after day the eel became less wary

⊕ A DEADLY BLUE RING OCTOPUS FLASHES ITS WARNING COLOURATION. (LEMBEH STRAIT, INDONESIA)

and swam even closer, until it finally dared to twine around our bodies in sinuous ecstacy. Therafter, as soon as we rolled into the water from our chase boat, our eel friend would swim almost to the surface, inspect our cameras, repeatedly twine itself around us and join us in the descent. [6]

Attacks by morays occasionally occur in locations where their natural patterns have been altered by divers feeding them. The eels are very shortsighted and can easily mistake a diver's hand for food. In 2005, British tourist Matt Butcher lost his thumb to a moray in Thailand. He was trying to feed it sausage-meat, and the moray latched onto his thumb instead. "I couldn't get my thumb out of its mouth once it started biting," said Matt. "Seconds later my thumb came off. The moray ate it and swam away." Morays usually let go when they make a mistake; most injuries come when divers jerk back their hands, lacerating their skin on the animal's teeth.

An octopus's garden

Another remarkable creature is the octopus. No diver who has ever met one underwater can fail to be impressed by the intelligence of this animal. Yet the octopus too has long been the subject of lurid horror fantasies – not least those of Victor Hugo:

No horror can equal the sudden apparition of the devil-fish, that Medusa with its eight serpents. The entire creature is cold, and it is with the sucking apparatus that it attacks. The victim is oppressed by a vacuum drawing at numberless points; it is not a clawing or a biting but an indescribable scarification. The monster clings to its victim by innumerable hideous mouths. The hydra incorporates itself with the man; the man becomes one with the hydra. He draws you to him, and while bound down, glued to the ground, powerless, you feel yourself gradually emptied into this horrible pouch, which is the monster itself. [7]

"No horror can equal the sudden apparition of the devil-fish, that Medusa with its eight serpents."

Victor Hugo

Octopuses are, of course, not fish. In fact they belong to a class of molluscs called cephalopods, which have a highly developed nervous system and remarkably good eyesight. Like morays, they are home lovers. But they have the advantage of eight arms with which to construct their lair, and will use anything from old shells, rocks and coral rubble to build it up until satisfied that they're safe. Sometime they even create a hidden back door through which to escape when threatened.

Octopuses are amazingly clever at finding food, whether it's hidden in a diver's BCD pocket or in a jam jar that they have to unscrew. They usually hunt by night, tracking down their prey and enveloping it in their tentacles, before eating it using their strong, parrot-like beaks.

Octopuses have many other tricks at their disposal. Since their bodies have only residual skeletons, they can mould themselves into any shape and squeeze through the smallest of crevices to avoid predators. They will also squirt black ink into the water to confuse enemies such as morays, sharks and other large fish, before making their escape. And octopuses are especially known for their pulsating colour changes – sometimes seen during mating rituals, when a pair will also caress each other extensively before the male extends a modified arm to deposit sperm in the female.

In fact, we're only just beginning to find out how ingenious these creatures really are. For instance, scientists have recently discovered one Indo-Malayan species that impersonates fish. We have long known that octopuses can change their skin colour and texture in order to blend in with the background, but this skill is of a different order of magnitude. This 30–45cm (12–18in) octopus, known as the Mimic Octopus, has been observed in the silty estuaries around Sulawesi, Bali and Papua New Guinea routinely changing posture, colour and motion to resemble lionfish, sole fish and sea snakes. By thus taking on the guise of venomous animals, this amazing creature is able to forage boldly in broad daylight.

The complex behaviour of octopuses leads many divers to attribute personalities to them. In a series in *Diver* magazine entitled 'Your Strangest Dives', Dan Blyth recounts this amusing tale of an octopus that was 'armed and dangerous':

Last summer I was working as a divemaster in the Canary Islands. One day while with two qualified divers I chanced upon an octopus sitting in a small

fortress of pebbles, its eyes visible over the top. One of the divers had requested a chance to see an octopus 'free swimming', so I decided to assist it in leaving its lair. The octopus always returns to its lair if the disturbance is minimal – I have handled hundreds and they generally always return within a minute or two. I took my diving knife out and, reversing my grip on it, started gently to disturb the sand in front of the 'pus, which is normally sufficient to persuade it to move out. But I discovered almost immediately that I had seriously underestimated the size of this one, as an enormous tentacle whipped out of the lair, around my wrist and took the knife out of hand before I could blink! The octopus then gave an excellent impression of smugness as it placed the knife beneath itself and sat there looking patiently at me. [8]

⊕ ⊕ AN OCTOPUS FINDS SHELTER IN A DISCARDED PINT GLASS.

⊕ A MIMIC OCTOPUS PERFORMS WHAT SOME BELIEVE TO BE AN IMPRESSION OF A FLOUNDER.

(BOTH IMAGES, LEMBEH STRAIT, INDONESIA)

⊖ AN OCTOPUS DIGS IN THE SAND FOR FOOD.

(SIMILAN ISLANDS, THAILAND)

⌐ A SQUID INVESTIGATES A DIVER'S FINGER. (ARMCHAIR REEF, GRAND CAYMAN)

"With the Caribbean squid, we mimic them by extending our hands and using our fingers like they use their arms and tentacles."

Guy Chaumette

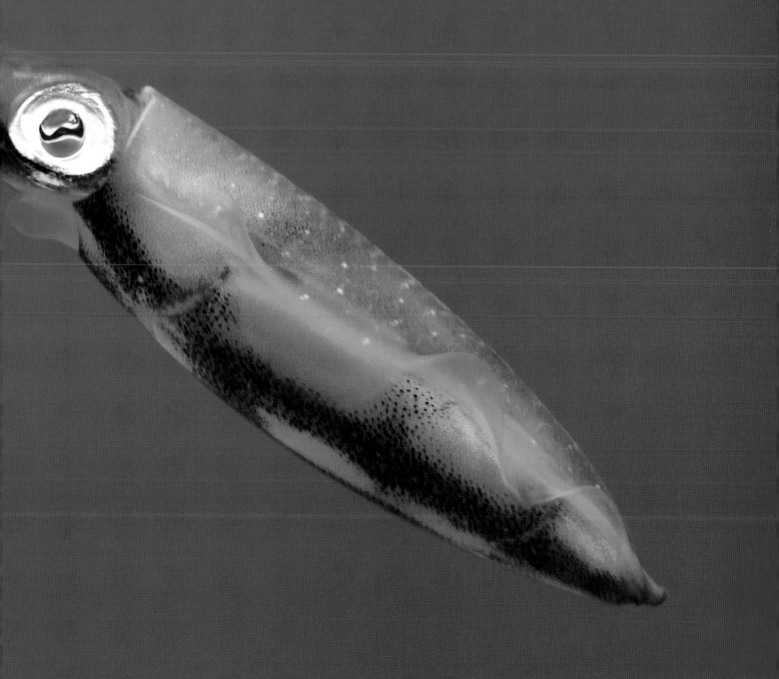

↑ AN OCTOPUS FINDS A HOME IN AN EMPTY BIVALVE SHELL.
(BALI, INDONESIA)

Clarke, "was the sort of rugged territory in which the giant cod, one of the most dangerous sea beasts, was likely to lurk," adding that," big groupers have jaws three or four feet across, and have been known to bite off legs and arms – and occasionally to bisect divers completely." [9]

Whether 'Art' had fallen for some Aussie leg-pulling who knows: although groupers are territorial and can seem threatening, there are no confirmed reports of one biting a diver in half. A grouper at the famous Cod Hole dive site is reported to have drowned a snorkeller by grabbing him and taking him underwater, and in 2002 a very aggressive grouper living on the wreck of the *Yongala* off Townsville Queensland, attacked two divers, taking the entire head of one of them in its mouth. The Marine Park Authority decided that this 80 year-old, two-metre (six-foot) long grouper must have been 'sick or injured'.

For the most part, however, stories of sea monsters simply represent a projection of our own fears onto harmless marine life. Cousteau was among the first to realise that the demonisation of sea creatures was exposed as mere superstition the moment we actually went underwater. "The villains of undersea myth are sharks, octopi, congers, morays, sting rays, Mantas, squids, and barracudas," he wrote. "We have met all but the giant squid, which lives beyond our depth range. Save for the shark, about which we are still puzzled, the monsters we have met seem a thoroughly harmless lot." [10]

Meetings with mammals

We terrestrial mammals may be proud of efforts to conquer the underwater realm by scuba, but we can hardly compete with those true marine mammals that have evolved for it naturally, namely the seals and dolphins.

Seals seem actively to enjoy frolicking with divers and snorkellers, performing acrobatics, blowing bubbles and generally behaving like delirious puppies given half the chance. Though wary of people on land, they become far more confident underwater where they seem to revel in demonstrating their prowess to divers. The 35 species found around the world comprise two distinct groups: 'eared seals', such as the Cape Fur Seal, which are also known as sealions; and 'earless' (or 'true') seals, such as our own

It took Blyth an "exasperating" ten minutes to trick the octopus into giving his knife back. Since octopuses are known for their tool-wielding skills, we can only imagine what might have happened had it kept it!

Harmless monsters

Groupers are not normally thought of as undersea monsters, and indeed most divers would consider them more of a pet than a threat (see p145). In Australia, however, it's a different story, according to science fiction guru and diving pioneer Arthur C. Clarke, who undertook an eighteen-month journey along the Great Barrier Reef in 1954-55. In *The Coast of Coral* he recounts a dive where his partner Mike and another diver hurriedly returned to the surface after discovering that they had strayed into an area known for its giant groupers. "This," explains

BOTTLE-NOSED DOLPHIN (STRAIT OF GUBAL, EGYPT)

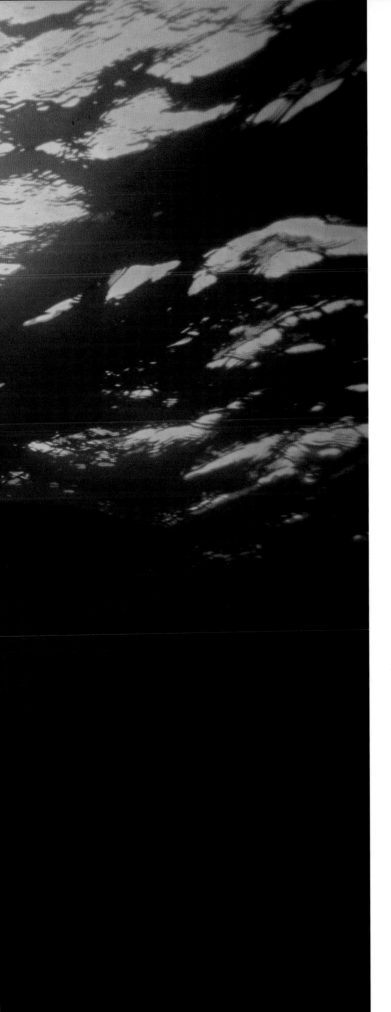

Grey Seal. Many live in temperate or polar regions, and are thus seldom encountered on reefs. But there are still many dive destinations where you can interact with these animals, including Britain, New Zealand, the Galapagos, southern Australia, the Cape coast of South Africa and the west coast of America.

Seals have a low boredom threshold, so you'll need to do something interesting in order to grab their attention. Turning somersaults, rolling over, or just sitting down and waving your fins around can all do the trick. Their natural curiosity and playfulness will quickly be roused.

For sheer speed and agility in the water, dolphins outdo even seals. But they are far less approachable and, unlike seals, don't like noisy, bubble-blowing scuba divers. However, these intelligent and curious mammals do love boats – or rather, riding their bow waves – and so it's from a dive boat that you're most likely to spot them. Underwater, you may well hear their distinctive clicks and whistles, but you'll seldom catch more than a fleeting glimpse of the dolphins themselves. I remember once hanging in the blue for a safety stop in Baja, California, when a pod of dolphins sped past: there was hardly even time to raise a camera. My friend and dive buddy Jo Dowle was luckier, when she had the following encounter with dolphins while on a dive in the Red Sea:

> *I was on a boat dive from Hurghada, and instead of going down to look at the reef we stayed on a sandy patch next to it and the dolphins just turned up as soon as we went down. So we abandoned our dive plan and just frolicked around with them for thirty minutes or so. There were at least ten dolphins. I remember having a lot of eye contact with them and thinking it was the best thing on earth.*

The best way to interact with wild dolphins is simply by snorkelling. On the Grand Bahama Bank offshore from Bimini, for instance, a pod of Spotted Dolphins arrives daily to play with snorkellers. They tend to ignore people who just float on the surface, so you need to put some effort into getting them interested: the sillier you look underwater, the more the dolphins like it, so free-diving down, doing handstands, making funny noises and turning somersaults are all good ploys. Dolphins love to play: whether watching the antics of a silly human, fooling around with a bit of seaweed or zooming after a DPV (diver propulsion vehicle), they're out to have fun and – it sometimes seems – to flaunt their superiority in their own element.

⌲ A SCHOOL OF SOUTHERN STINGRAYS MAKES AN IMPRESSIVE SIGHT. (STINGRAY CITY, GRAND CAYMAN)

the spirit of the seas

"As life itself began in the sea, so each of us begins his individual life in a miniature ocean ... from gill-breathing inhabitants of a water world to creatures able to live on land."

Rachel Carson

LIFE ON EARTH BEGAN IN WATER SOME 3,500 MILLION YEARS AGO, WHEN MICRO-ORGANISMS SIMILAR TO SINGLE-CELLED BACTERIA OR ALGAE BEGAN TO GROW IN THE PRIMAEVAL OCEANS. BY 3,000 MILLION YEARS AGO, SOME OF THESE CELLS DEVELOPED THE ABILITY TO ABSORB ENERGY FROM SUNLIGHT AND EVOLVED INTO PLANTS; OTHER ORGANISMS, LACKING THE ABILITY TO PHOTOSYNTHESIZE, GREW BY FEEDING ON THESE PLANTS. FROM THESE SIMPLE, ONE-CELLED BEGINNINGS, JELLYFISH, SPONGES, WORMS, SEAWEEDS, CORALS AND OTHER SEA LIFE BEGAN TO DEVELOP.

For millions of years, as life in the ocean continued to evolve, there was still nothing on the land. By 500 million years ago, in the Cambrian Period, marine invertebrates such as corals, arthropods and crinoids were the dominant forms of life on the planet, and the earliest vertebrates – simple fish with body-armour plates – had appeared. The first primitive plants and fungi began to colonise the land, followed 50 million years later by the first air-breathing arthropods – spiders, mites and millipedes. By the Devonian period, when terrestrial insects and amphibians were evolving, there were already sharks in the seas.

Over aeons, as amphibians, reptiles and finally mammals slowly evolved on land, they carried in their bodies an essential part of the sea – a chemical heritage that even now links us to our watery beginnings. Human blood flows with almost the same proportions of sodium, calcium and potassium as seawater, while over 70% of an adult body is composed of oxygen and hydrogen, combined in that unique substance known as water. "When they went ashore, the animals that took up land life carried with them a part of the sea in their bodies," declared Rachel Carson in *The Sea Around Us*, "a heritage which they passed on to their children and which even today links each land animal with its origin in the ancient sea." This journey from ocean to land, believed Carson, is one that we all replicate in our lives:

> As life itself began in the sea, so each of us begins his individual life in a miniature ocean within his mother's womb, and in the stages of his embryonic development repeats the steps by which his race evolved, from gill-breathing inhabitants of a water world to creatures able to live on land. [1]

At the time of the first dinosaurs, in the early Triassic Period, land animals started returning to the oceans. The first to take the plunge were reptiles. We can still see their descendants today, the turtles, encased in protective shells that have changed little in basic design for over 200 million years. With the demise of the dinosaurs at the end of the Cretaceous Period, 65 million years ago, mammals began to proliferate. Soon the first fully aquatic mammals, the whales, evolved, and by 25 million years ago the seas were teeming with mammalian life, including dolphins, dugongs and seals.

Given this heritage, it is little wonder that water plays such a major part in the great spiritual traditions. 'By means of water, we give life to everything', says the Koran (21:30), which sets out the rules for bathing and immersion (*ghusl*) on ritual occasions. During the *Kumbh Mela* festival, up to ten million Hindu pilgrims take part in ritual bathing and spiritual purification at Allahabad, where the holy waters of the Ganges meet those of the Jumna. In Christianity, baptism with water symbolises entry into the religious community, while in Judaism, the *mikvah* is also an important ritual immersion.

Man as aquatic ape

In other cultures, ancient creation myths speak of the ocean as the mother of all life and all creatures of the earth as children of the ocean. It isn't such a giant leap from these beliefs to the idea that humans actually *did* have an aquatic phase in our history. This is the so-called 'aquatic ape' theory.

This theory was the brainchild of marine biologist Sir Alister Hardy, following his field trip to the Antarctic in 1929. Reflecting on the smooth skin and subcutaneous blubber of whales and seals, it occurred to him that there was more similarity between these and human physiology than there was between humans and the hairy apes. He began to speculate whether competition for food on land had driven humans to the sea, where they had adopted a semi-aquatic lifestyle. Fearful of jeopardising his scientific standing by broadcasting this outlandish notion, Hardy kept quiet for 30 years and didn't publicise his ideas until 1960, when he was invited to give a talk to a British Sub-Aqua Club conference in Brighton. If he imagined that his fanciful musings to a bunch of divers were likely to

$\rightarrow$
COULD ENTERING
THE OCEANS MARK
AN UNCONSCIOUS
DESIRE TO
RETURN TO OUR
EVOLUTIONARY
ROOTS? (FELIDHOO
ATOLL, MALDIVES)

"A dive is also an inner experience because the outside world, no matter what its form, is a reflection of your inner world."

go unnoticed, he was wrong: there was an outcry in the popular press and Hardy was invited by the *New Scientist* to explain himself. He did so, in an article published on March 17, 1960: "My thesis is that a branch of primitive ape-stock was forced by competition from life in the trees to feed on the seashores and to hunt for food, shell fish, sea-urchins etc. in the shallow waters of the coast," he wrote. "I am imagining this happening in the warmer parts of the world, in the tropical seas where man could stand being in the water for relatively long periods, that is, several hours at a stretch."[2]

Humans started by foraging in the shallows, suggested Hardy, and then gradually learned to catch fish with their hands and swim down to the seabed to harvest crabs and bivalves. Although they would have had to return to the beach to sleep and find drinking water, these 'aquatic apes' would have spent at least half their time in the sea, gradually learning to stand in an upright position as the water supported their weight.

The ability of babies to swim from birth gave Hardy further proof of our aquatic past: "Does not the vogue of the aqua-lung indicate a latent urge in Man to swim below the surface?" he wondered. He even thought that the hairs on our body are orientated for this purpose. "All the curves of the human body have the beauty of a well-designed boat," he wrote. "Man is indeed streamlined."[3]

Hardy's ideas were widely ridiculed at the time, but that didn't stop them being taken up from the 1970s onwards by an American writer, Elaine Morgan, who popularised them in a series of books that includes *The Descent of Woman* and *The Aquatic Ape Hypothesis: Most Credible Theory of Human Evolution*.

Back to the sea

The aquatic ape idea is an appealing one, but unfortunately it doesn't stand up to scientific scrutiny. Being hairy is not necessarily a hindrance in the water, and would in fact help retain heat: otters, beavers and fur seals have all kept their fur, and swim much better than us. And we're not really covered in a layer of fat, like seals and whales: we just have fatty deposits, due mostly to our sedentary lifestyles. Although humans can learn to swim (and babies take to the water easily enough), it's not an innate skill and has to be learned. Even elephants, which use their

trunks as a snorkel, are better swimmers than us. In fact, most other terrestrial mammals can swim instinctively. They float horizontally, with their nostrils out of the water, whereas we humans tend to float vertically with our nostrils submerged – a much more impractical position.

"If we were descended from a truly aquatic ape," asks Trevor Norton in *Underwater to Get Out of the Rain*, "why are we not endowed with the essential attributes of a diving animal, such as a waterproof skin that doesn't go wrinkly after ten minutes in the bath, effective insulation, a body with a large mass and small surface area, and eyes that can see underwater?"[4]

Another piece of evidence used to support the aquatic ape theory is what's known as the mammalian diving reflex: in most mammals, when the face is immersed in water, the heart rate slows down and there is a reduced blood flow to the body's extremities. However, this reflex only comes into play in *cold* water, so it is more likely to be a survival mechanism to combat hypothermia than anything else.

So, although chimpanzees and gorillas are occasionally known to wade upright through swamps and rivers, it seems that the only genuine aquatic ape is the one that goes underwater in scuba gear. But even if there was no 'swamp period' during our evolution, this doesn't stop us resonating with a deep-felt sense of belonging to the ocean. We can often feel so comfortable and at ease in the water that it feels as though we're returning to where we came from – a sensation perfectly evoked by Osha Gray Davidson, in his book *The Enchanted Braid*:

I floated there at the reef's edge. It was the cusp of day and night. Below me was a perfect living circle of slender-branched corals, their tiny, gelatinous tentacles just now beginning to emerge for their nighttime feeding from a colony that was precisely my size. Above, if I turned my head, I could see a faint few stars venturing out, like the coral polyps below, into the tropical twilight. And rather than feeling alien in this exotic world, I was filled with the opposite sensation: I felt completely, if inexplicably, at home, as if I belonged there as much as the fishes or the sea cucumbers or the corals. It was if all those years on land had been the sojourn in foreign territory and now, on the reef, I had arrived back home. What lay behind those feelings, so irrational and yet at the same time to strong? All I know was that in that moment I didn't want to return to land, ever.[5]

⬆ THE OCEAN CAN BE A SPIRITUAL ENVIRONMENT .
(PEPPERMINT REEF, GRAND CAYMAN)

Spiritual scuba

This sense of re-entering the sea, of reclaiming our watery heritage, has led to the development of a new approach to scuba diving that places specific emphasis on the spiritual aspects of being underwater. It has been called Zen diving, spiritual scuba, aquatic yoga, yoga scuba and yoga diving, and has inspired courses in places as far apart as Egypt, Mexico, Turkey and the Caribbean.

The first of these courses was in the Red Sea resort of Dahab, just over 100 kilometres (62 miles) north of Sharm-el-Sheikh in Egypt's Sinai peninsula. This is where American-born instructor Monica Farrell teaches yoga diving. Monica has worked in the Red Sea since 1998 and is an advanced technical diving instructor with over three thousand dives under her weightbelt. Significantly, she has also studied yoga in India. "I began by trying out yoga techniques in my diving classes," she explains. "I noticed straight away how the *asanas* [yoga postures] helped with general fitness as well as helping to cope with the different technical skills that you need to learn on the diving course." She also became aware of how the breathing exercises lowered stress levels for divers of any ability, and how students who practised just the most basic yoga techniques found themselves more comfortable in the water and seemed to get more from their dives.

Thus was born yoga diving, in which the combination of the two skills emphasizes how a physical experience – like an *asana* posture or a dive – can also become an inner one. "My experience is that your ability to stay in the moment – the blue, the colour, the fish, the feeling of floating, your own breathing – that experience of being in the present can be heightened," explains Monica, adding that, "diving can act as a window for expanding consciousness." And whether you're free-diving, snorkelling or on scuba, the essential idea remains the same: namely that being outside your normal environment can release the mind and enable you to connect with your inner self: "You can drop the 'I'," says Monica, "whether that 'I' is a doctor, traveller or whatever – drop the 'I' and then you're nobody, there's just the sea, and light and water."

Another important aspect of yoga and meditation is their non-competitive nature. This makes for very safe diving – there's no rushing around (or down) to beat records – and is the antithesis of the tick-box mentality (ticking off species seen, for example). "For me, diving should be less of a goal-oriented activity," she says, "and focused more on relaxation and being involved

Could it be, wonders Davidson, that we have retained some genetic memory from our amphibian ancestry? Hans Hass had no doubt that the 'manfish' had evolved a set of external organs that would allow him to re-enter the sea: "I now developed a form of diving gear which would turn us into fishlike creatures," he pronounced. And he saw evidence all around him: "Everywhere, people equipped themselves with flippers, donned diving masks, and discovered the bottom of the sea, their one-time kin, their one-time home. Man, in an artificial fish shape, went back into the sea."[6]

⊕
DIVING CAN ACT
AS A WINDOW FOR
AN EXPANDING
CONSCIOUSNESS.
(HIGH ROCK WALL,
GRAND CAYMAN)

*"By means
of water,
we give life to
everything."*
The Koran (21:30)

⟵ FLOATING IN THE 'NOW' IS A
MEDITATIVE EXPERIENCE.
(DAHAB, EGYPT)
⟶ THE PULSE OF LIFE EBBS AND
FLOWS THROUGH THE OCEANS.
(SIMILAN ISLANDS, THAILAND)

holistically with the aquatic world." She maintains that this approach sets you on the way to meditation:

Because you're floating weightless in a womb-like environment, with your focus naturally on your breathing, then the relaxation of the mind is happening automatically. So, you're getting a taste of meditation without even trying – and the more you can become aware of it, however subtle the effect, then the more this will happen. You are being totally in the present underwater, since all your normal cares to do with your family, job, relationship or whatever, are fairly distant. This being in the 'now', and the quietening of the mind, is what Zen and meditation are all about.

Bending myself into a yoga *asana* under the shade of a palm tree on the Dahab shoreline prior to a dive with Monica, I felt very focused on what lay ahead. My body felt more prepared when I eventually donned my kit, and once I was underwater the whole dive became a very relaxed experience. A friend who also took the course over several days, London-based photographer Henrietta Van den Bergh, says that it helped her to become more balanced and relaxed underwater. "I found I gained a more sensual understanding of the diving environment and was diving in a much calmer manner," she says, She describes how slowing down made her more aware of the rhythm of the reef, and enabled her to spot elusive and camouflaged creatures, such as frogfish, that would previously have remained hidden. There were other benefits, too: "My diving improved," she adds, "which was even noticed by my dive buddy!"

*"All life on land
is a life in exile."*

Hans Hass

↑ THE REVERSAL OF AIR AND WATER GIVES PAUSE FOR REFLECTION. (SENTINEL ROCK, GRAND CAYMAN)
← HAPPINESS IS FLOATING WEIGHTLESS INTO A WARM OCEAN. (DOC POLSON WRECK, GRAND CAYMAN)

Holistic diving

You don't have to be into new-age spirituality to enjoy the benefits of super-relaxed diving. Many divers are already practising this kind of diving, despite having never heard of an *asana*. The best divers are already in a Zen-like state: calm, controlled and centred on the experience. The idea of yoga diving is to increase your quotient of the here-and-now, and to move from a linear approach – pursuing a set route around the reef, for instance – to a more holistic consciousness of the ocean.

Try it for yourself. Look for a spot on the seabed that you can return to repeatedly. Here you can observe or meditate on what's going on around you, and the seabed becomes like an underwater temple or shrine. You will soon relax and feel the focus shift to your inner world.

Many divers are reluctant to admit to experiencing the spiritual side of being underwater – even if they're vaguely aware that they have touched something deeper, as it were, than the reading on their depth gauge. "I do think a lot of divers are quite nervous about either exploring those thoughts or acknowledging them," says Tim Ecott, "because it's a bit too poetic and bit too sensitive."

For many divers trained in warmer waters, diving in temperate seas doesn't seem particularly appealing. However, for *Diver* columnist Louise Trewavas it's precisely the qualities that would deter most people (such as low visibility) that she finds compelling: "People think, 'oh, that's not a very attractive place to dive'," she says. "but actually it's the absence of distraction which is the point. When you go diving, it fills everything you do, it involves your whole body and you're not thinking about anything else at all. It's very therapeutic, it's like a break from all the worries and concerns that fill up your head."

Similarly, diving is an escape for thriller writer Frederick Forsyth, who describes it as being like entering an underwater cathedral, where emptiness and silence reign. "Silence is something that has almost ceased to exist in our world," he claims. "For most of our lives there is never a moment without sound, but you get down there

and it is absolutely quiet apart from the sound of your own heartbeat, and your breathing. There are no computers, no mobiles, no phones, no cars, no jets, no noise – complete silence."

Possibly it's the unique combination of floating in an entirely different environment, amidst beautiful marine wildlife, that gives diving a spiritual dimension few other activities can match. "I shall never forget diving at Sipadan once and seeing giant columns of fish, almost like a column in a temple," says writer Anthony Horowitz. "It really was for me the moment of 'And God Created Fish'," he adds. "I'm not that sort of person, but diving is as close to spiritual as I ever get – it's that sense of perfect contentment, that sense of floating and watching and being – and feeling very much connected to the planet."

Mind, Body and Spirit diving

Alex and I are on the deck of a small day boat off the West End of Grand Cayman. We're diving with Ocean Frontiers, but before we can even think about getting in the water we're having a gentle stretch. At least, we're trying to: there's not much room on the deck, what with everybody's gear all over the place. But instructor Steve Schultz isn't letting us slacken off: he's devised a set of stretches for divers, specially designed for the confined space of a boat deck. "Stretching helps to condition the body, loosen up before a dive and avoid the strains associated with physical activity such as lifting tanks," says Steve. He points out that a lot of the muscles used in diving are not normally used in everyday activities, so they are often tight and cold when you start the dive and are more easily injured as a result. This explains why divers often complain of bad backs, leg cramps, tense neck muscles and so forth.

The stretches we're doing are part of a course called Mind, Body and Spirit diving (MBS). It brings Schultz's experiences with transcendental meditation, martial arts and other disciplines into this PADI speciality, which he has already taught in the Caymans, Turks & Caicos, Bonaire and on board the *Belize Aggressor*. "Early on in my experience as a diver I found that there were ways to step over into the realm of the momentous almost every time I dived," he says. He also explored yoga, hypnosis and sports training in search of that same sense of well-being. But when he started teaching scuba, he became alarmed by the high drop-out rate among new divers; it seemed that these

⬆ MONICA FARRELL PRACTICES YOGA ASANAS BESIDE THE RED SEA. (DAHAB, EGYPT)

divers somehow never really reached the point of real comfort and exhilaration. So he set out to design a system that would apply gentle discipline and spiritual impetus to the whole process in order to make each dive a more meaningful experience.

The techniques involved in MBS scuba include meditation, breathing, visualization and yoga and stretching exercises. These enable you to decrease your air consumption, increase your comfort levels and enhance your interaction with marine life. The process can re-invent your diving, claims Schultz, by turning it into something much more personal and spiritual. "You can increase your enjoyment," he says, "and even have the opportunity to touch into religious and mystical experiences that are only limited by your faith and imagination."

Like Monica Farrell, Steve Schultz believes we get too caught up in task-oriented diving. He points out that the very spirit of MBS is to be able to enjoy diving without a goal, and that sometimes a passive dive – with no photos to shoot or species to tick off – is just what the doctor ordered. "Every now and then," he suggests, "you should just kick back and enjoy a dive for diving's sake."

All in the mind

Visualisation is a key component of the MBS course. The main aim is to create a positive attitude when diving by visualising a successful outcome to the dive. This can be useful when dealing with tasks that might be worrying you, such as clearing your mask. Schultz describes how, when working with students who have problems of this kind, he first gets them to relax through meditation so that they step aside from the fear and emotion of the problem. He then works through a visualisation exercise that breaks the task down into individual steps so that the students can 'see' themselves performing it without fear or worry. Affirmations also help to reinforce the students' belief that they will succeed without problems.

Visualisation and affirmation, according to Schultz, can also be useful for improving specific skills, such as underwater photography or wreck penetration. "They are very powerful tools used by world class athletes and performance coaches worldwide," he explains. "They are subtle techniques in that, rather than actively teaching, the teacher empowers students to work through his or her

"And God Created Fish ... I'm not that sort of person, but diving is as close to spiritual as I ever get." **Anthony Horowitz**

⬆ YOGA HELPS YOU RELAX AND LOOSEN UP BEFORE A DIVE. (DAHAB, EGYPT)

own issues, whether that's mask removal, first deep dive, first night dive, or whatever. I once had a diver who was afraid of seeing fish," he recalls. "We worked together to get her over it."

Another way of tackling fears and phobias associated with diving and being underwater is a technique called Neuro-Linguistic Programming, or NLP. This method is designed to replace automatic responses and unwelcome feelings with more empowering thoughts. NLP expert Brendan O'Brien claims that it can be used to calm nerves, conquer fears and help divers feel confident about their ability to cope with problems. This can be particularly useful for beginners, whose perfectly natural fears are often unwittingly exacerbated by their instructors. "It's the most unnatural thing in the world to do," says O'Brien. "Put this thing in your mouth, stick your head underwater and breathe through it – it runs contrary to all our natural instincts." Trying to calm a beginner by telling them

"Meditation allows the diver to still the mind and enhance the relaxed brain patterns that are associated with peak performance."

Steve Schultz

And it's not just beginners who can benefit from NLP techniques. "Certainly, if you're planning to do a deep dive in cold water, or something that's really quite challenging," says O'Brien, "then it can be useful to run through the plan in your mind, to visualise it beforehand." This is the philosophy behind a school of diving known as DIR, or Do It Right, who pre-plan their technical dives and often run through the drills on dry land before entering the water. And, as we have seen in *Chapter three*, diver training agencies also recommend using visualization as a means of making your diving safer.

MBS diving also uses meditation to help create a calm mental state, allowing you to visualise mastering tricky skills or overcoming phobias. "Meditation allows the diver to still the mind and enhance the relaxed brain patterns that are associated with peak performance," says Steve Schultz. And, he claims, fish can tell the difference:

Changes that occur when you are in a higher state of consciousness include slower, smoother breathing, slower heart rate, lower blood pressure, enhanced alpha brain wave patterns and less muscle tension. Some of these things fish can sense with their eyes and lateral line sensory systems. When you appear relaxed and in control, fish see you as less of a threat and approach you more.

For Schultz, it's all about trying to arrive at that place during a dive where you have left the outside behind and become more deeply connected to the environment. "The more intense the connection that I have with the underwater environment," he told me, "the stronger the spiritual experience."

that there's nothing to fear, explains O'Brien, can have precisely the opposite effect. "It's all about the power of suggestion," he says. "If you say to someone 'don't worry', actually what you're inviting them to do is to worry."

Instead, instructors should be setting their pupils up for success with simple strategies, such as asking them on the way to the pool what they're good at. "By suggesting things that give you confidence," says O'Brien, "then you start wiring the brain for confidence."

STEVE SCHULTZ MEDITATES UNDERWATER IN THE CAYMAN ISLANDS. (HIGH ROCK WALL, GRAND CAYMAN) ↗

"The idea is to turn diving into something much more personal and spiritual."

Steve Schultz

Fooling around

Like Steve Schultz, Monica Farrell worries that instructors are often not trained to deal with beginners' phobias. But she approaches the problem from a slightly different perspective. After yoga to help with relaxation, Farrell takes her students into the ocean with the idea of *play* uppermost – suggesting, for instance, that they play with their masks or buoyancy jackets. Any notion of 'skills tests' that must be passed or failed can wait until the students are already competent at the task. "If you start with the idea that it's simply enjoyable play," she says, "then the 'performance levels' tend to take care of themselves."

In this way, Farrell recognizes an essential aspect of Zen diving: namely the importance of cultivating a 'playful mind'. And performing underwater manoeuvres such as swimming upside down or looping-the-loop is a good way to start.

The much-respected *Scuba Diving* magazine ran a cover story (when it was still *Rodale's Scuba Diving*, in 2003) on '137 Ways to Play Underwater'. This included ideas and techniques on how to kiss underwater (plan it beforehand, and make sure you synchronise your regulator removal); how to drink a soda at 30 metres (give it a good shake before descending, pop the top off and suck while crushing the can); and even how to dive naked. For the last of these, it quoted Frank Lombino of the Nautical Nudists Dive Club in Land O'Lakes, Florida, who insisted that people like being taught in the nude but that conditions must be just right: "Hell yeah, you can get injured!" he warned, "I worry about the coral more than the fish. You don't want to be around any fire coral, for instance."

Playing around underwater is a good way to improve your confidence and aquatic skills. Children do it naturally. Recently I went underwater with my two sons, Luke and Oscar, while they learned to dive on a junior open water course in the Red Sea. I felt like a wise, ponderous marine mammal as I finned along calmly and slowly beneath them while they frolicked energetically around a shallow reef like a couple of baby seals, chasing fish.

A 'playful mind' could also include listening to music underwater. Take a waterproof MP3 player, for instance, and dive with Handel's *Water Music*, or an aria from Bizet's opera, *The Pearl Fishers*. Or you could join in with the annual Lower Keys Underwater Music Festival off Big Pine Key, Florida, when over six hundred divers descend with everything from guitars to trombones to help the fish dance.

⊖ IF YOU BREAK AN EGG DEEP UNDERWATER THE PRESSURE WILL HOLD IT TOGETHER. (JACK MCKENNY'S WALL, GRAND CAYMAN)

⊖ GOING FOR A STROLL IS A GREAT WAY TO TAKE A BREAK FROM ESTABLISHED DIVE PATTERNS. (TURTLE FARM REEF, GRAND CAYMAN)

A walk on the wild side

There are other ways to change your perspective, to make that slight shift that takes your diving into another zone. One is to slip out of your fins and go for a walk. Yes! Take an undersea stroll. Why not? All we normally do is swim, swim, swim. Find a nice big sandy patch or lagoon-type environment, take off your fins, tuck them under your arm and give it a go. This is called 'moon-walking' and with good reason, since you bounce around on the seabed just like an astronaut on the moon. Try some big bunny hops and indulge that wonderful, free-floating sense of weightlessness.

Moon-walking is easiest if you're negatively weighted, so take extra. Normal weights may give you just a bit too much bounce, and there is the risk of an uncontrolled ascent. Most confident divers will get the hang of it after just a step or two. But try to avoid areas with steep topography or strong currents. If in doubt, consult your dive guide and practise under supervision.

Taking off your fins can be a very liberating experience. Conversely, putting them back on again afterwards is also illuminating, giving you a new appreciation of just what wonderfully efficient tools dive fins are for underwater propulsion. Making this switch – from finning to walking and back again – increases your awareness of the ways in which you move through water, as well as the power of finning. It's a great exercise in Zen diving.

One of the immediate advantages of walking on the seabed is that you are able to control your movements more precisely, both in terms of how and where you place your feet, and how quickly you can stop. When swimming, there's a motive force behind your movements, which can make it tricky to slow down if you spot an interesting creature. By contrast, walking allows you to stop dead in your tracks – and the creature will be less afraid of you, since you are not a wheezing, puffing, sand-stirring monster. Just breathe calmly, and watch what's going on right in front of your face. If it's easier, you can drop onto one knee, or kneel down altogether. This is something you can do much easily than while wearing fins: you don't have to worry about what your fins are hitting behind you, and you can fit into a much smaller space with less disturbance.

Ⓚ TRY CULTIVATING A PLAYFUL MIND UNDERWATER. (STINGRAY CITY, GRAND CAYMAN)

↧ GO MOONWALKING WITH YOUR BUDDY. (DAHAB, EGYPT)

Does it look silly? Probably yes, and passing divers might well be chuckling into their regs. Let 'em! I'll bet they'll give it a go when they think no-one's looking. In Dahab once I was buddied up with someone I had only just met who knew nothing about Zen diving. We had a perfectly normal dive until I spotted a sand patch and, unable to resist, slipped my fins under my arm and did a few somersaults. Before I knew it, my buddy had taken off her fins and was space-hopping all over the place. "God, that was so much fun!" she said when we surfaced. "At first I thought you'd gone nuts – but then I thought 'Oooh, I want to do that!'"

The easiest way to deal with your fins is to tuck them under your arm, then you can pop them back on whenever you want. Alternatively, you could hand them to your buddy or guide. You can also put them under a convenient rock (taking good care not to disturb any marine life), or take a mesh fin bag down with you, plus an additional weight to secure it. A fin bag can be fixed to your BCD or the anchor line with a clip. You'll be amazed at how effective normal breast-stroke is on scuba gear without fins. In fact, it's the best way to travel when you're not actually walking or bouncing around.

"Does it look silly? Probably yes, and passing divers might well be chuckling into their regs. Let 'em! I'll bet they'll give it a go when they think no-one's looking."

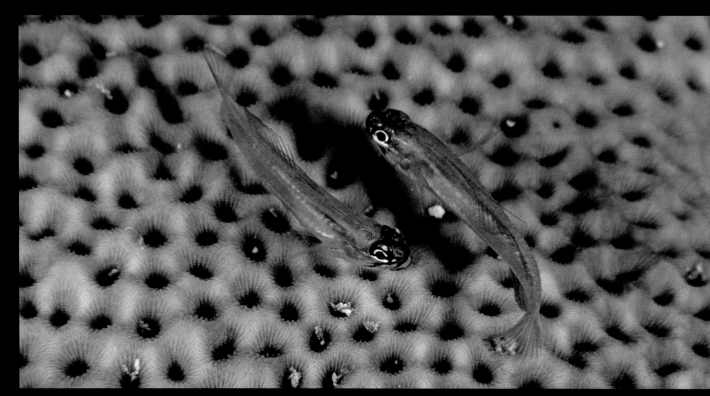

① THE YIN AND YANG OF THE OCEAN. (THE MAZE, GRAND CAYMAN)

Being playful is also a way of being subversive; of changing the way we perceive things. A German diver, Hermann Gruhl, describes what happened on an ice dive in a frozen lake when he discovered the joys of bouncing around upside down without his weight belt: "I gave up my camera and weighted belt to the outside world and stumbled around upside down under the surface of the ice, pushed upwards by strong buoyancy," he wrote. "With a bit of practice you learn to stand erect and run around on the ice, head downwards, with big jumps. The Antipodes game! My example inspired the others and soon everybody was hopping and slithering, it's sheer joy. I wonder if we can get away with it?"[7]

A sea change

Being underwater can change you, often profoundly. For Hans Hass, paradoxically, it led him to stop diving for a decade. "My many years of diving undoubtedly wrought a kind of change of consciousness," he wrote. "Underwater you have a strange freedom which is not possible on land. Down there you gain a detachment from the human world such as is scarcely to be found elsewhere." This detachment led him into a ten-year study of human evolution during which he sold his beloved

boat, *Xarifa*, and immersed himself in politics, economics and law. "This happened because I still remained underwater in principle," declared Hass. "Our watery abode, the starting point for this whole development, remained constantly before my eyes and virtually forced upon me a different and unaccustomed way of looking at things."[8]

Whether we're connecting with our inner selves or merely pondering the seeming infinity of the oceans, a return to the sea has primal echoes that evoke for us the origins of life. Rachel Carson reflected that humans, being unable permanently to re-enter the sea like the seals and whales, have used ingenuity and reason to "re-enter it mentally and imaginatively." Mankind's search beneath the oceans, she concluded, is a search for "a world long lost, but a world that, in the deepest part of his subconscious mind, he had never wholly forgotten." As we race around our cities and towns, worries Carson, we may forget that we live on a watery planet. But on a long ocean voyage, with only the stars and the sea for company, man discovers the truth: "that [our] world is a water world, a planet dominated by its covering mantle of ocean, in which the continents are but transient intrusions of land above the surface of the all-encircling sea."[9]

the art of
freediving

"They're taking to a high art the sensation of freeing up your brain by being immersed in water."

Tim Ecott

A FREEDIVER
RETURNS TO
THE SURFACE
AFTER A DIVE. (OFF
THE NORTH WALL,
GRAND CAYMAN)

A SLIGHT CHOP ON THE SURFACE IS MAKING IT HARD TO CONCENTRATE ON MY *PRANAYAMA* BREATHING – BREATHE IN FOR TEN SECONDS, HOLD IT FOR TWO, BREATHE OUT FOR FIVE SECONDS, HOLD IT FOR TWO – DESIGNED TO SLOW THE HEART RATE PRIOR TO A FREEDIVING DESCENT. A CROWD OF CURIOUS ONLOOKERS HAS GATHERED AT THE END OF THE JETTY, WONDERING WHAT THESE TWO PEOPLE – INSTRUCTOR ANDY LAURIE AND MYSELF – ARE DOING, BOBBING AROUND IN THE SWELL OF THE SOUTHERN RED SEA. THEY'RE BOUND TO BE DISAPPOINTED: FREEDIVING JUST ISN'T A GREAT SPECTATOR SPORT. ONE MINUTE SOMEONE'S FLOATING ON THE SURFACE, THE NEXT MINUTE THEY'VE DISAPPEARED – ONLY TO POP UP AGAIN A FEW MINUTES LATER. END OF STORY. EXCEPT FOR THE FREEDIVERS THEMSELVES, OF COURSE, FOR WHOM THOSE FEW MINUTES ARE THE WHOLE STORY, AN UNDERWATER ADVENTURE OF GREAT SKILL AND DARING, AND – FOR MANY – EVEN A JOURNEY INSIDE THEMSELVES.

My four minutes of *pranayama* is up, and I'm ready. I exhale three times with a loud 'whoosh', take a final deep breath and signal to Andy Laurie. It's the end of the 'breathe-up' and we duck dive and start to descend. I pull myself slowly, steadily down the line. As a scuba diver, the contrast in pace was one of several things that surprised me during my two-day freediving course with NoTanx freediving. You don't swim frantically downwards to reach your goal: everything is very slow and deliberate in order to conserve oxygen. I was also surprised by how hard it is to do a proper surface dive: we're used to a rudimentary duck dive, sticking our legs in the air to descend when snorkelling, but the freediving technique is much more precise, involving raising just one leg and then sliding under. I confess it took a lot of pool sessions before I got it right – you're meant to leave just a tiny ripple, not the tidal wave I was creating.

Still descending, Andy and I pass ten metres...fifteen metres...and finally encounter the seabed just short of twenty metres (65 feet). I release the rope and swim briefly around the reef before the pressure in my lungs starts sending me warning signals. I reach for the rope and start to climb again. Calmness and economy of effort are essential at the turn-around point, I had been warned, in order to conserve oxygen and keep the pulse rate low. And there were other surprising instructions for the ascent: don't exhale ("You need all the air you can get," Andy had said); don't look up – it can stop the blood flow to the brain and lead to a shallow water blackout; and don't get faster towards the end. Above all – never panic.

These instructions run through my head and I try to stay relaxed, doing my best not to think about the fifteen metres still to go. To save energy, I stop finning at ten metres (33 feet) and let my natural buoyancy and momen-

tum carry me up. Finally I break the surface, fix my eyes on the horizon and take several deep breaths. Andy has followed me all the way and he makes sure I give him the 'OK' sign before we both relax. He knows that most freediving accidents happen in those last few metres.

Going deeper

My lessons continued. Together we worked through some of the 17 basic safety rules of freediving, which include never diving alone, never freediving after scuba and never exceeding your limits. I learned the differences between using my diaphragm and my intercostal muscles to breathe; how chemoreceptors tell the body when its oxygen levels are too low; and how to watch out for signs of a 'samba' – loss of motor control underwater. I also began to learn more about the strange and intense world of the freediver.

Freediving for economic reasons – in search of pearls, sponges, shellfish or other commodities – has been around for centuries. Back in the time of Homer, men used a heavy weight to help them descend 30 to 35 metres (98 to 115 feet) to pluck sponges from the seabed. Sponge diving still takes place in the Mediterranean and the Caribbean. All over the Pacific, people have plunged underwater in search of pearls, clams, and other valuable products since before recorded history. In Korea and Japan, female divers known as *Ama* collect edible seaweeds and clams at depths of 20 metres (65 feet) or more. But the idea of freediving as a recreational activity only really took off in the 1960s. At the same time as the early 'gogglers' were honing their spearfishing skills in California and the South of France, another set of divers was taking a

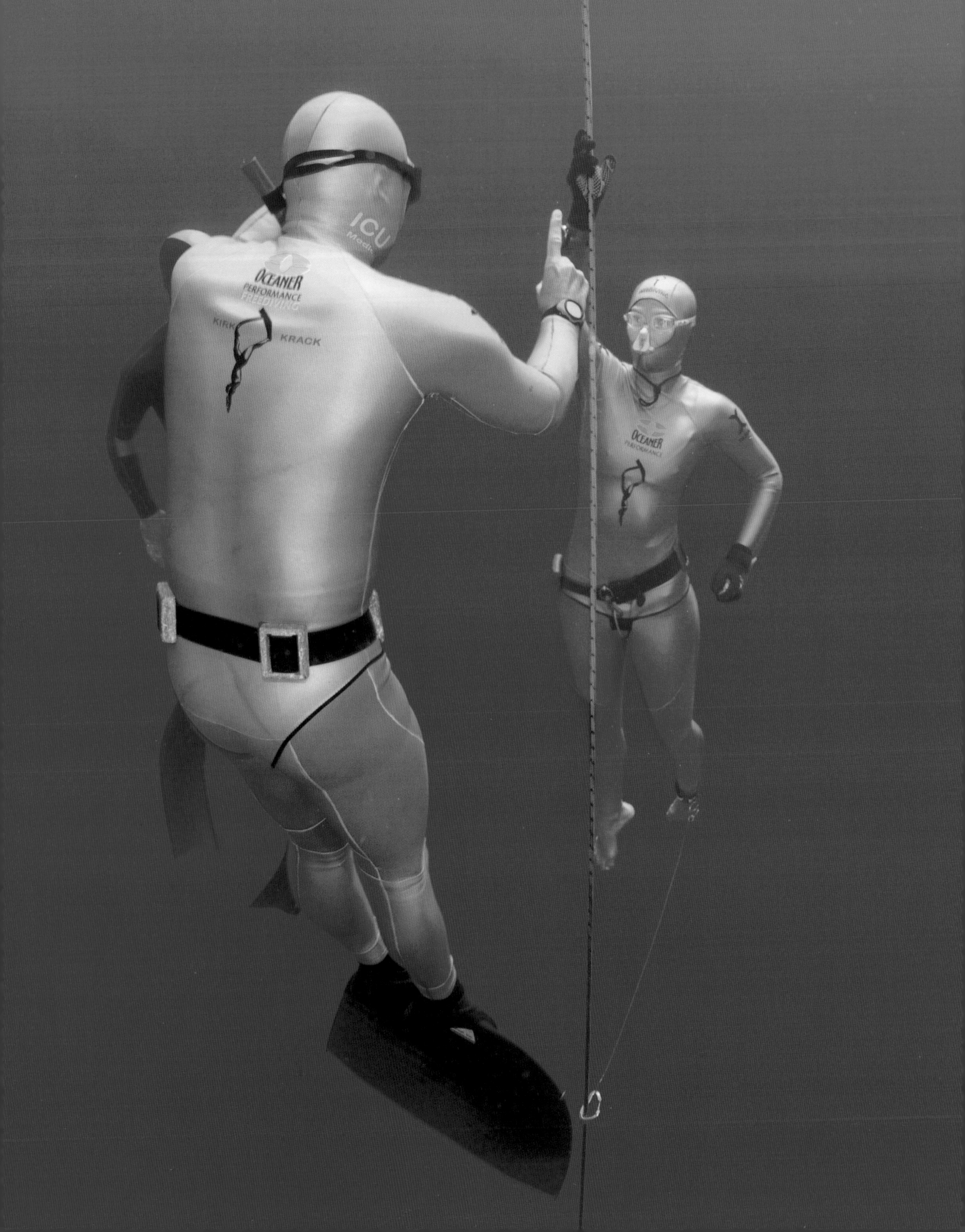
ICU
OCEANER
PERFORMANCE
FREEDIVING
KIRK
KRACK
OCEANER
PERFORMANCE

"Compared to scuba divers we're very lean and sleek and smooth in the water, and there's a fluidity about our motions."

Kirk Krack

different route into the underwater world. At first the idea was simply to hold onto something heavy and sink as far as possible. Today the techniques have become rather more advanced and free diving has evolved into a competitive sport, complete with sophisticated equipment, high-profile sponsorship and major international stars.

The first real freediving celebrity was Jacques Mayol, who became world champion in 1974. Alongside Enzo Maiorca of Italy and Bob Croft in America, Mayol blew apart our notions of what the human body was capable of achieving. He finally broke the 100-metre (327-feet) barrier in 1976, using a mechanical sled to go down and a balloon to pull himself back up again. The jockeying for position between Mayol and Maiorca was immortalised in Luc Besson's fictionalised film *Le Grand Bleu* (The Big Blue), released in 1988. The film, which achieved cult status among freedivers, was a cinematic hymn to their obsession with the blue depths. It also exposed the bitter rivalries between competitive divers, and cemented the symbolic connections that freedivers like to believe exist between themselves and dolphins (at the end of the film, the character of Jacques swims off after a dolphin, leaving the world of air-breathing mammals behind). Mayol himself even wrote a book called *Homo Delphinus*.

The record breakers

"Dolphins are what we all want to be," says Andy Laurie, as I sit in a classroom practising static apnea (breath-holding) at the start of my freediving course. The carbon dioxide build-up in my lungs is telling me to breathe, but the trick is not to listen to your body: focus instead on a poem, a song or anything other than what your lungs are telling

you. Later we move on to static apnea in the pool and it somehow seems a whole lot easier: my timed breath-hold gradually increases as I learn to override the signals from my body and move into another, calmer mindset.

During the 1980s the freediving world was taken by storm when an Italian, Umberto Pellazzari, arrived on the scene and proceeded to break all previous records. In 1988 he set his first world record by holding his breath for an astonishing five minutes and thirty-three seconds. Frenchman Philippe Goasse soon beat him with five minutes fifty seconds, so Umberto surpassed this with six minutes and three seconds in 1990. Another Frenchman, Michael Bader, took the record to six minutes 40 seconds, so Umberto upped the stakes again by passing the seven-minute barrier.

By the end of the decade Pellazzari held all the records, including a depth of 150 metres (490 feet) in the No Limits category. But here's the thing about freediving: there's always someone else coming up behind to push the boundaries of the possible even further. Pellazzari was eclipsed by the charismatic Cuban, Francisco 'Pipin' Ferreras, and his partner Audrey Mestre. Mestre set a new women's record with a dive to 125 metres (409 feet) in June 2000 off La Palma in the Canaries, but she was overtaken by the glamorous Tanya Streeter, who broke the No Limits record in 2003 with a descent to 160 metres (523 feet) – beating the men's record, too. The following year, Tanya was ousted from the podium by the French free diver, Loic Leferme, who reached 171 metres (559 feet) in October 2004.

Just when nobody thought humans could go any deeper, Patrick Musimu – born in Kinshasa, Zaire, but now living in Belgium – stunned the freediving world by reaching 209 metres (683 feet) during a dive off Hurghada in the Red Sea on 30th June, 2005. He achieved this amazing feat using a specialised technique to flood his Eustachian tubes and sinuses with seawater during the descent, instead of equalising using the Valsalva manoeuvre (whereby you exhale against a closed glottis or closed mouth and nose).

Ⓔ KIRK KRACK ENCOURAGES MANDY-RAE CRUICKSHANK AS SHE RETURNS FROM A WORLD RECORD FREE IMMERSION DIVE TO 74 METRES (242 FEET). (OFF THE WEST WALL, GRAND CAYMAN)

"Nothing is absolute," he said after the dive. "The only barriers are in your mind." Unfortunately Musimu's dive isn't classified as an official record because there were no observers present from the sport's governing body, AIDA (the Association for the International Development of Apnea). He also needed to spend time in a recompression chamber for a suspected bend after the dive, which added to the controversy surrounding this attempt.

Musimu's equalisation technique was just one part of a complex training programme that prepared his body for the dive. "At those depths," he remarked, "something very weird happens to the human organism." And it was not merely a physical sensation: "I found peace down there," he added, "and feel blessed for what I have been able to experience deep inside of me."

Inner journeys

Freedivers often frame their experiences in terms of reaching inner depths, of being on a journey with spiritual dimensions. Many mention the mammalian reflex, the origin of life in the seas and the aquatic ape hypothesis (*see Chapter 5, The Spirit of the Seas*) when staking their claim for a trancendental connection with our deep blue world.

This attitude has, until recently, made freedivers an easy target for mockery by scuba divers. "Free divers are sometimes even more reluctant to discuss this side of things than divers," says Tim Ecott, "because it's incredibly easy to take the mickey out of them when they're waxing lyrical about the Zen of inner space." But he points out that freedivers use *bona fide* meditation techniques to get themselves into the right state of mind to slow their breathing, and that top freedivers are actually expert yogis:

> They're taking to a high art the sensation of freeing up your brain by being immersed in water. Some of them are interested in getting records but actually it's the mental side of free diving which makes people really want to get into it and pursue it at the senior level.

The problem, believes Ecott, is that until you've experienced freediving for yourself, you can't understand what it's all about; and once you have, it becomes all too easy to slip into mumbo-jumbo when trying to express your feelings about it. I can't say that I returned from my dives with any last-

ing sensation apart from deep gratitude for being back on the surface breathing air again, but many others have experienced a profound transformation. Among them is Renden Sullivan, who was training in Maltese waters under Chris Cardona of the Maltese national team when he underwent a dramatic, mind-altering experience on one of his deepest dives. At first it seemed inexplicable but he later found out that a handful of other freedivers had experienced the same thing. The sensation, of unified space and time, seemed to Renden to resemble the mental states experienced in mystical and religious traditions – in particular the Buddhist idea of Sartori. At first he believed that it was due to hypoxia (lack of oxygen), but gradually he understood that it was closer to the 'flow' state experienced by athletes at the height of their performing powers. "It was one of the most profound experiences of my life," said Renden, whose experiences were made into a film, *The Greater Meaning of Water*.

Musimu echoes this perspective. "Your body starts talking to you in a way that it doesn't when you're outside the water," he told me. "You start feeling everything: your heartbeat, the contraction of every tiny muscle in your legs and arms and toes." He describes every sensation as 'amplified', but hastens to add that he feels no pain when going down. "The deeper you go," he says, "the deeper you start feeling your inner self."

The first time this happened, Musimu experienced a sensation of paralysis and had to wiggle his fingers just to prove that he was in control of his body. "Normally when you're freediving at depth your body feels completely different," he told me, "but there it had just gone, it had completely disappeared and I was just a brain." He recalls how the record attempt began to lose any significance as he started going deeper and deeper, and he was unable to express himself each time he returned to the boat. "The two or three minutes that I spent down there felt like hours," he told me. "It was like being in a different dimension. I felt like I had touched paradise, I had flirted with the Gods. It was beautiful."

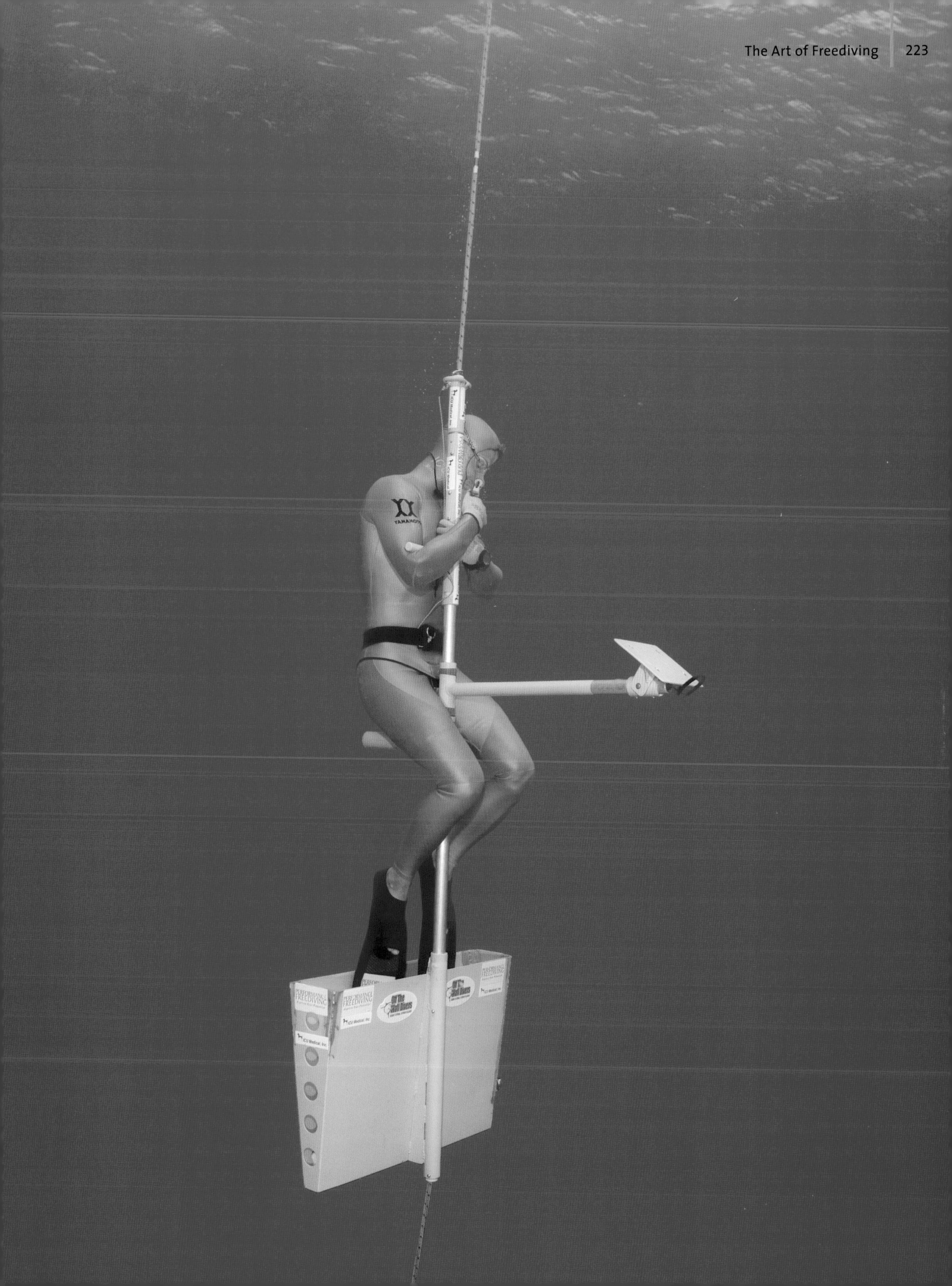

A FREEDIVER PREPARES METICULOUSLY AT THE SURFACE BEFORE DIVING, AND AS A RESULT OF
THEIR CONSIDERED APPROACH THEY ARE OFTEN MORE CONNECTED WITH OCEAN DURING THEIR DIVES . (DORSET, ENGLAND)

↑ FREEDIVER PREPARES ON THE BACK OF A DIVEBOAT. (DAHAB, EGYPT)

← SCUBA DIVERS CAN LEARN MUCH FROM THE FREEDIVER'S ATTITUDE TO DIVING. (OFF THE NORTH WEST WALL, GRAND CAYMAN)

Underwater compositions

Record-breaking French diver Loic Leferme likens his freediving to 'composing with the elements'. Leferme's sports career began in rock climbing and it was only later that he switched to free diving in the bay of Villefranche-sur-Mer, a picturesque Mediterranean port to the east of Nice. "I began freediving in the same way that I was climbing," he recalls, "that is, very simply." Leferme describes how free climbing offers a powerful contact with nature and the elements, and sees his freediving as a natural underwater extension of this. "Being very close to the elements is very important to me, that's why I'm doing freediving," he says. He likens it to a martial art, in that you have to go with the flow and work with the elements. To do otherwise, believes Leferme, means that you will lose; the water will break you. "You need to go where the water wants you to go," he says. "If I'm not flexible and I go in the water, then I will feel the pressure. But if I'm flexible, stretching my lungs and my frame, then I will be able to go deeper."

Canadian free diver Kirk Krack, who manages the Performance Freediving team, endorses the view that flexibility is the key. "Clear your mind of anything you know about being in the water and understand that the biggest thing you can do is relax," he says:

The water is a huge, powerful medium. If it's between you and the water, the water will always win. When you're descending and the water wants to compress your lungs, you can't resist that. You need to be like a flexible sponge and just let yourself relax into it, let the chest walls compress and don't fight that. But most importantly open your ears, go at your own pace and don't put expectations on yourself.

Part of the attraction of freediving, claims Leferme, is the release it offers from the sanitized constraints of modern everyday life. "A lot of people want to feel their existence through the elements," he says. "The elements are very powerful, and that's why [in freediving] you're very close to the basic things such as life, death, fear and cold." Though freediving, believes Leferme, you can get to know yourself better, and forge a stronger connection with your own body than scuba diving ever allows.

Leferme began his training under the great free diving teacher Claude Chapuis, who founded AIDA. "I just kept going deeper and deeper, and then one day – it really was like this – one day we realised that I was as deep as the world record, and that's how I did it," he says. So if you want to train for a world record, he claims, it's best to set your sights elsewhere. Otherwise the sea will "kick your ass."

The relaxed approach

"Loic's approach is very different to other freedivers," says Marcus Greatwood of NoTanx freediving, who trained with him and Chapuis in Nice. "It's based on being relaxed in the water. So basically fun comes before depth and time. The mainstream way is to set targets and push yourself to those targets," he says, "whereas their way is to enjoy themselves training and the targets are a by-product." NoTanx freediving follows the same philosophy in its own training. "It's a longer process, but it's a lot more true to my idea of what freediving is all about," says Marcus. "We never push ourselves, and we don't use computers because depth isn't important either. If you come up and you're smiling," he says, "then that's a good dive." This approach also reduces the likelihood of the dreaded shallow-water blackout, which is the biggest hazard that freedivers face.

Most recreational freediving is similar to what's known as 'Constant Weight': basically, swimming down and back up a vertical line anchored on the seabed. 'Free Immersion' is more or less the same, except without using fins; you just pull on the rope with your hands. Then there is 'Static Apnea', where you hold your breath for as long as possible (freediving is sometimes simply called 'apnea' from the Greek for 'want of breath') – with the world record standing at almost nine minutes. 'Dynamic Apnea', which usually takes place in a swimming pool, is swimming as far as possible underwater while holding your breath.

But the disciplines which attract the most attention, and which have put freediving in the media spotlight in recent years, are the 'Variable Weight' and 'No Limits' categories. In the former, the freediver descends feet-first on a weighted sled that runs along a rope. On reaching the

target depth, he or she returns to the surface by finning up and/or pulling on the line. Although this requires exceptional breath-holding and equalisation abilities, it's the No Limits diving that makes the greatest demands of the human body. In this form, the freediver descends on a weighted sled that incorporates an air cylinder and a large air bag. On reaching the target depth, the diver inflates the airbag from the cylinder and allows it to carry him upwards. The speed of ascent can be as high as three to four metres (10 to 13 feet) per second, and consequently there's a risk of decompression sickness. To reduce these risks, the diver usually releases the airbag at around 20 to 30 metres (65 to 98 feet) and then ascends under his or her own steam for the rest of the way. This is the riskiest form of freediving, a fact that was highlighted by the tragic death of Audrey Mestre while attempting a new No Limits world record in October 2002.

Freediving just for the fun of it doesn't require any kit at all except for your mask, snorkel and fins. In fact there are probably more recreational freedivers in the world than there are scuba divers, since snorkelling effectively becomes freediving once you go below the surface. Admittedly the holiday tourist finning gently over a shallow coral reef doesn't bear much resemblance to the sleek, silver-wetsuited, seal-like beings descending to fantastic depths in freediving's world championships, but the two are essentially at different ends of the same spectrum. Serious freedivers, however, do use more refined equipment, including lower volume masks and carbon-fibre fins. And many never use a snorkel.

A different awareness

What can scuba divers learn from freedivers? Kirk Krack believes that you can gain greater 'water awareness' by freediving. "Compared to scuba divers we're very lean and sleek and smooth in the water, and there's a fluidity about our motions," he says. It's certainly true that, unencumbered by bulky scuba gear, freedivers move differently. "There's definitely a sense of freedom – not just with the equipment but with the style of movement through the water," adds Kirk. He recommends that any diver would benefit from a freediving course, even if freediving were not their primary goal:

FREEDIVERS DELIBERATELY SLOW THEIR PHYSIOLOGICAL RATES WHILE DIVING. (RAS MUHAMMED, EGYPT) ➔

A FREEDIVER DESCENDS INTO THE OCEAN. (OFF THE WEST WALL, GRAND CAYMAN)

"Dolphins are what we all want to be."

Andy Laurie

⊝ FREEDIVER DESCENDING. (OFF THE WEST WALL, GRAND CAYMAN)

Think of it as cross training for scuba diving. It gives you a sense of water awareness and how to be efficient in the water. The focus is all on energy conservation and relaxation – you only have so much oxygen, so you have to use it efficiently. Being efficient with our kick and our body movements through the water are very important. The breathing exercises are also helpful in terms of using oxygen efficiently.

Tanya Streeter has a similar message. "It will make you a much safer, much more aware scuba diver," she says. "You're more than likely to consume a lot less air than you did before," she adds. Mandy-Rae Cruickshank, also part of the Performance Freediving team, echoes this belief. "I was always good on air when I was on scuba," she says. "But after learning proper breathing techniques for freediving my air consumption was just incredible – I can spend three times as long down there as anybody else on one tank."

Cruickshank held the Constant Weight women's record until she was beaten by the Russian Natalia Molchanova, who dived to 80 metres (262 feet) at the first Individual Freediving World Championship in Villefranche in September 2005. A PADI Course Director, Mandy-Rae teaches in Vancouver, British Colombia, and says that being a freediver makes a big difference to her comfort levels on scuba. "When you can do 100 to 130 feet on a free dive, and you go back to scuba," she says, "all of a sudden you're thinking that this isn't very deep anymore. You know you can handle yourself, and even if all your equipment fails, you know you can make it back up."

Wildlife encounters

While scuba divers may accept that freediving has advantages in terms of air consumption and safety, they are often sceptical about the ability of freedivers to get close to marine life. After all, even the best freedivers in the world have to surface after just a few minutes. It's an impression that freedivers are keen to dispel. Marcus Greatwood describes how, while freediving in the Red Sea, a scorpionfish appeared just inches from his mask and started hunting. "He fed right in front of me," recalls Marcus, "a fish came along and he ate it. You just wouldn't see that on scuba, even on a rebreather."

⊕ DEVELOPING SIMPLE SNORKELLING SKILLS CAN ALLOW
EVERYONE TO EXPERIENCE THE ADVANTAGES OF FREEDIVING.
(POOH CORNER ,GRAND CAYMAN)

⊕ FREEDIVING MAKES SHY CREATURES EASIER TO APPROACH.
(LEMBEH STRAIT, INDONESIA)

Mandy-Rae Cruickshank is equally positive about the benefits of free diving with wildlife. "It's true that you've only got a couple of minutes down there before you have to come back up again, so you can't investigate underwater quite as well," she says. "But then there are a lot of animals that won't interact with you if you're on scuba that will if you're on breath-hold." She describes how the Harbour Seals in Vancouver wait for the freedivers at the bottom of their line: "You go down to 60 or 100 feet and they'll just be sitting there," she says. "They're very curious creatures and basically they're just waiting to play." And she describes how turtles in the Caribbean will let you swim right alongside them, whereas the bubbles exhaled by a scuba diver would soon scare them away. "Once I was in Aruba on my way up," she adds, "when I found myself right in the middle of about two hundred parrotfish. If I had exhaled they would all have scattered. But because I was

"Every now and again I find myself in the middle of nowhere diving with some beautiful animal and I feel like all my hours in the gym have paid off."

Tanya Streeter

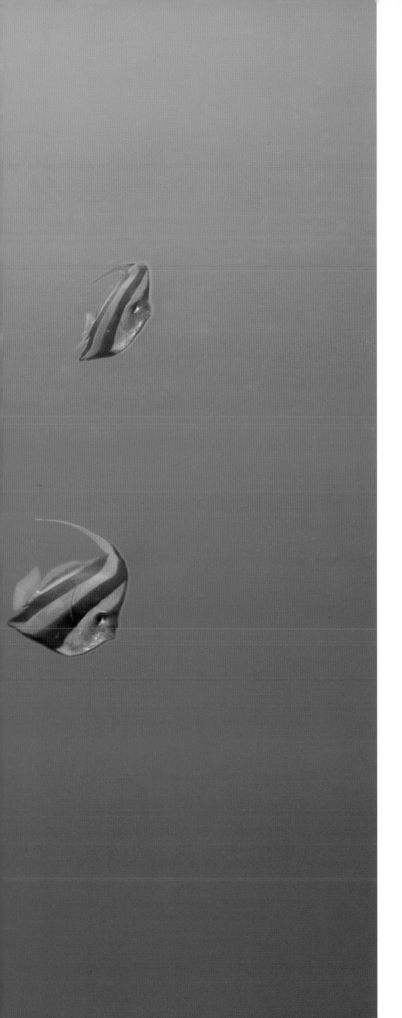

"Once I was in Aruba when I found myself right in the middle of about two hundred parrotfish. If I had exhaled they would all have scattered. But because I was on breath-hold I was really bumping into them all, right in the middle of this school."

Mandy-Rae Cruickshank

← BANNERFISH SCATTER AS A DIVER EXHALES.
(SOUTH MALE ATOLL, MALDIVES)

⤢ A LARGE SCHOOL OF BOHAR SNAPPER STREAM PAST. (RAS MUHAMMED, EGYPT)

on breath-hold I was really bumping into them all, right in the middle of this school."

Tanya Streeter, holder of ten freediving world records, has recently developed her career by becoming a television presenter, principally for the BBC. Her focus is now on wildlife encounters, and she is finding this new challenge just as rewarding as her old competition days. In the Galapagos, where she dived with penguins, marine iguanas, turtles and sea lions, she found that many of these animals, having never been threatened by human beings, were 'surprisingly accommodating'.

In the Maldives, she freedived with Whalesharks and Mantas for the BBC (like Alex and myself, she was on board the *Sea Spirit* for these encounters). And in the Silverbanks, an area offshore from the Turks and Caicos, she even got to dive with the whales for which the area is renowned. "This is something I will never get used to," she says. 'It really is such an enormous privilege to find yourself swimming next to a Humpback Whale. It's magi-

Encounters with whales and Whalesharks are generally governed by regulations to ensure that the animals are no disturbed, so scuba is rarely allowed. It's in these sort of situations that the training for freediving can really pay off. "If you've got a certain skill level in freediving then you're going to have better encounters," says Tanya. "Any time that you're in the water with marine mammals, you can control your movements better but also stay down a bit longer, so your encounter is going to be that much more comfortable."

Like most competitive freedivers, Tanya follows a strict training regime before record attempts. Now she seems to be reaping the benefits in new ways:

Every now and again I find myself in the middle of nowhere diving with some beautiful animal and I feel like all my hours in the gym have paid off. I never think twice about having a world record but I do think two, three, four and five times about being able to

⊖
A GROUP OF
FREEDIVERS
RETURNS FROM
A DIVE.
(OFF THE WEST
WALL, GRAND
CAYMAN)

⊕ MANY SKILLS LEARNT THROUGH FREEDIVING CAN BE APPLIED TO SNORKELLING. (RIDGEFIELD REEF, GRAND CAYMAN)
⊛ A FREEDIVER AT THE SURFACE. (DAHAB, EGYPT)

The future for freediving

There are many inherent contradictions in freediving: you're free to move gracefully underwater without scuba gear, but not free to stay down as long as you want. Competitive divers claim to be lured by the deep blue, but then many make their descents with their eyes closed, seeing nothing. Other freedivers profess to be interested in inner exploration, but end up being more aware of the contents of their depth gauge than of themselves. Plenty of freedivers think they're dolphins, but couldn't care less about other life in the sea.

The truth is that freediving, like scuba diving, attracts people for all sorts of different reasons – from snorkellers who want to dive deeper in search of fish, to budding yogis after a short cut to Nirvana. And like scuba diving, it will continue to grow and develop precisely because it *does* embrace so many different approaches.

During the 2005 Individual Freediving World Championships, a 29-year-old Venezuelan, Carlos Coste, reached 105 metres (343 feet) on a Constant Weight dive

– that is, just a man and his fins. This was the same depth reached in 1983 by Jacques Mayol, except that he used a sled. And Musimu, meanwhile, has passed 200 metres (654 feet) with a sled. New records are established every year, and as freediving continues to evolve there are surely further surprises in store. With training becoming increasingly available in dive resorts, more people are taking up freediving as an adjunct to scuba or snorkeling, thus bringing it into the diving mainstream. Already, freediving is widely practised as a means of getting closer to big marine wildlife and this too will continue to grow, as more marine parks encouraging these encounters are developed.

At the end of my freediving course I knew I would come back to it, if only to experience that sense of joy at being in the water unencumbered by kit; the pure sensation of just me and the elements. Perhaps after all it is freediving that best allows us to understand what Jacques Cousteau's meant when he claimed that: "underwater, man becomes an archangel."

the fate of the oceans

"The world we have created today as a result of our thinking thus far has problems which cannot be solved by thinking the way we thought when we created them."

Albert Einstein

IN A DOCKYARD IN LA ROCHELLE HARBOUR ON FRANCE'S ATLANTIC COASTLINE, JUST PAST THE FLOAT-ING MARITIME MUSEUM, LIES A RUSTING HULK OF A BOAT. ITS BROKEN LADDERS, SMASHED PORTHOLES, FLAPPING SHEETS OF CANVAS AND LAYERS OF PEELING PAINT ARE A SAD TESTAMENT TO THE ONCE-PROUD SHIP THAT WAS FAMILIAR TO MILLIONS OF TELEVISION VIEWERS WORLDWIDE. THIS IS *MV CALYPSO*, COUSTEAU'S FLAGSHIP FOR SEVERAL DECADES, A STURDY CONVERTED MINESWEEPER THAT PERFORMED STERLING SERVICE ALL OVER THE BLUE PLANET. CAUGHT UP IN A LEGAL DISPUTE BETWEEN COUSTEAU'S SURVIVING DESCENDANTS, THE SHIP IS NOW GENTLY ROTTING AWAY.

But something curious is happening in the dockyard. As I sit in the afternoon sunlight contemplating the detritus strewn across *Calypso*'s deck – old workbenches, discarded air cylinders, rusting motors and the like – a steady procession of people wanders down the quayside to take a look at the boat. There are no signposts, it's certainly not on any tourist maps, and there's not even a name on the boat – and yet all these people know exactly what it is.

Cousteau's legacy is gigantic. Even posthumously he remains the best-known diver in the world, and his work has left a lasting influence on the marine environmental issues of today. His great talent for self-promotion ensured that he generated huge interest in diving, spurring on a whole generation to explore the underwater world. That generation has automatically donned the mantle of Cousteau's environmentalism, sharing his deep concern for the changing fortunes of our oceans.

We know little about what the oceans were like in ancient times – or, for that matter, just a century or two ago. But it's probably safe to assume that they were once rich in much of the megafauna that is so scarce today. In Roman times, for instance, the Mediterranean abounded in Monk Seals, most of which were exterminated by commercial sealing in the 17th century. Today there are only a hundred of these critically endangered animals left. Tens of thousands of Sea Otters once inhabited the Californian coast, until they were almost exterminated for their pelts. In the last century, commercial whaling devastated populations of all the great whales. Today dolphins are dying *en masse* in fishing nets, while sharks are being slaughtered in their millions to satisfy commercial greed. Meanwhile we are catching fish such as marlin, tuna and cod in such numbers that many species are spiralling towards extinction; scientists estimate that we've lost around 90 per cent of the ocean's larger species already.

The fate of the Green Turtle illustrates the destruction we've wrought on ocean ecosystems in the past 500 years. When Columbus sailed through the Caribbean, it was recorded that he had to stop his ships for a full day to let a migrating stream of turtles pass. Dr Jeremy Jackson, a biologist with the Scripps Institute of Oceanography in La Jolla, has estimated that more than 35 million turtles once roamed the Caribbean – until people developed an appetite for them. Unfortunately the turtle's shell, such a good protection against other predators, effectively turned it into tinned food for sailors, who carried the marine reptiles on board ship for weeks on end as a ready supply of fresh meat. Now only a few hundred thousand green turtles remain in the Caribbean, and all seven species worldwide are endangered or threatened.

Another major herbivore that would have been present in huge numbers in the Caribbean during Columbus' time is the West Indian Manatee. Today this rare creature exists only in a few isolated pockets. The fate of its relative, the Steller's Sea Cow, was even worse: during the 18th century this giant sirenian went from discovery to extinction in a record-breaking thirty years.

Reefs in trouble

Anecdotal evidence of the contemporary decline of marine life abounds. In the 1960s Arthur C. Clarke found himself diving among vast numbers of fish. "They crowded around us so closely," he wrote, " that we could see nothing but a solid wall of scales, and had literally to push our way through it."[1] In the same decade, Sylvia Earle was on expedition to the Indian Ocean. "Everywhere we dived," she recalls, "we found fish curious and unafraid, a pristine sea, the distillation of millions of years of history preceding that moment."[2]

Today, sadly, it is more common to hear divers lamenting the lack of fish. "When I first went diving in Puerto Rico in

⬅ ALL SEVEN SPECIES OF TURTLE ARE ENDANGERED OR THREATENED. (SOUTH MALE ATOLL, MALDIVES)

⬅⬅ CORAL REEFS ARE UNDER THREAT WORLDWIDE. (BALI, INDONESIA)

"They crowded around us so closely, that we could see nothing but a solid wall of scales, and had literally to push our way through it."

Arthur C. Clarke

the 1960s," Alina Szmant tells me, "there were giant barracuda living on each fern groove, green morays everywhere, and lobsters and schools of snappers and groupers hiding under the overhangs. Go out there now, and it's all gone." In the thirty years that photographer Jeff Rotman has been working underwater, he's noticed major changes too. "I've seen it disappear right in front of my eyes," he says. "We've removed so many of the populations and we know that many will not be able to return to healthy levels."

Coral reefs are particularly vulnerable to human impact. Reef fisheries are an important source of protein for coastal communities in tropical countries, but exploitative fishing (which includes overfishing and destructive fishing) is damaging the long-term sustainability of this resource. Marine scientists estimate that 36 per cent of the world's reefs are already suffering from overfishing. Destructive fishing, which destroys fish habitat, is also widespread: 56 per cent of reefs in South-east Asia are at risk. The two most damaging practices are poison fishing (where bleach or sodium cyanide is used to stun the fish, making them easier to catch but killing corals in the process) and dynamite fishing – the latter being widely practiced in South-east Asia, Oceania and East Africa.

Unplanned coastal development is another threat to reefs. The construction of airports, hotels, jetties and other forms of tourist infrastructure can cause significant damage, while the attendant sedimentation, sewage effluent and industrial run-off increase the degradation. In addition, corals, molluscs and fish are often removed for the souvenir and aquarium trades, causing more damage in the process.

On a much larger scale, human-induced global warming now poses perhaps the most serious threat of all. Sea levels are expected to rise as a result of climate change by anything from 15 to 110 cm (6–37.5 inches) over the next century. This is faster than the vertical growth of coral, so corals will be left deeper, receive less sunlight and grow more slowly – greatly reducing their effectiveness as shoreline protection.

Corals are also very sensitive to temperature change: if the water warms up, the coral polyps – stressed by heat or ultraviolet radiation – expel the symbiotic algae that live in their tissues. This leaves the corals appearing white or 'bleached'. Corals can recover after short periods of bleaching but they will die if it continues for too long. An epidemic of bleaching in the 1990s caused more coral to die in that decade than from all other causes to date. As sea temperatures continue to rise, the problem is expected to spread.

A threat that reefs have always faced is the regular battering by storms and cyclones – but even this may now be exacerbated by global warming. Researchers from the Australian Institute of Marine Science have discovered that Cyclone Ingrid, which hit Australia's eastern seaboard in March 2005, damaged at least ten per cent of the Great Barrier Reef. Eighty individual reefs that bore the brunt of the cyclone may take decades to recover, they have warned. Tropical storms have doubled in destructive potential over the past 30 years as ocean surfaces have got warmer; the devastation caused by cyclones in the Gulf of Mexico in 2005 may be some indication of what is to come.

Corals also have to cope with natural disturbances such as disease and attacks from predators (including the voracious Crown-of-Thorns starfish). Alex explains that reefs can usually handle these reasonably well, but may struggle to cope when they are combined with manmade disturbances. "Problems start when different factors come together," he explains. "A reef already stressed by pollution will be less well-placed to cope with a hurricane, for instance." For reefs already facing stress from exploitative fishing, pollution and tourism, climate change could thus be the final straw.

The value of reefs

Although coral reefs account for only one per cent of the ocean's surface area, they have a disproportionate value as an economic resource. One study[3] estimated the annual economic value of reefs for tourism, fisheries and coastal protection worldwide at around US$375 billion.

The role of coral reefs in protecting vulnerable coastlines from storms and wave action was highlighted during the devastating tsunami that struck the Indian Ocean in December 2004. In the Maldives, a study by WWF (Worldwide Fund for Nature) found that: "damage from the tsunami could have been much worse if the government's policy of protecting the network of coral reefs that buffer the islands from the open sea hadn't been so diligent." Conversely, a joint study by US and Sri Lankan researchers showed that the illegal mining of reefs in south-western Sri Lanka meant that the destruction and

→ THE DIVING INDUSTRY ADDS SIGNIFICANT ECONOMIC VALUE TO REEFS. (FELIDHOO ATOLL, MALDIVES)

→ → REEFS PROVIDE VALUABLE HABITATS FOR SPECIES SUCH AS THIS SLENDER FILEFISH. (LEMON REEF, GRAND CAYMAN)

"By exploring this fantastic realm, we cannot help but become touched by the beauty and fragility of the diverse life it cradles."

Fabien Cousteau

MARINE PARKS
HELP PROTECT
BIODIVERSITY.
(RAS MUHAMMED,
EGYPT.)

loss of life there was far greater in areas where the reef had been destroyed than where it was still intact. Globally, WWF estimates that coral reefs save US$9 billion of the costs associated with coastal protection.

Reefs may also have other benefits for humanity. Because so many reef creatures rely on toxins to protect themselves, they represent a valuable resource in the search for new drugs. In the US, the National Cancer Institute is currently investigating the potential of around 50 compounds derived from marine organisms in the treatment of conditions as diverse as leukemia, lung cancer and Alzheimer's disease. A painkiller derived from the venom of the cone snail is currently under development; it is fifty times stronger than morphine, but without being addictive.

But, sadly, the degradation of coral reefs worldwide has now reached a critical stage. As President of the Ocean Futures Society, Jean-Michel Cousteau has (like his father) spent a lifetime campaigning on environmental issues. He believes that reefs are in trouble. "Coral reefs are dying very fast," he says. "In the last 20 years or so, 25–30 per cent of the coral reefs have died. If nothing changes, it will be up to 60 per cent." Cousteau believes that we're heading towards major problems, both in terms of coastal protection from tsumanis and hurricanes, and of the economic consequences of losing such a major resource for the developing world.

Protecting reefs

Will reefs survive? We don't yet know. There is some evidence that corals that become bleached and then recover develop more resistance, while certain species show far greater tolerance to climate change and bleaching than others. Meanwhile staghorn and elkhorn corals have started to grow offshore from Fort Lauderdale, Florida, which is further north than their usual range. Broadly speaking, it seems that reefs will probably change rather than disappear entirely.

The creation of marine parks and marine protected areas goes some way towards reducing local and regional impacts on reefs. Good management and planning can protect biodiversity and help create a sustainable resource from which everybody can benefit. Worldwide, there are around 660 marine protected areas that contain coral reefs and 685 that contain mangroves. Examples of good practice abound – from community-based marine

reserves in the Philippines, to the enormous and much more sophisticated Great Barrier Reef Marine Park. Diving tourism can be a significant factor in marine parks, bestowing economic value on protected areas and creating local employment. Tourism revenue in Hawaii brings in US$8.6 million per square mile of coral reef. Divers and snorkellers are generally willing to pay a premium to visit pristine reefs, generating vital income for the management of marine parks.

As a diver, you can do your bit by supporting marine parks and following guidelines for visitors. Problems caused by divers and snorkellers include stirring up sediment and breaking corals. These are usually due to poor buoyancy control, careless fin kicking or standing on the reef – with novice divers and underwater photographers generally having the greatest impact. You can avoid causing damage by taking a few basic precautions, including ensuring all trailing items (such as gauges) are well secured; ensuring you are neutrally buoyant at all times; practising buoyancy tests away from the reef; never touching corals; choosing entry and exit points with care; knowing where your fins are at all times; and always moving slowly and deliberately in the water.

Also, think about the operator with whom you're diving. Try to choose one whose boats make use of available moorings and who dispose of garbage correctly. And, when underwater yourself, make a habit of collecting recent litter – particularly plastic bags – from the reef (although you should leave anything older, such as a glass bottle, that already has growth on it).

Our impact on land is also important. Try to choose environmentally-aware hotels or resorts that recycle and treat waste responsibly. Think about what you're eating and drinking. Choose items made with local ingredients, rather than exotic imports which have accumulated thousands of 'food miles' to get there. Eat in local restaurants, buy local handicrafts, and donate to community development funds where possible. You could also leave behind something at the end of your trip, such as an old piece of dive gear or a reef identification book, so that local dive guides can benefit.

Divers can also help by joining schemes to monitor reefs, contributing potentially valuable information to scientific surveys at the same time as enhancing their own knowledge of marine life (ReefCheck is the best known of these – see Appendix). Today many volunteer programmes offer opportunities to become part of an exciting conservation expedition.

The cost of flying

How we travel to dive resorts also has an impact. A return flight from London to the Maldives, for instance, emits 2.3 tonnes of carbon dioxide *per passenger*. Thus by flying to the Maldives we are effectively helping to sink them. To give another example, a return flight from Chicago to Brisbane would add to the stresses on the Great Barrier Reef by pumping just over four tonnes of carbon dioxide into the atmosphere – again, that is *per passenger*. We are killing coral reefs in the very act of flying to visit them on holiday; we are, literally, loving them to death.

This huge problem is being exacerbated by the growth in low-cost airlines within Europe. There are now, at any one time, around 400,000 people airborne in the skies over Europe. 'Low-cost' is a misnomer: there's an enormous cost, and we're all going to pay it whether we fly or not. Greenhouse gases from UK flights alone have doubled in the past 13 years, and have now reached 40 million tonnes annually.

As passengers we can help compensate for our flights by contributing to carbon offset schemes such as those run by the CarbonNeutral Company and Climate Care (*see Appendix*). One tree absorbs about a tonne of CO_2 per year – so for a return flight from Britain to the Red Sea you would need to pay to plant at least one tree. However, whether this is really enough, or whether it is an effective means of atoning for our polluting habits, remains open to question.

Samantha Pollard, Director of Conservation at the Marine Conservation Society, believes we need to think about our whole 'ecological footprint' if we're to make any difference. "I'm as guilty as anybody in taking up the opportunities offered by cheaper flights," she admits. "I do have a conscience about it and I'm sure that for divers the link between flying, climate change and the future of coral reefs will start to become more and more obvious." She believes that we must all address this issue seriously: "People will maybe need to start thinking about limiting their trips, or reducing their whole ecological footprint," she says, "so if you do get on a flight, then you'd better not get in your car for several thousand miles to compensate for it!" Air travel is the only form of transport in the world that pays no taxes or duties on the fuel it consumes. "Despite their bleating about rising fuel costs," says *Lonely Planet* publisher Tony Wheeler, "airlines get a free ride when it comes to fuel." A true ecotourist, so the saying goes, would never get on a plane.

What should divers do?

I asked many of the people involved with this book what action they would like divers all over the world to take in order to secure a sustainable future for our oceans and coral reefs. This was no methodical survey or rigorous policy analysis, but it provided an interesting snapshot. Almost everybody I talked to felt that divers had a special role to play in broadcasting the message that the oceans are in trouble. Journalist John Bantin was in no doubt about divers' responsibilities:

For most people, what goes unseen has no importance. Divers are the tiny minority who witness the wonders of the underwater world and understand its importance to the health of our planet. We need those who dive constantly to remind everyone else that the oceans cannot be plundered without enormous cost; neither are they available simply as a dumping ground for things we no longer need. The health of the oceans is an indicator of the health and future of our whole world.

Shark Trust founder Jeremy Stafford-Deitsch is of a similar opinion, and believes divers should act as ambassadors for the oceans, explaining to the general public "the realities of the underwater world" and "the warped, myopic and destructive practices of commercial fishermen." Author Tim Ecott also wishes that divers would be more evangelical about the seas:

Underwater, we see things that most people on this planet will never see at first hand, and I think we owe a debt of gratitude to the liquid world. Divers need to talk loudly about their love for the marine environment, and make choices that respect it: think about eating sustainably produced seafood, be less wasteful of all natural resources, and explain to people who don't dive why their actions have an impact upon the marine world. Commercial fishing practices are very often destructive and wasteful and lobbying for a ban on fishing endangered species is essential. Consumer power can be a wonderfully positive thing, especially when you decide what not to buy.

⊖ STRICT CONSERVATION POLICIES HAVE ENSURED THAT THE CAYMAN ISLANDS HAS A BOOMING ECONOMY BASED ON MARINE TOURISM. (STINGRAY CITY, GRAND CAYMAN)

⬆ WILDLIFE ENCOUNTERS SUCH AS THOSE AT STINGRAY CITY, GRAND
CAYMAN, HELP PEOPLE APPRECIATE THE OCEANS.

Marine reserves are an important means of protecting coastal areas from pollution, and provide replenishment zones for local fisheries. "We should be getting governments, particularly our own, to seriously support marine reserves around our coast rather than just paying them lip service," adds BSAC former National Training Officer Lizzie Bird. "What really concerns me is that all the warning signs are there but governments merely waffle. By the time they get around to doing anything it will be too late."

Incredibly, there are only two marine reserves in the whole of the British Isles.

Publisher of marine books Helmut Debelius wants governments to take more action. "What I would like to see is the only realistic action possible: the decision for a sustainable future of the oceans will be made on a much higher level than in diver circles," he says. "Before elections, divers should petition the representatives of their party to force a future government to take action on these

membership; ongoing financial contributions for ocean protection at whatever level you can comfortably afford; and vigorous communication with your political representatives to support pro-ocean government legislation."

Mark Caney of PADI International believes that actually getting politicians underwater can have a significant effect. "In my experience the best thing we can do is to train as many people as possible," he says, "because that way you are inevitably going to train some of the decision-makers." He explains how taking a politician diving can give them a much greater understanding of the issues and a much greater interest in resolving them. "Otherwise," he says, "governments tend to view the ocean as a carpet under which they can sweep various problems." The PADI database, he tells me, features "a lot of key names you'd recognise, both in the UK and the US."

Marine conservation begins at home

The link between what happens in our backyards and what happens in our oceans was one that many respondents made explicit. "As a keen diver I realise that only a small fraction of my life can be spent underwater," says Our World – Underwater scholar Jade Berman. "So remembering the four "R's" (Reduce, Reuse, Recycle, and Reclaim) and applying these to everyday life," she says, "would lead to significant reduction in pollution levels both above and below the surface." Similarly, digital film-maker John Boyle would like us to ask ourselves a few basic questions: "Do I really need to make that car journey? Do I really need all those plastic bags every time I visit the supermarket? Do I really need products with all that packaging?" He points out that what we do in the heart of the city can have just as much impact on the fragile oceans as the care we exercise while swimming over a reef.

Fabien Cousteau believes that diving creates a bond that binds us to the fate of the oceans. "By exploring this fantastic realm," he says, "we cannot help but become touched by the beauty and fragility of the diverse life it cradles." He believes that this consciousness should inform our everyday actions so that future generations may enjoy the treasures we have been taking for granted. "Each decision by every individual on this planet, such as throwing a wrapper in the garbage can or choosing a sustainable fish on the menu," he argues, "will help ensure that we keep enjoying the privilege of everything the ocean affords us."

issues." Filmmakers Guy and Anita Chaumette believe that individuals, when acting together, can make a difference. "The pressure of the public on the decision-making leaders and politicians," they say, "is vital for laws and measures to be enforced."

Photographer Cathy Church agrees, and suggests that the best way to do this is through pressure groups. She advocates that we all join and vigorously support three environmental organisations. "By support," she explains, "I mean

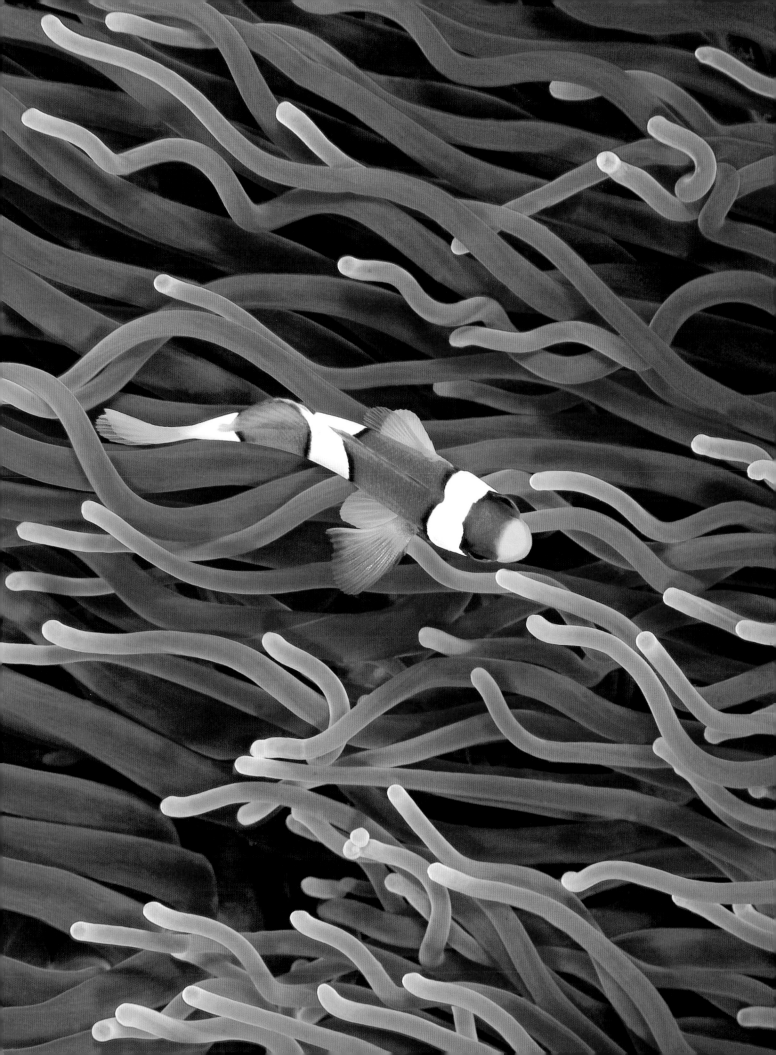

Steve Schultz, founder of Mind, Body, Spirit scuba, puts the case for this connection equally eloquently:

We must convince our fellow divers, and everyone else for that matter, that our everyday choices – of what to eat, what products to buy and how to use resources in general – all have powerful ripple effects upon our planet and the people around us. When people show the awareness to buy environment-friendly products, to consume conservatively, and to treat every piece of trash, every opportunity to recycle, and every purchase as a chance to effect the world in a positive way, that is when we will truly be able to affect our environment for the better. The ripple effect reminds us that it's all connected – not only how we act when in cities, on land and in the ocean, but also how we affect the ocean, the land, and the air. If people can grasp that everything we do matters and affects everything else, divers will act in positive ways both when they are under the water and on the surface.

Our informal survey elicited many other suggestions for divers. Guy and Anita Chaumette urged that we should never leave *anything* behind after our trip, and should bring back suntan lotion, batteries and waste since these may otherwise be disposed of in the ocean, polluting the water and eventually the coral reefs and marine life. Tim Ecott, meanwhile, would like us to be more pro-active with tourist boards, campaigning against coastal developments near sensitive areas, such as mangroves, hatcheries and reefs, and writing to tourist boards to express our dismay at what we have seen.

Yoga diving instructor Monica Farrell believes that there need to be changes in the way that diver training is organised. "As I see it, divers are not taught proper buoyancy skills to prevent them from damaging the reefs," she says. "Part of the problem is that divemasters cannot supervise large groups of novices – both in terms of safety for divers and the environment." Better and more thorough diver education is needed, she believes, in order to help beginners stay off the reefs. "You have to give divers the skills and awareness they need – and this includes dive professionals as well."

Ⓔ AN ANEMONEFISH SWIMS OVER A PURPLE TENTACLES.
(LEMBEH STRAIT, INDONESIA)

Divemaster Patrick Weir wants us to be much, much more careful of our buoyancy – even if we think we know what we're doing. "As a dive master I watch people diving every day, and even the 'good divers' touch things," he says. "Most of the time they don't even know they're doing it – especially the ones with cameras." he advises all divers not to touch, and to be more aware of their movements. "It's very easy to see the impact we have on the reef. We have to take greater care!"

The bigger picture

While it is good to learn how to dive responsibly, we must not lose sight of issues that affect marine life on a grander scale. Alex points out the inherent contradiction in a diver who is ultra-careful underwater, but then orders grouper for their evening meal. "It's important that we understand that factors such as overfishing and carbon dioxide emissions are far more critical than cosmetic diver damage," he says, adding: "Of course that doesn't excuse us from making small changes on a personal level."

Filmmaker Howard Hall echoes this belief with a call for divers to focus on what really matters. "I would like to see sport divers organize against commercial fishing interests," he says. "Commercial fishing is sweeping our oceans clean of wildlife. Not only are targeted fish populations in drastic decline, but the impact on incidental kill is largely unnoticed, unstudied and unknown." He points out that populations of many marine species discarded as a 'by-catch' – especially sharks – are collapsing. "Unfortunately, the sport diving community is so busy punishing its members for touching coral or petting Manta Rays," claims Hall, "that it has no time left for addressing significant environmental problems." Thus, while agreeing that divers should avoid damaging coral and harassing marine life, he believes that our energies should also be directed against the slaughter of marine life by commercial and sport fishing boats operating in the same area – often just a few hundred yards away.

Overfishing is undoubtedly one of the biggest problems facing the world's oceans today: we are simply eating our way through the planet's marine wildlife. "The world's fisheries and fishing communities face an unprecedented crisis," claims WWF. "Fish stocks are overfished and important habitats are being lost or degraded at an unprecedented rate. The increasing number of people living on the coasts and the continuing rise in consumer demand for fish threaten marine biodiversity across the oceans."[4]

TOXINS FOUND IN MANY REEF
CREATURES ARE TODAY BEING
DEVELOPED FOR MEDICINES. THIS
HUNTING LIONFISH DISPLAYS ITS
POISONOUS FINS.
(RAS MUHAMMED, EGYPT)

 EXPLOITATION OF THE OCEANS IS DECIMATING MANY FISH SPECIES. (SINAI, EGYPT)

Many in the diving community advocate immediate action to address the problem of overfishing. "We need to be looking at fishing policies around the world," said Lizzie Bird, "and supporting those countries that have sustainable policies." Others drew attention to our role as individual consumers, suggesting that we should boycott endangered species sold in markets and restaurants, and instead choose fish that are harvested sustainably. "Boycott any fishing that does not employ one man, one hook techniques," urged Douglas David Seifert, taking this one step further. Certainly we should all be aware of how the choices we make as consumers affect the broader environmental picture, and it is worth consulting consumer guides produced by such bodies as the Marine Conservation Society and the Monterery Bay Aquarium (*see Appendix*).

Any consideration of the overfishing problem must, however, take into account the differences between commercial fishing and local, small-scale subsistence fishing. The relationship between divers and local fishing communities is often hostile, but divers – who are often from privileged developed countries – need to understand that subsistence fishing is often the only livelihood for many people in developing countries. Divers can't expect local people simply to abandon the reef because they want to go diving there; and it's pretty hypocritical to complain about the local who's trying to catch his lunch off the beach, then go out to a restaurant and eat a meal of commercially caught seafood.

Charles Clover's powerful book *The End of the Line - How Overfishing Is Changing The World And What We Eat*[5] is a scathing indictment of current fisheries policies. In it he argues that: "Fishing with modern technology is the most destructive activity on Earth." He goes on to chronicle, in painful detail, just how exhaustively we are exploiting the world's oceans. The UN Food and Agricultural Organisation warns that 75 per cent of the world's fish stocks are fully exploited, over-exploited or significantly depleted. "This is about as strong as a pro-fisheries organisation is going to get to saying that the world's fish stocks are going down the plughole forever unless we do something about it," says Clover. The current unsustainable approach is partly due to what's known as the 'tragedy of the commons' – meaning that, since no-one owns the sea, no-one is interested in preserving it for the future and fishermen will therefore take as much as they can with impunity in case someone else catches it instead.

The arguments over fishing and ownership rights are complex, but what they boil down to, says Clover, is that citizens need to reclaim their stake in the future of the oceans. When politicians pander to the power of the fishing lobby, sustainability is the main casualty. "Sooner or later, people will realise that their birthright, a healthy ecosystem, has been stolen and they will want it back," says Clover. We need to reclaim the sea before it's too late, he believes, and this involves allowing more influence from people other than fishermen; people such as divers. "In future that's where divers need to stick up for themselves," Charles told me, "by asserting that they have interests too."

Fighting back

One small organisation, set up by three diving friends shows just how divers can make a difference when they work together. Bite-back is a small, web-based campaigning group which within the space of just over a year has achieved several major successes in altering the buying habits of Britain's supermarkets and some restaurant chains. Through email campaigns they have persuaded Tesco, Asda and Sainsbury's to remove pelagic fish such as swordfish and marlin from their stores. Asda has stopped selling Bigeye Thresher Shark and Mako Shark and noodle chain Wagamama has also been cajoled into taking shark off the menu. Bite-back's website is now receiving around 10,000 hits a month from divers (and many others), who find it a powerful vehicle through which to channel their marine conservation concerns directly to the supermarkets.

"I wanted to harness the support and passion of the diving industry and give them a voice," says Bite-back's founder Graham Buckingham. He believes that if divers agree with their message and get behind them, they can overturn the whole dynamics of the fishing industry. "The scuba diving community knows that it has the best ambassadors for the world's oceans," says Graham. "There's so much passion there. We've given people a voice and they can see the results." Divers, he believes, can make a real difference to marine conservation:

If what is happening in the oceans was happening on land, there would be a public outcry. But I am sure we will see a change in people's understanding of the oceans. I keep coming back to the fact that divers are some of the luckiest people on God's earth – what we see underwater just blows me away. Somebody has got to stand up and say 'No' to the destruction. Not just because it's our playground, but because we actually care what goes on down there.

Safe havens

It was only around a hundred years ago that humanity woke up to the need to protect our natural landscapes and wildlife habitats, and the process of creating national parks began. Today, around 12 per cent of the Earth's land surface is protected. Some environmentalists claim that's not enough – but compared to the oceans, of which just one per cent is protected, it seems huge.

Around 65 per cent of the world's ocean currently lies outside the Exclusive Economic Zones of coastal states, and these vast areas must be protected from commercial fishing, mining, oil and gas exploration and pollution. "The international community needs to act," says WWF, which is campaigning for a series of High Seas Parks in order to manage these areas for future generations.

First, more work needs to be done to make existing marine parks more effective: of 285 marine protected areas in the Caribbean, a survey found that only six per cent were managed effectively. Second, many need to be enlarged, and to be made part of carefully designed networks to make sure that connected ecosystems are protected. Larger, linked networks of marine parks would allow migratory species to move unhindered between protected areas (in the same way that land corridors link terrestrial parks in so-called 'Trans-Frontier Conservation Areas'). Marine scientists have identified 'hotspots' in the open oceans where key species such as marlin, tuna and swordfish are concentrated. Such parks would allow populations of these species to recover.

The tide of public opinion is changing, believes Charles Clover. We have seen it on land in the growing distaste for industrialised food and modern farming practices. Now we are beginning to see a similar transformation in attitudes towards fisheries and the oceans. "What we need are marine reserves that are biologically representative of the species we've got," he says, "and we want them to be large enough to be actually capable of conserving those species." There are already signs of progress. "Marine parks and 'No-take' areas do actually work," says Dr Elizabeth Wood, Coral Reef Conservation Office with the Marine Conservation Society, "and local communities are really looking after and managing them." She explains that much more effort is now being made to set up protected areas, and to link them across boundaries and between nations.

The Great Barrier Reef Marine Park is a good example of a large, linked network where commercial activities are allowed in some areas and not others. Another is the Mesoamerican Barrier Reef project, one of the largest reef conservation projects in the world. The Mesoamerican Reef extends from the Yucatan Peninsula in Mexico through Belize and Guatemala to the Bay Islands of Honduras. Home to 66 species of coral and more than 400 species of reef fish, it is an important economic resource for coastal populations.

Sylvia Earle is one of our generation's leading oceanographers and conservationists. Currently National Geographic's Explorer-in-Residence, she recently discussed the future of the oceans at the 2005 Celebrate the Sea Festival in Singapore. "There's still a chance," she said. "I get excited about the concept that we can do for the ocean what's been done for the land in terms of protecting areas of national parks." It's not too late to turn the tide, claimed Earle: "We must, at this stage, seize the opportunity that we have now, but won't have for much longer."[6]

In this book we've celebrated many of the different underwater environments so beloved by divers: deep reef walls, sandy seagrass beds, hidden caves, big seamounts, swaying kelp forests, spooky shipwrecks, gorgeous shallow reefs and more. We've marvelled at everything from the tiniest blenny to the mightiest Whaleshark. Like most divers, I would love my children and even my grandchildren to share the joy of these discoveries and experiences. There's no reason why they shouldn't – but it's up to us, this generation of divers, to make changes. We must make our leaders and politicians, all over the world, sit up and listen. "The next ten years," says Sylvia Earle, "may be the most important decade for the next thousand years." Next time you go underwater, remember those words.

⊖ A BUBBLE CORAL SHRIMP. (BUNAKEN ISLAND, INDONESIA)
⊖ ⊖ MALE ROCK BEAUTY NUZZLES A FEMALE DURING SPAWNING.
(SUNSET HOUSE REEF, GRAND CAYMAN,)

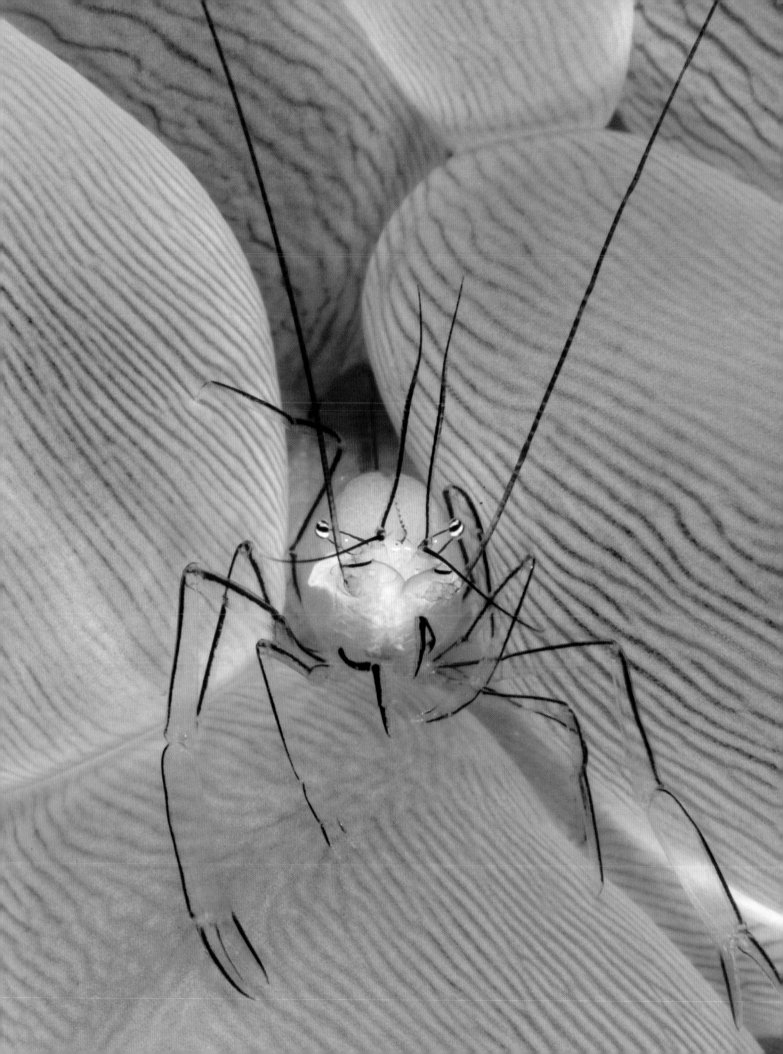

"I get excited about the concept that we can do for the ocean what's been done for the land in terms of protecting areas of national parks."

Sylvia Earle

marine organizations

Oceans

www.savethehighseas.org

The **Deep Sea Conservation Coalition** brings together around 30 conservation groups worldwide in an attempt to halt trawling and damage to seamounts, cold water corals and other deep sea ecosystems.

www.fish4ever.org

Fish 4 Ever is a global email campaign calling for the urgent implementation of sustainable fisheries and the creation of a network of marine parks to safeguard the future of the world's oceans.

www.greenpeace.org

Greenpeace runs international campaigns on a variety of marine issues including pollution, whale and dolphin conservation, and deep sea trawling.

www.oceana.org

Oceana works in North America, South America and Europe on issues including oil pollution, destructive trawling and seafood contamination.

www.oceanconservancy.org

The **Ocean Conservancy** coordinates international coastal clean-ups (covering 90 countries) and campaigns on a range of marine issues.

www.oceanfutures.org

Jean-Michel Cousteau's **Ocean Futures Society** focuses on four main areas: clean water, coastal marine habitats, marine mammals and sustainable fisheries.

www.panda.org

WWF (formerly World Wildlife Fund) runs a Global Marine programme that sponsors research and publications as well as campaigning on a wide range of marine conservation issues.

Coral reefs

www.coralreefalliance.org

Coral Reef Alliance works with divers, snorkellers, local communities and governments to protect and manage coral reefs and promote marine parks. It produces an excellent and comprehensive set of guidelines on good environmental practice for diving, snorkelling, and managing an 'underwater clean-up'.

www.reefcheck.org

ReefCheck, founded in 1996, is dedicated to saving coral reefs globally and temperate reefs in California. It works in over 80 countries with volunteers, local communities, governments and businesses to monitor, restore and maintain coral reef health.

www.reef.org

The **Reef Environmental Education Foundation** is a fish monitoring programme for divers, in which information is fed into a publicly-accessible database.

www.reefkeeper.org

ReefGuardian International focuses on reefs and marine life.

Sharks and whales

www.csiwhalesalive.org

The **Cetacean Society International** campaigns on whale conservation.

www.ecocean.org

Ecocean campaigns for increased protection for Whalesharks in Western Australia's Ningaloo Marine Park.

www.cethus.org

Fundación Cethus is an Argentinian organisation dedicated to researching, conserving and providing public education about the dolphins and whales of the south-western Atlantic.

www.sharktrust.org

The **Shark Trust** works to promote the study, management and conservation of sharks, skates and rays in the UK and internationally.

www.wdcs.org

The **Whale and Dolphin Conservation Society** is one of the leading international voices for the protection of whales, dolphins and their environment.

www.whalesharkproject.org

The **Whale Shark Project** is a joint campaign by the Shark Trust and PADI Project AWARE to create a Whaleshark photo-identification database.

Regional organizations

www.asoc.org

The **Antarctic and Southern Ocean Coalition** brings together NGOs from more than 430 countries to fight unsustainable fisheries and other threats to the Antarctic and surrounding seas.

www.amcs.org.au

The **Australian Marine Conservation Society** works on a range of regional marine issues, including marine parks, fisheries, threatened species and land-based pollution.

www.deepwave.org

Deep Wave is a German ecology group working on a range of marine issues.

www.ecologyaction.ca

Ecology Action campaigns on sustainable fisheries, oil and gas exploration, habitat protection and other marine issues affecting Nova Scotia, Canada.

www.livingoceans.org

Living Oceans campaigns on fisheries, aquaculture and marine protected areas in British Columbia, Canada.

www.mcsuk.org

The **Marine Conservation Society** is a UK-based charity dedicated to protecting the marine environment and its wildlife. MCS organises an annual beach clean up and publishes the *Good Beach Guide* and the *Good Fish Guide*.

www.marviva.org

MarViva is a Spanish-based organization that works with local communities and governments to protect marine and coastal resources across the eastern tropical Pacific and Caribbean.

www.reef-doctor.org

Reef Doctor is a UK-based programme helping to restore coral reefs in Madagascar.

www.sanctuaries.noaa.gov

The **US National Oceanic and Atmospheric Administration** (NOAA) has a national marine sanctuaries programme.

www.gbrmpa.gov.au

Australia's **Great Barrier Reef Marine Park Authority** has a huge amount of information about the world's largest marine protected area.

Consumer issues

www.bite-back.com

Bite-back has successfully campaigned to persuade supermarkets and restaurants in the UK to stop selling shark products. It has since also campaigned on other non-sustainable fisheries, including those for marlin, swordfish, monkfish and Orange Roughy.

www.fishonline.org

The UK-based **Marine Conservation Society** has an on-line guide to help consumers choose fish from sustainable sources. (Internet version of their *Good Fish Guide*.)

www.msc.org

The **Marine Stewardship Council** is an independent, non-profit organization that promotes responsible fishing practices through the MSC sustainably-fished labelling scheme.

www.mbayaq.org/cr/seafoodwatch.asp

The **Monterey Bay Aquarium** publishes seafood guides.

www.oceansalive.org/eat.cfm

US-based **Oceans Alive** publishes another seafood selector guide.

www.seafoodchoices.com

The US-based **Seafood Choices Alliance** helps fishermen, chefs and restaurant-goers make sound seafood choices.

Conservation expeditions

www.amca-international.org

Access to Marine Conservation for All helps disabled divers participate in conservation expeditions.

www.coralcay.org

Coral Cay Conservation manages reef and rainforest conservation projects in Fiji, Honduras and the Philippines.

www.earthwatch.org

Earthwatch, established in 1973, runs a wide variety of volunteer expeditions, including marine surveys for snorkellers and divers in the Bahamas, Jamaica and Belize.

www.greenforce.org

Greenforce offers marine expeditions, including programmes in Fiji, the Bahamas and Borneo.

www.opwall.com

Operation Wallacea began with marine surveys in Indonesia but now encompasses diving expeditions to South Africa, Honduras, the Red Sea and Cuba.

www.raleighinternational.org

Raleigh International is a youth development charity that works on environment and community projects worldwide, including helping to build artificial reefs in Costa Rica.

www.i-to-i.com

i-to-i offers a wide-ranging programme of travel and work experiences, including fish conservation in Thailand, turtle conservation in Sri Lanka, Guatemala and Kenya, and shark research in South Africa.

Carbon offset schemes

www.carbonneutral.com

Formerly known as Future Forests, the **CarbonNeutral Company** also allows you to calculate your emissions from flights, domestic travel or from your home, and to offset them in various ways.

www.climatecare.org

On the **Climate Care** website you can calculate the carbon cost of flights or the day-to-day emissions from your car and home. You can then offset your carbon usage by donating to reforestation or projects to reduce greenhouse gas emissions at source.

references

Chapter 1

1. Trevor Norton, *Stars Beneath the Sea* (Arrow Books, London, 2000).
2–3. William Beebe, *Beneath Tropic Seas* (Putnam's, New York, 1928).
4–5. Norton, *op cit.*
6–7. Eugenie Clark, *Lady with a Spear* (Heinemann, Oxford, 1954).
8. Norton, *op.cit.*
9–10. Jacques-Yves Cousteau, *The Silent World* (Hamish Hamilton, London, 1953).
11. Hans Hass, *To Unplumbed Depths* (Harrap, Edinburgh, 1972).
12–16. Cousteau, *op. cit.*
17. Captain Philippe Tailliez, *To Hidden Depths* (William Kimber, London, 1954).
18. Hans Hass, *Conquest of the Underwater World* (David & Charles, Newton Abbot, 1975).
19. Axel Madsen, *Cousteau – An Unauthorized Biography* (Robson Books, London, 1989).
20–21. Cousteau, *op. cit.*
22–24. Sylvia Earle, *Sea Change – A Message of the Oceans* (Fawcett Books, New York, 1995).
25. Beebe, *op. cit.*
26. Trevor Norton, *Under Water To Get Out Of The Rain* (Century, London, 2005).

Chapter 2

1. M.D. Spalding, C. Ravilious and E.P. Green, *World Atlas of Coral Reefs* (University of California Press, 2001).
2. Annemarie and Danja Köhler, *The Diver's Universe – A Guide to Interacting with Marine Life* (New Holland, London 2003).
3. Osha Gray Davidson, *The Enchanted Braid: Coming to terms with Nature on the Coral Reef* (John Wiley, Chichester, 1998).
4. Darwin, Charles, *The Voyage of the Beagle*, (first published 1845; reprinted, Heron Books, London, 1968).
5. Davidson, *op. cit.*
6. Jacques-Yves Cousteau with Philippe Diolé, *Life and Death in a Coral Sea* (Cassell, London 1971).
7. Hans Hass, *Conquest of the Underwater World* (David & Charles, Newton Abbot, 1975).

8. Account of the filming of *Deep Sea 3D* at www.howardhall.com
9. Tim Ecott, *Neutral Buoyancy* (Michael Joseph, London, 2001).
10. Eugenie Clark, *Lady with a Spear* (Heinemann, Oxford, 1954).
11. Rob Palmer, *Deep Into Blue Holes* (Media Publishing, Nassau, 1989).
12. Trevor Norton, *Under Water To Get Out Of The Rain* (Century, London, 2005).
13. Cousteau and Diolé *op. cit.*
14. Norton *op. cit.*
15. Earle *op. cit.*
16. Arthur C. Clarke, *The Treasure of the Great Reef* (The Scientific Book Club, London, 1964).
17. Kendall McDonald (ed), *The World Underwater Book* (Pelham Books, London, 1973).

Chapter 3

1. Lou Fead, *Easy Diver* (Waterlou Enterprises, Fort Lauderdale, 1983).
2. Robert N. Rossier, *Dive Like a Pro* (Best Publishing Company, Flagstaff, 1999).
3. Hans Hass, *Conquest of the Underwater World* (David & Charles, Newton Abbot, 1975).
4. Jacques-Yves Cousteau, *The Silent World* (Hamish Hamilton, London, 1953).
5–6. Tim Ecott, *Neutral Buoyancy* (Michael Joseph, London, 2001).
7. Sylvia Earle, *Sea Change – A Message of the Oceans* (Fawcett Books, New York, 1995).

Chapter 4

1. Ned DeLoach and Paul Humann, *Reef Fish Behavior* (New World Publications, Jacksonville, 1999).
2. Helen Buttfield, *The Secret Life of Fishes* (Harry N. Abrams, New York, 2000).
3–6. DeLoach and Humann *op. cit.*
7. *Guardian*, September 2003.
8. Keven N. Laland, Culum Brown and Jens Krause, 'Learning in fishes: from three-second memory to culture', *Fish and Fisheries*, 4, 3, 2003.

9. Kendall McDonald (ed), *The World Underwater Book* (Pelham Books, London, 1973).

10–11. Jacques-Yves Cousteau with Philippe Diolé, *Life and Death in a Coral Sea* (Cassell, London, 1971).

12. Cyber Diver News Network (www.cdnn.info), 23 November 2003.

13. DeLoach, *op. cit.*

14. Sylvia Earle, *Sea Change – A Message of the Oceans* (Fawcett Books, New York, 1995).

15. Trevor Norton, *Under Water To Get Out Of The Rain* (Century, London, 2005).

16–17. DeLoach, *op. cit.*

Chapter 5

1. Thor Heyerdahl, *The Kon Tiki Expedition* (George Allen & Unwin, London, 1950).

2. Jacques-Yves Cousteau, *The Silent World* (Hamish Hamilton, London, 1953).

3. Hans Hass, *Conquest of the Underwater World* (David & Charles, Newton Abbot, 1975).

4. Ichthyology at the Florida Museum of Natural History (an online resource at http://www.flmnh.ufl.edu/fish).

5. Cousteau, *op. cit.*

6. Annemarie and Danja Köhler, *The Diver's Universe – A Guide to Interacting with Marine Life* (New Holland, London 2003).

7. Victor Hugo, *Toilers of the Sea* (Thomas Nelson & Sons, Edinburgh, 1866)

8. Dan Blyth, in 'Your Strangest Dives' , *Diver* Magazine, July 2003).

9. Arthur C. Clarke, *The Coast of Coral* (Ibooks, 2002).

10. Cousteau, *op. cit.*

Chapter 6

1. Rachel Carson, *The Sea Around Us* (Staples Press, London, 1951).

2–3. Professor Sir Alister Hardy, 'Was Man More Aquatic in the Past?', *New Scientist*, 17 March 1960.

4. Trevor Norton, *Under Water To Get Out Of The Rain* (Century, London, 2005).

5. Osha Gray Davidson, *The Enchanted Braid: Coming to terms with Nature on the Coral Reef* (John Wiley, Chichester, 1998).

6–8. Hans Hass, *Conquest of the Underwater World* (David & Charles, Newton Abbot, 1975).

9. Carson, *op. cit.*

Chapter 8

1. Arthur C. Clarke *The Treasure of the Great Reef* (The Scientific Book Club, London, 1964).

2. Sylvia Earle, *Sea Change – A Message of the Oceans* (Fawcett Books, New York, 1995).

3. Sue Wells, 'Breaking Waves: shoreline protection and other ecosystem services from mangroves and coral reefs', UNEP-World Conservation Monitoring Centre, Cambridge, December 2005.

4. WWF Global Marine Programme (www.panda.org/downloads).

5. Charles Clover: *The End of the Line: How Overfishing Is Changing The World and What We Eat*, (Ebury Press, London, 2005).

6. Sylvia Earle, *X-Ray* Magazine, August–September 2005.

photographic notes

⤒ NICK HANNA BRUSHES SAND OFF THE MIRROR. (DAHAB, EGYPT)

Divers and photographers have been taking pictures in the ocean since well before the advent of scuba, and they have produced many stunning images. My main aim for the collection of images in this book was to photograph many of the familiar sights of diving with a fresh interpretation and to give these classic scenes a new twist. Just as Nick has done with the text it was my objective to show that there is much more to diving than simply learning how a regulator works.

With my marine life images I have tried to show the personality and also the natural behaviour of creatures. And with my people pictures I hope I have conveyed divers as humans – enjoying themselves, playing and expressing themselves underwater as people always do. Throughout I have tried to capture images that are a little different from the norm, which I feel gives them some visual integrity as a coherent collection, despite the diverse subject matter.

We regularly dived together during this project, as Nick says in the introduction, but during these dives I was often struck how different an experience a writer and a photographer have underwater. He would often get the sense of a dive quite quickly and be relaxing underwater, whereas I would want to spend every minute I could working hard to get my shots. Invariably Nick would have more fun diving than me! That said, this project was a true team effort. Just as I have been able to suggest directions for Nick to explore in the text, he gave me many ideas for my images (as well as appearing in plenty of them).

I am not a photographer who travels with masses of equipment. I dive with only one camera. But I am a control freak, and I like my camera to do exactly what I tell it to – so almost every images in this book was shot on manual exposure (although this was often set from the camera's metering) and with manual flash settings (no TTL). However, I only ever use auto-focus and do not even own manual focus gears. The main cameras used in this book were both digital: a Nikon D2X during 2005, and a Nikon D100 during 2004 and 2003. Both cameras were used in underwater housings made by Subal.

I have not included detailed photographic captions in the main text of the book, as I did not want to distract the reader from the proper text of the book. All this information AND MORE is available online on the Art Of Diving website: **www.artofdiving.com** which I hope expands your enjoyment of this book.

Alexander Mustard

⤓ SAFETY DIVERS POSITION A MIRROR. (DAHAB, EGYPT)

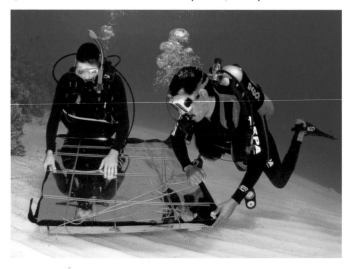

index

Page numbers in **bold** refer to illustrations.